THE POSTWAR EPOCH

THE POSTWAR EPOCH:
PERSPECTIVES ON
AMERICAN HISTORY SINCE 1945

Edited by
Allen Yarnell
University of California, Los Angeles

HARPER & ROW, PUBLISHERS
New York   Evanston   San Francisco   London

57785

57785

The Postwar Epoch: Perspectives on American History Since 1945

Copyright © 1972 by Allen Yarnell

Printed in the United States of America. All rights reserved. No part of this book may be used or reproduced in any manner whatsoever without written permission except in the case of brief quotations embodied in critical articles and reviews. For information address Harper & Row, Publishers, Inc., 10 East 53rd Street, New York, N.Y. 10022.

Standard Book Number: 06-047324-X

Library of Congress Catalog Card Number: 72-84324

For my parents and Pat

Contents

The Foreign Policy Scene

Preface

This book is the result of my attempts to find suitable material for use in the last parts of survey and twentieth-century United States history courses. The collection was crystallized when I began offering senior seminars in the post-World War II period at UCLA. Now, as new courses focusing on post-1945 events are developed, I hope that this anthology will be able to serve both students and instructors.

Most of the selections have been shortened, and most have had footnotes deleted. I hope that, in my capacity as editor, I have not done an injustice to any of the authors whose work I have used.

THE TOTAL PERSPECTIVE

The United States Since 1945
ALLEN YARNELL

Not long ago courses in United States history concluded with a discussion of World War II or perhaps entered into the 1950s. For many, the very recent past was not considered history and was completely ignored. However, the situation has changed dramatically today. There is a heightened awareness of the legitimacy and importance of the years since 1945 as a period for study. Furthermore, there are few who would deny the excitement or flux of the post-World War II era.

Following the end of World War II the United States emerged as the most powerful and prosperous nation in the world. Yet the American people were unsure about what peace would bring them. Would there be a postwar depression or would wartime prosperity continue? And what of atomic power? Technology had produced a weapon of such magnitude that one explosion could devastate a city. If scientists could do this, what kinds of miracles could they perform for a country at peace?

The year 1945 saw not only the cessation of hostilities but it also brought a new leader to the forefront of American politics. Harry S Truman assumed the Presidency and the task of directing postwar America after the death of Franklin Roosevelt. He had a firm commitment to the New Deal and quickly made clear his desire to follow FDR's policies. Yet there was great uncertainty about this untested and untried President. Could he rise to the demands that would be facing him? Only time would tell.

For better or worse, Harry Truman did rise to the occasion of the Presidency. The decision to drop the atomic bomb was made by the new President, as were other crucial decisions that helped shape the nature of post-1945 America. However, not long after he took over, Truman encountered difficulty with the body politic. Reconversion, that is, moving the American economy to a peacetime footing, was a complicated job and many felt that the President lacked the sophistication necessary to cope with it. This lack of confidence became blatantly obvious when the Republicans won control of the Congress in the 1946 elections. By 1948 a Republican Presidential victory seemed a certainty. But an upset occurred;

the polls predicted that Thomas E. Dewey would be the new President, but Truman thought otherwise. Although his campaign gave all appearances of being a one-man show, it was actually very well planned and coordinated. Truman's victory was due largely to the desire of the American people to see a continuation of New Deal policies. In addition to this, he had developed a tough bipartisan Cold War foreign policy that had the support of most Americans, and from 1945 on he was seen as standing up to Russia and preventing that country's attempt at world domination.

Truman's second term in office was beset by the emergence of McCarthyism. In February 1950 Senator Joseph R. McCarthy began accusing the State Department of having become infiltrated by Communists, an assault that was to last into 1954. He received wide press coverage and important Republican Party support, both of which helped make his name a household word in the United States. Finally, though, as millions watched on television, the Senator went too far in his confrontation with the Army, and McCarthyism faded from the national spotlight.

The Truman administration met the issue of Communism with the firm conviction that its spread had to be halted. During the 1940s the Truman Doctrine, containment, the Marshall Plan and the Berlin airlift became part of the Cold War. But in June 1950 the Cold War turned hot. Harry Truman's response to the North Korean crossing into South Korea was swift and decisive. Immediately, the United States took military action (through the United Nations) and the country was once again involved in a war. At home the American people had a hard time understanding the war. It was a limited effort, quite different from World War II, and the administration was never fully able to explain its intentions to the people.

This was especially evident when Truman, as commander-in-chief, felt compelled to remove General Douglas Mac-Arthur from his post as head of American forces in the Far East. Not only was the Korean War unpopular, it also kept the administration from becoming fully involved in the pursuit of social welfare policies at home. Joe McCarthy and Korea spelled doom for the Democrats.

As the 1952 Presidential campaign approached, the Republican Party was in an excellent position. Truman had decided against running for another term, and the Democrats had chosen Governor Adlai Stevenson of Illinois as their candidate. Stevenson was a proven vote-getter with solid liberal credentials, but he had trouble reaching some elements of the society. Many felt him to be aloof and too intellectual for their tastes. The Republicans, on the other hand, had selected Dwight David Eisenhower, an overwhelmingly popular military hero, as their candidate for the nation's highest office. And with Eisenhower the Republicans chose a young California senator, Richard M. Nixon, to seek the Vice Presidency. From the outset the campaign was personality oriented. Surprising as it may seem, Stevenson and Eisenhower had very similar views on foreign policy, both being staunch anti-Communists, but the decisive issue of the campaign was image. For the first time, television played a major role in American politics and Eisenhower came across as having the qualities that Americans wanted in their President. The results of the election showed an impressive Republican victory. The GOP not only won the White House but it also captured control of the Congress.

The 1950s have had many epithets attached to them, most of which have been negative. Yet a closer look at the Eisenhower years reveals that much more was taking place than has been acknowledged. First, the Korean conflict was brought to a halt. Second, in the field of civil rights, the Supreme Court—with an Eisenhower appointee as Chief Justice—ruled in 1954 that the policy of separate but equal facilities in the field of education was in violation of the law. Further, Eisenhower as Chief Executive followed up that decision by using federal troops in Little Rock, Arkansas, in 1957 to enforce the law. And in 1957 the first Civil Rights Act since the Reconstruction period was passed. If there was indeed activity, why are the 1950s viewed in such a dismal perspective? The answer lies in the overall quality of American life in that decade.

While some problems were addressed, other major ones were pushed aside. Poverty and hunger were virtually ignored, as were the living conditions of minority peoples in American society. The white middle class wanted to sit back and enjoy the good life rather than blaze new trails. The 1950s were years when the generation that had fought World War II sought to reap the benefits of what they had fought for. The movement to the suburbs symbolized the achievement of some material wealth. In the business world the "organization man," a type that would blend and become part of the team, developed. Television presented shows like "Father Knows Best," which emphasized the qualities Americans wanted to possess. There were some rebels in the culture, most notably the "beats," but on the whole the fifties were years of tranquillity because the people wanted them to be that way. To be sure, there was some activity, but compared to the 1960s it was minimal.

As the 1960s began the Democrats felt they had a chance to recapture the White House. Eisenhower had won a second victory over Adlai Stevenson in 1956, but in 1960 the General was ineligible to run again because of the two-term amendment of the Constitution. Instead, the Republican Party chose Vice President Nixon as its standard-bearer. For the Democrats, the first indications were that a full battle royal would take place, but that threat ended when Senator John F. Kennedy of Massachusetts showed his strength in primary victories. Kennedy had qualities that made him very appealing as a Presidential candidate—a distinguished war record, many years in the Congress, a liberal background, and most important of all a good television style. Working against him was the fact that he was a Catholic; however, his triumph in the West Virginia primary removed that obstacle from his path.

While "Ike" himself remained very popular, many Americans had become disenchanted with Republican policies. An economic recession in 1957 and 1958 had thrown a sizable number of people out of work. In foreign affairs the administration had suffered a number of embarrassments, beginning with the Russian launch of Sputnik in 1957 and concluding with the U-2 spy incident of 1960. This gave John Kennedy a perfect opportunity to challenge the administration's policies in the Presidential campaign.

Kennedy was an avowed anti-Communist, as Eisenhower had been and Nixon was. Anti-Communism had been a constant since the end of World War II, and Kennedy was not about to change that stance. Yet in 1960 John Kennedy appeared to differ from Richard Nixon on this issue even though there was agreement on fundamentals. On most issues, in fact, the two candidates had similar moderate views. However, Kennedy maintained that the United States had to regain its position in the world vis-à-vis the Soviet Union. In the end it was a very close contest with the outcome in doubt until the final moment. But the voters had decided that John Kennedy should lead the nation into the 1960s.

The early 1960s seemed to bring a change to the United

States. The appearance of a young energetic leader brought a kind of excitement that had been missing in the previous decade. Perhaps the country was on the move again. The rhetoric of the new administration was very liberal, but its actions on the domestic scene were extremely cautious. Very quickly, the nation was made aware of the problems plaguing it—poverty, hunger, and civil rights inequities, to name just a few—but the Kennedy administration lacked the power necessary to get laws passed to remedy the situation. On the domestic front Kennedy was most successful in focusing attention on serious problems and laying a groundwork for potential problem solving. However, it is in the realm of foreign policy that the administration is most remembered. The most notable success in this area was the Nuclear Test Ban Treaty of August 1963. But the Cuban missile crisis, probably the most dramatic confrontation ever to take place between the United States and Russia, stopped the world for a few days in 1962. In analyzing this episode, it is worth noting that the country was brought to the brink of war by a "liberal" administration. Liberalism and anti-Communism had fused to such an extent in the early 1960s that they could not be divorced from each other.

John Kennedy's tragic assassination on November 22, 1963, left the reins of government in the hands of Lyndon Baines Johnson, who immediately promised to push ahead with the slain President's programs. His was a style quite different from Kennedy's. Johnson lacked Kennedy's sophistication in dealing with intellectuals, but as a politician in the White House he was eminently successful in pushing through a vast amount of domestic legislation.

By 1964 the Republican Party had been taken over by its conservative wing, which fostered the nomination of

Senator Barry Goldwater of Arizona. Goldwater was a champion of conservatism, and many in the GOP felt he was their only hope for beating the Democrats. However, in retrospect, Goldwater's pronouncements on domestic matters were less important than his stance on foreign policy. The country's involvement in Vietnam became the key issue in the contest, and Lyndon Johnson was seen as the "peace" candidate, with Goldwater wanting to escalate the war. The President won an enormous victory, giving him the power he needed to carry on his programs. Through 1963 and 1964 Johnson had centered his attention on passing the legislation that had been pending when Kennedy was killed. After his election Johnson began pushing his own programs (called "the Great Society") through the Congress. Generally speaking, the Johnson domestic program was an extension of the New Deal, bringing it into the 1960s. Medicare, federal aid to education, the 1965 Voting Rights Act, and antipoverty programs are just some of the things that the administration will be remembered for.

However, even with all this legislation there were real problems. Many Americans living in the 1960s began to question whether these kinds of programs could bring about a truly better America. Students, members of minority groups, women, and citizens from the intellectual community began to argue that liberalism had lost its vitality. The days of a large federal bureaucracy administering to the needs of the people were over. Programs based on new ideas were called for, but they were not forthcoming from the administration. Americans looked around them and were horrified at what they saw. Cities were unfit to live in and were erupting in violence. Minorities, especially the nation's black population, had become very vocal as they took to the streets to demand change. Racism was acknowledged to be an unsavory part of

American life. On college campuses students were challenging traditional ways of doing things, and universities began to reel from the attacks. Finally, the people realized that our environment was a national disgrace and was becoming worse all the time. Added to all of these problems was the persistent war in Vietnam.

As one looks at the second half of the 1960s, the over-whelming issue that emerges is the United States involvement in Southeast Asia. At first a small "advising" mission, the Vietnam war turned into a major disaster for the country. Not only had this war to contain the spread of Communism in Asia polarized American opinion but at the same time it had exaggerated and made worse the problems present in domestic America. The country's blacks wondered why they could not attain first-class citizenship at home while having to bear a disproportionately high percentage of the fighting. The "guns and butter" economy could not stand the tremendous drain of the war and a spiraling inflation resulted. It became apparent that the Johnson administration could not continue its energetic activities in the domestic field while the war was being pursued.

Lyndon Johnson's Vietnam policies have been criticized at great length and for a variety of reasons. The President never fully leveled with the American people as to the aims of this country's involvement. Further, as the years went by and the administration hinted at victory (whatever that was perceived to be), Americans became more and more disillusioned with the war and the President's conduct of it. In 1968 the Democratic Party divided on the issue of the Southeast Asian war. A group led by Senator Eugene McCarthy of Minnesota began to urge an immediate end to the conflict. The Democrats had a real dilemma. McCarthy entered the New Hampshire Presidential primary and showed unusual strength. Senator

Robert F. Kennedy announced his intention to seek the Presidency too. And on March 31, 1968, Lyndon Johnson told a national audience via television that he would not be a candidate for the Presidency again.

The unmistakable highlights of the 1968 campaign were the acts of violence that took place. In June Robert Kennedy was shot to death on the night he won the California Democratic Presidential primary. A stunned nation watched as the brother of John Kennedy was laid to rest—like his brother the victim of an assassin's gun. Then in late August protesters and police battled in Chicago as the Democratic convention nominated Vice President Hubert Humphrey to run against Richard Nixon. Humphrey represented the administration position on the war, and even if he personally wanted to end the conflict he was tied to Johnson's policies. Nixon, on the other hand, said that he would bring about an "honorable" peace. In a campaign that saw television used more than in any other campaign Richard Nixon just barely defeated Hubert Humphrey.

The Nixon administration, as the transitional government from the 1960s to the 1970s, faced a difficult task. Between 1969 and 1971 the President succeeded in pulling a great many troops out of Vietnam and bettering the country's relations with Communist China, yet the Southcast Asian war dragged on. The economy became so depressed that wage and price controls had to be ordered in August of 1971. Most important of all, strong executive leadership did not emerge from the White House during the first three years of Nixon's Presidency.

Has the United States changed that much from 1945? By the end of the 1960s the country was sending men to the moon. The media, especially television, had become so perfected that the Vietnam war was being shown to the American people almost as it was taking place.

Technologically the nation had progressed tremendously since the days of World War II. And superficially a new lifestyle seemed to have emerged. Clothing in the late sixties and early seventies was much more colorful and dramatic than the garb of the forties and fifties. On the music scene rock blasted through radios and stereos, bringing a freedom that had not been present in earlier decades. And in the 1970s white middle class America discovered a drug problem in its midst, as compared with the forties, fifties, and early sixties when drugs had been almost entirely confined to the "seamy" side of town.

That change has occurred, then, is a given, but has the United States been altered very much? One has only to look at the country in the early 1970s to see what the answer is. The fundamental beliefs and values of most Americans have remained the same. The political system is based on two parties that by and large have the same tone that they did following the end of the war. Anti-Communism is still a firm part of American life and remains the major guidepost of United States foreign policy. "Law and order" may have been the Republican political slogan of 1968, but it also represents a constant in American life. Stability is a quality that people seek, and there is antipathy toward any force that may alter the existing framework. By and large then, the United States in the 1970s is quite recognizable to those who were part of the society in 1945.

And what of those forecasters who speak of the development of a counter-culture or a new emerging revolutionary society? Only time will tell if their perceptions are correct, but for the moment it seems that most members of American society are wedded to the existing system. People may want modifications and changes, but only a handful seem to gravitate to real revolution.

THE SETTING

Mood Maybe

ERIC F. GOLDMAN

Eric Goldman's The Crucial Decade—and After *has for many years been considered the standard survey of the post-World War II period. In the following selection from his book, Goldman, as a historian, informs his readers as to the mood and spirit of the United States upon the completion of the war. And Goldman, as a participant in the events described, represents a liberal's reflections on the end of the war.*

A U.S. radio monitor in a little frame house in Oregon caught the first hint. The Japanese were interested in peace, the Domei broadcast said, provided that the prerogatives of the Emperor would not be "prejudiced." Then came two days of diplomacy, a few hours of false armistice, more waiting through an interminable weekend. Finally, on Tuesday, August 14, 1945, reporters were summoned to the Oval Room of the White House. President Truman glanced at the clock to make sure he was holding to the agreement of simultaneous announcement in Washington, London, and Moscow. At exactly 7 p.m. he began reading: Late that afternoon a message had been received from the Japanese Government which "I deem . . . full acceptance of . . . unconditional surrender."

Across America the traditional signs of victory flared and shrieked. In Los Angeles, yelling paraders commandeered trolley cars, played leapfrog in the middle of Hollywood Boulevard, hung Hirohito from scores of lampposts. Salt Lake City thousands snakedanced in a pouring rain and a St. Louis crowd, suddenly hushing its whistles and tossing aside the confetti, persuaded a minister to hold services at 2 a.m. New York City, hardly unaccustomed to furor, amazed itself. With the first flash of V-J, up went the windows and down came the torn telephone books, the hats, bottles, bolts of silk, books, wastebaskets, and shoes, more than five thousand tons of jubilant litter. Whole families made their way to Times Square until two million people were milling about, breaking into snatches of the conga, hugging and kissing anybody in sight, greeting each twinkle of V-J news on the *Times* electric sign with a cheer that roared from the East River to the Hudson. The hoopla swirled on into the dawn, died down, broke out again the next afternoon, finally subsided only with another midnight.

•   •   •

Peace had not come to the nation with the soothing coo of a dove. Instead it came in swift hammer blows of news, smashing old sure stand-bys. Four months before the Japanese surrender, cerebral hemorrhage struck down Franklin Roosevelt, a second father to millions of Americans during their worst depression and their worst war. Another three months and the British were sweeping out of office Winston Churchill, doughty symbol of steadiness to much of Western Civilization. Eleven days later, just before V-J, President Truman announced: "An American airplane [has] dropped one bomb on Hiroshima. . . . It is an atomic bomb. It is a harnessing of the basic power of the universe."

Over all the victory celebrations, the fact of the atomic bomb hung like some eerie haze from another world. Americans tried to make jokes. The Japanese were suffering from atomic ache, people giggled to each other. Or when God made Atom, he sure created a handful for Eve. Americans were sententious. The bomb meant the end of civilization and atomic energy was certain to usher in a golden age of peace and plenty. Americans argued furiously. John Foster Dulles intimated that atomic bombs and "Christian statesmanship" were hardly compatible and scores of leaders answered hotly that a truly Christian nation ended wars as quickly as possible. Somehow neither the arguments nor the jokes nor the sententiousness meant much. People fumbled along, trying to comprehend the incomprehensible, to fit a sense of terrifying newness into their accustomed ways of thinking. And in almost every American mind, there was one corner that could respond to the words reported from a European prison cell. "A mighty accomplishment," the captured Nazi leader Hermann Göring said. "I don't want anything to do with it."

• • •

Worriedly, yearningly, the liberal leaders were talking of sixty million jobs, the figure that Franklin Roosevelt had used in his vista of the postwar. Sixty million jobs, the argument ran, were a symbol of the full employment and social advances which could be; they were also a measuring-rod that would warn of oncoming disaster. And this time, a thousand New Deal commentators added, failure to solve America's domestic problems would mean something worse than hard times. As the end of World War II neared, *Harper's Magazine*, certainly a restrained liberal journal, was running an article which argued that "the veterans are not going to accept unemployment with the bewildered docility which was characteristic of most of the jobless in the last depression. . . . What action will result from that attitude . . . ? Nobody knows, of course. But we have some hints, and they are hints which should make any American start worrying. One of them is the report of a historian who watched fascism rise in Italy and Germany after the last war."

• • •

The anti-New Dealers, the people who more and more were coming to be called "conservatives," had their portentous reading too. Late in the war, the University of Chicago Press published *The Road to Serfdom*, by an Austrian-born economist, Friedrich A. von Hayek. The Press knew well the usual fate of scholarly treatises; it printed only two thousand copies. But Hayek had set his scholarship within a general proposition that caught perfectly the mood of much of American conservatism. Nazism, he contended, had not grown up in opposition to New Deal-type liberalism; such liberalism and Nazism came from the same roots. All Western Civilization had been relying increasingly on ideas of national economic planning, and the ideas, whether called liberalism, Nazism, socialism, or Communism, led inevitably to totalitarian serfdom. Hayek's volume was scarcely in the bookstores before the University of Chicago Press discovered that it had published not only a scholarly monograph but a manifesto for American conservatism. Hailed by anti-New Deal publications, purchased in quantity by a number of American corporations, *The Road to Serfdom* promptly made its way to the best-seller list and stayed on month after month into the V-J period. The severely intellectual Hayek, dumfounded at the sales of the volume and half-protesting that he did not want to be a spokesman for any political group, found himself lecturing up and down the country to rapt anti-New Deal audiences.

. . .

Some American conservatives were avid for an all-out effort to get rid of the New Deal and turn America back toward unregulated capitalism. Others acquiesced in what the New Deal had done but insisted upon drawing a stern line, beyond this not one step further. Both conservative groups often talked a formula that was decades old but now had a fresh significance and a new name, "welfare capitalism." Industry itself, the formula ran, should protect the welfare of its employees to such an extent that social legislation, and perhaps unions, would lose their appeal. Whatever the emphasis, conservatives joined with liberals in considering the postwar a battleground on which domestic issues of far-ranging significance would be fought out, with results that could mean heaven or hell.

At V-J, the field of foreign policy brought its own sense

of great possibilities for good or evil. Throughout the war, most liberals had been little bothered by the alliance with the Soviet Union. After all, they argued, the Soviet stood for anti-fascism, for collective security against aggression, and for the betterment of the underprivileged. With patience, Russia could be brought more and more to the ways of democratic nations; besides, if the United States did not co-operate with the Soviet, how could it win the war? Many liberals went beyond these sidewise justifications to the argument that the Soviet alliance was a positive good. It meant a peace that would endure because it would be built on unity between the powers that counted, the United States and Russia; it foreshadowed a postwar in which, through the pressure of both New Dealism and Communism, social reform would become a prime concern of world leadership.

During World War II, only a minority among the conservatives sharply differed with the liberal attitude toward the Soviet alliance. Stalin's public statements and actions seemed devoid of double-dealing; the Russians were obviously saving American lives by smashing Nazi divisions; the fierce Soviet holding operation at Stalingrad and then the hammer blows back across Russia had a heroic quality about them which won general American admiration. Public-opinion polls indicated that most business executives were thoroughly optimistic about Russia's postwar intentions. The powerful anti-New Deal Luce publications were explaining away the Russian secret police as "a national police similar to the FBI," with the job of "tracking down traitors," while the high-Republican Main Line filled the hall with cheers when the Philadelphia Orchestra introduced the new Russian anthem, "Hymn to the Soviet Union." The Yalta Conference of February, 1945, seemed a triumph of Allied unity for purposes on which all groups in the United

States could agree, and the Yalta communiqué was greeted by almost unanimous praise in the United States.

Yet beneath the conservative acceptance of the Soviet alliance ran irritations and misgivings. The man who had long considered the New Deal dangerous radicalism hardly took real pleasure in joining hands with out-and-out Bolsheviks. He was the more edgy because the camaraderie was being promoted by Franklin Roosevelt. He could not help but feel that a peace built on a Com-munist-New Deal understanding would move everything away from the kind of pattern he considered sensible and decent. This underlying disturbance of the conserva-tives over the Soviet relationship was especially marked in the Midwestern Republican faction led by Senator Robert A. Taft. "It's all very well to win a war with socialist New Dealers and Bolsheviks having a love feast," Senator Kenneth Wherry of Nebraska expressed the at-titude, "but what follows then?"

As the war drew to a close and the day approached when Russian divisions would no longer be needed, the conservative restiveness mounted. It was further in-creased by headlines which began breaking soon after the Yalta communiqué of February, 1945. The news was revealed of a secret Yalta agreement, easily deemed favorable to the Soviet. The Russians made moves in flagrant violation of the Yalta provisions for free elec-tions in the liberated countries of eastern Europe. Stalin seemed to speak contempt for the whole idea of world peace by announcing that he would send merely an underling of his Foreign Office to the San Francisco con-ference for setting up the United Nations—a decision that was reversed, it was widely assumed, only by strong pressure from President Truman.

At the time of the Japanese surrender, most liberals were still optimistic about American-Russian relations;

if they doubted, it was largely because Franklin Roosevelt had been removed from the negotiating table. But
many an anti-New Dealer was beginning to wonder aloud
if the whole Roosevelt policy had not been a tragic
blunder. Some conservatives, particularly the Taftian
Republicans, were projecting into the V-J air doubts
whether peace itself could long endure between the
United States and the Bolsheviks.

Russians or no Russians, Hayek *vs.* the New Dealers,
atom bomb or not, World War II was over, and all
America joined in a sense of coming home. At V-J, the
first groups of veterans were already fidgeting in trains
and buses, straining for some half-remembered clump of
billboards, a bed of petunias, a funny-shaped building
that meant they were almost there. Defense workers
were pulling out of the Quonsets in Los Angeles and Detroit and Hartford, heading back to Alabama, Oklahoma,
and the hills of Maryland. Men and women who had
taken the same commuter train, prepared dinner in the
same kitchen, punched the same time clock for twenty
years, were coming home too. At last they could fill their
gasoline tanks, use a second chunk of butter, watch the
long lazy curl of a fishing line flicker in the sunlight, or
get royally tight, without feeling that they were cheating
some GI in the flak over Berlin or on the bloody ash of
Iwo Jima.

It was good to be home; for millions, it was better still
to be in what home had become. The America of V-J was
prosperous, more prosperous than the country had been
in all its three centuries of zest for good living. The boom
rolled out in great fat waves, into every corner of the
nation and up and down the social ladder. Factory hands,
brushing the V-J confetti out of their hair, laid plans for
a suburban cottage. Farmers' children were driving to
college classes in glossy convertibles. California border

police, checking the baggage of Okies returning east, came across wads of hundred-dollar bills.

* * *

The sense of wonderful possibilities ahead kept breaking into every part of living. In the year when man mastered the atom, a good many people did not smile at the feature-page stories which predicted that the average American would soon work twenty-five hours a week, return to a dinner cooked by the flick of a single button, educate his children through the finest authorities televised into a sun-heated livingroom, and take his vacation a continent away. In a period when medical research had just produced the yellow magic of penicillin only to have it promptly topped by streptomycin, it did not seem utopian to talk of conquering tuberculosis, infantile paralysis, even cancer. As for the bread-and-butter of living, the U.S. Director of War Mobilization and Reconversion, Fred Vinson, was saying: "The American people are in the pleasant predicament of having to learn to live 50 percent better than they have ever lived before." From somewhere deep in the national psychology came the surest affirmation of tomorrow. Throughout the depression days of the 1930's, well into the war period, millions of couples had made the decision against children or ventured only as far as a single son or daughter. Now a rampant birthrate was turning community life into one vast gurgle.

* * *

A zest in today, wondrous hopes for tomorrow—but always, in the America of V-J, there were shadows. A nation accustomed to the categorical yes and no, to war or peace and prosperity or depression, found itself in the nagging realm of maybe. The liberals worried over the conservatives and the conservatives watched the liberals with an uneasiness akin to dread. Conservatives, liberals, and the half of the nation which was not really either asked: Would events follow the same pattern as during the last postwar? Was unprecedented boom to bring unprecedented delights only to turn into unprecedented bust? Was peace just a prelude to another war?

•   •   •

THE POLITICAL SCENE

The 1948 Presidential Election
CABELL PHILLIPS

Journalist Cabell Phillips has analyzed why Harry S Truman won the presidential election of 1948. According to Phillips, shrewd planning by Truman's chief political advisor, Clark M. Clifford, and the President's support of traditional New Deal policies were key ingredients in the victory. Phillips, writing in 1966, was one of the first to dispel the myth that Harry Truman had waged an unplanned, off-the-cuff campaign. The excerpt presented here demonstrates the kind of carefully planned battle that was fought and the way in which it paid off.

Reprinted with permission of The Macmillan Company from *The Truman Presidency: The History of a Triumphant Succession* by Cabell Phillips. Copyright © by Cabell Phillips, 1966. (Title supplied by editor.)

If ever a successful political campaign was patched together with scissors and paste and sheer bravado, it was
that incredible effort of 1948 when Harry Truman upset
not only his Republican rivals but the massed forces of
the nation's press, public opinion polls, and political experts, including his handlers and seconds. He was seeking vindication of his record by winning the Presidency
in his own right. Not only did he have a host of issues
raised against him by the Republicans, but he faced a
two-pronged revolt within his own party—the Wallace
Progressives on the left and the Thurmond Dixiecrats on
the right. Moreover, a sense of defeat overhung the
Democratic organization from coast to coast like a para-
lyzing miasma. The party's morale was shot and its
treasury worse than broke. In the final week before
election day, Mr. Truman was the deadest of ducks to
just about everybody except candidate Truman himself.
Because he stubbornly refused to lie down, he wrought
the greatest coup d'état in all the history of Presidential
politics.

When and how did he decide to take this riskiest of
gambles? In his many recollections about it, Truman
leaves the impression that from 1947 onward his mind
was made up, however reluctantly, to run. There was
still "unfinished business" from sixteen years of Democratic reforms to be completed, he has said, and the
Republicans in the Eightieth Congress had demonstrated
both their disinclination and their inability to carry them
out or even to deal adequately with the newly arising
problems at home and abroad. He was not blind to the
mountainous obstacles in his way, but "I was not brought
up to run away from a fight when the fight is for what

is right. Supposedly scientific predictions that I could not win did not worry me one bit."

Two other little-known circumstances may have had a bearing on that decision.

The first one: Truman offered, as late as the autumn of 1947, to step aside for Eisenhower if the General would accept the Democratic nomination, while Truman would take the No. 2 position on the ticket as Vice President.

Ever since the 1946 election, Eisenhower's name had acquired a growing and irresistible magic to the politicians of both parties. The General's preference as between the GOP elephant and the Democratic donkey was unknown, but in the declining light of Truman's popularity he looked like a sure winner on any ticket for 1948, and he was assiduously courted by emissaries from both sides. This courtship grew in ardor as 1947 wore on.

One day in the fall of that year Kenneth C. Royall, Secretary of the Army, came to see the President. With some trepidation he told Mr. Truman that, if Eisenhower, who was then Chief of Staff, did become a candidate under either party's banner, he could not, in conscience, work against the General, whom he so greatly admired. The Secretary asked, Would it not be the best thing for him to resign quietly now before the issue had to be faced?

Not a bit of it, the President replied. On the contrary, he had a countersuggestion to offer. He would like to have Royall go in deepest confidence to Ike and tell him that, if he were receptive to the Democratic nomination for President, he, Truman, would not only help him get it but would offer to be his running mate as Vice President.

The incredulous Secretary did as he was bidden. He had some difficulty in persuading the equally incredulous

General that the President was in earnest. But Eisenhower at that time was just as earnest about staying out of politics as others were to get him in, and this message was then conveyed back to the White House with, of course, hearty expressions of gratitude.

The implication of this incident is clearly that Truman, even in the later months of 1947, doubted his ability to win reelection and possibly even the nomination. But rather than forfeit the Presidency to the Republicans he was willing to make a personal sacrifice such as no President before him had ever ventured. When his strange gambit failed, he was ready to go it on his own.[1]

The second circumstance: Mr. Truman's decision was ultimately shaped by the cogent and persuasive reasoning of Clark Clifford and the secret political strategy board. Late in November of 1947, Clifford put in the President's hands a 40-page analysis of the status of Truman and the Democratic party that should rank as one of the great dissertations on the art of politics. It did not promise Mr. Truman he could win. What it did do was to cut down to size some of the mountainous imponderables of his situation and to suggest that he did not have to lose.

---

[1]This incident is published here for the first time. The writer submitted the facts to the three principals involved and received the following comments: Secretary Royall wrote that the account was "substantially correct" but denied that he was unprepared to support Mr. Truman if he should become the candidate. He adds: "Mr. Truman was a realist and from time to time doubted whether he could win in 1948. But he never gave up trying." General Eisenhower wrote: "Your letter involves an action by an individual who is still alive and active. It is my conviction that in writing about words or actions of such a person, you should contact him directly." Mr. Truman wrote: "That story about which you wrote me has been going around and around. I never agreed to help Ike get the Democratic nomination. There is nothing to the story."

As an extraordinary example of the kind of political perception that underpins a Presidential election campaign, this study is worth summarizing at some length.

The aim of the memorandum was "to outline a course of political conduct for the administration extending from November 1947 to November 1948." Its basic premise, as stated, was "That the Democratic Party is an unhappy alliance of Southern conservatives, Western progressives, and big city labor. . . . The success or failure of the Democratic leadership can be precisely measured by its ability to lead enough members of these misfit groups to the polls" on election day of 1948.

What were the "probabilities" of the opposition to be encountered in that effort?

First of all, Dewey was almost certain to be the Republican nominee—"a resourceful, intelligent, and highly dangerous candidate . . . with an extremely efficient group of men around him."

Second, the only safe assumption to make about Wallace was that he would run as a third-party candidate, in spite of all the talk about the "futility" of such a gesture. If he should do so, and then draw 5 to 10 percent of the vote in a few key states, this might throw the victory to the Republicans. There was no question about the strong Communist influence at work in the Wallace ranks, or that Moscow would delight in seeing the Truman administration pulled down. "The best way it can achieve that result and hasten disintegration of the American economy is to split the independent and labor vote between Truman and Wallace, and thus assure the Republican candidate's election." To ignore the Wallace threat would be "extremely unrealistic." Every effort should be made to dissuade him from running, and if that fails, "to identify him and isolate him in the public mind with the Communists."

Third, "The South, as always, can be considered safely Democratic." That (mis)calculation left the administration free to concentrate on the large bloc of western states that the party had carried in 1944. The two blocs, combined, should yield 216 of the required 266 electoral votes, leaving only 50 to be picked up in doubtful states of the Middle West and East. If that could be brought off, "We could lose New York, Pennsylvania, Massachusetts, Ohio, and Illinois—all the big states—and still win." (Clifford was looking into his crystal ball three months before the submission of Truman's 1948 civil rights program, which galvanized the Dixiecrat revolt. But the other half of his postulate was correct.)

There then followed a long analysis of the major voting blocs. The No. 1 priority should be the farmers, who were enjoying a high rate of prosperity and whose Republican moorings were already loosening. The labor vote was crucial in most big states, and it almost certainly would suffer some inroads from the Wallaceites. The same was true of the Negroes, and strong emphasis on civil rights would be necessary to hold them in line. Jews held the key to New York, and the key to the Jewish vote was what the administration would do about Palestine.[2]

As to issues, the President had a majority of the people with him on his handling of foreign policy, the degree of assent fluctuating pretty much in accordance with the fever chart of U.S.–Soviet relations. On domestic problems, the Republican Congress would almost certainly block him on every major maneuver, so that Congress itself became the overriding issue for the President.

Finally, the Clifford memo urged a prompt and drastic

[2] On direct orders of President Truman, United States recognition was extended to Israel eleven minutes after it proclaimed itself a government on May 14, 1948.

overhaul of the Democratic Party organization. "The blunt fact is that the party has been so long in power that it is fat, tired, and even a bit senile." A new chairman should be brought in to start rebuilding "from the ground up." Moreover, the Truman "image" could stand a little face lifting. To add a new dimension to the popular conception of him as "a man of the people trying to do his best," he might consider an occasionally well-publicized lunch "with an Einstein or a Henry Ford, or to speak out now and then about an important current book he is reading."

Above all, he should get out of Washington more, to be seen and heard by the people in the flesh.

> Since he is President, he cannot be conspicuously active politically until well after the convention. So a President who is also a candidate must resort to subterfuge. He cannot sit silent; he must be in the limelight. . . . He must resort to the kind of trip Roosevelt made famous in the 1940 campaign—the "inspection tour." . . . No matter how much the opposition and the press pointed out the political overtones of those trips, the people paid little attention, for what they saw was the Head of State performing his duties.

What direct effect this document had on Truman's ultimate decision to take the plunge in 1948 has never been stated. But that its influence was substantial, and perhaps decisive, can hardly be doubted.

Weighing against all the negative political snares that lay in Truman's path were two positive factors of his own temperament and personality. First, his instinctive response to a challenge was to fight back; he was not, in this case, going to take repudiation lying down. Second, he was convinced that the forces arrayed against him,

Democratic as well as Republican, were intent on rolling back the liberal accomplishments of his and the Roosevelt administrations. And his belief that he alone could thwart that design grew in direct proportion as the campaign to deny him the opportunity intensified.

Given these subjective compulsions "to show those s.o.b.'s who's right," the Clifford memo provided Harry Truman with a practical rationale and a strategy to underpin his natural impulse. It resolved whatever misgivings he was still harboring as 1947 drew to a close and the year of decision dawned. And its traces are strikingly evident in all that he did subsequently.

•　•　•

Truman launched his campaign with a Labor Day speech at Detroit, which has become a ritual for Democratic candidates ever since. The event set a pattern that he was to follow almost without deviation for the next eight weeks.

The "Truman Special," with eighty-odd reporters and photographers, details of Secret Service and Signal Corps men, a dozen White House aides and secretaries, and the President and his daughter, Margaret, aboard (Mrs. Truman was attending a christening in Denver), pulled out of Washington's Union Station at 3:40 on the afternoon of Sunday, September 5. It was a sixteen-car train with sleeping and dining cars, a work car for the reporters, a communications car for the Signal Corps and Western Union, and, at the end, the *Ferdinand Magellan*, a Pullman specially adapted for Presidential use in the days of FDR. The *Magellan* contained its own galley and dining area, two spacious bedrooms, and a combination salon and office. An oversized platform at the rear, with a protective striped canopy and a public address system, served as a stage for the endless repetition of a seriocomic folk drama with which hundreds of thousands of Americans were to become familiar in the next two months. A typical day went like this:

The "Truman Special" rolled onto a siding at the station in Grand Rapids, Michigan, shortly before 7 o'clock on a Monday morning. Several hundred people lined the station platform, cheering and shouting a welcome. The local leaders and politicians—among them an ambitious newcomer to Democratic politics in Michigan, one G. Mennen Williams,[3] who was running for the governorship —packed into the President's car for handshakes and coffee, and then into open automobiles for a parade to the town square. Although it was the breakfast hour and Grand Rapids was a heavily Republican city, 25,000 people jammed into the area to hear and see the President and to give him a warm welcome.

Within an hour the train was under way again. At crossings and way stations knots of people were on hand to wave to the President as he whizzed by and get a wave in return. Several times the train stopped briefly at stations where crowds of a few hundred to a few thousand had assembled, and the President stepped out on the back platform to speak for four or five minutes and to shake some of the scores of hands thrust up eagerly toward him. He was genial and good-natured, full of quips and folksiness, and even when he warned them of the perils of sending another Republican Congress to Washington, or electing another Republican governor of Michigan, it was in a joshing, half-serious vein free of venom. Everywhere the people responded warmly, sometimes enthusiastically, occasionally with shouts and whistles of genuine fervor.

[3]No one thought he had much of a chance in his campaign, but he won that year and four successive terms as well—a Michigan record.

Detroit, where the party arrived about noon, wore a carnival aspect, with marching bands, flags flying, and masses of cheering people along the streets. This was labor's city, labor's holiday, and labor's candidate, and approximately a quarter million working men and their wives and children were packed in Cadillac Square to give the President a noisy workingman's greeting. And he gave them what they had come to hear.

Two years ago, he said, the people had dropped their guard and elected a Republican Congress.

"The Republicans promptly voted themselves a cut in taxes and voted you a cut in freedom. They put a danger-our weapon in the hands of the big corporations, in the shape of the Taft-Hartley law, I vetoed it, but they passed it over my veto."

If the same forces that created Taft-Hartley, he went on, are allowed to stay in power and to elect a Republican President, "labor can expect to be hit by a series of body blows—and if you stay at home as you did in 1946, and keep these reactionaries in power, you deserve every blow you get."

There were roars of assent and shouts of "Pour it on," "Give 'em hell, Harry!" The crowd was with him as he went on to excoriate "that do-nothing Eightieth Republican Congress" for high prices and for blocking minimum wage and Social Security improvements and low-cost housing legislation. He lambasted the "gluttons of privilege" in the Republican Party, and, making it clear he had Dewey in mind, said they were men "with a calculating machine where the heart ought to be."

The yells and applause coming wave upon wave filled Cadillac Square and rattled from radio sets in living rooms, union halls, taverns, and picnic grounds all across the United States. This was not just another Labor Day speech by a President. It was the opening attack in a go-for-broke election campaign. It *had* to be good. It *had* to go over. And it was aimed as much at New York, Pittsburgh, Dallas, and Seattle as it was at Detroit. In the anxiety-ridden Democratic strategy, this was *it*.

·   ·   ·

What happened? How did this greatest of political miracles come to pass?

The Presidential vote statistics are as follows:[4]

Candidate	Popular Vote	Electoral Vote	States
Truman	24,045,052	304	28
Dewey	21,896,927	189	16
Wallace	1,137,957	—	—
Thurmond	1,168,687	38	4
Others	240,594	—	—
Total	48,489,217	531	48

The vote for Congress was as follows, with figures in parentheses showing the previous membership:

	Democratic		Republican	
Senate	54	(45)	42	(51)
House	263	(188)	171	(246)

It was the closest Presidential election since 1916. Truman's margin over Dewey was 2,148,125. He won by a plurality, not by a majority. His percentage of the popular vote was 49.5; Dewey's, 45.1. In a general way, each man lost where he assumed he was strongest, and won where his prospects seemed thinnest. Dewey swept

[4]All figures from *The World Almanac, 1949.*

all of the industrial Northeast, from Maryland through Maine, except for Massachusetts and Rhode Island. This was traditional Democratic territory. Truman captured many of the important farm states, most notably Wisconsin, Iowa, and Colorado, which were traditionally Republican. In addition, he swept the whole tier of eleven western states (excluding Oregon), in which, though they are traditionally Democratic, the Republicans had confidently expected to make important gains. Thurmond deprived Truman of four states in the once-solid South—South Carolina, Alabama, Mississippi, and Louisiana. And Wallace certainly robbed him of New York (the Progressive Party total there was approximately twice Dewey's winning margin), and probably of New Jersey.

What were the factors in this upset?

There were many, but in this writer's view the controlling one was this: Truman had, in the November 1947 memorandum by Clifford and the political strategy board, a basic campaign strategy that was unique to his needs and to his capacities, and he stuck with it. It was a strategy for go-for-broke; of recognizing that he was the underdog and that he had little to lose and much to gain; of seizing the initiative and pressing it with every weapon and against all risks. His banner was the New Deal; his targets were familiar and well defined; and the obstacles were starkly and realistically portrayed. The strategy called for courage and persistence, which Truman supplied in absolute measure. He did not deviate essentially from his master plan throughout the campaign. The result was that he knew what he was doing every step of the way.

Three voting blocs supplied the margin for Truman's victory: labor, Negro (plus other minorities), and farm. Throughout the campaign Truman had emphasized day after day his fights with the Eightieth Congress over civil rights for the Negroes, housing, minimum wages, and his veto of the Taft-Hartley Act. When the votes were counted, he had carried the thirteen largest industrial cities, where labor and Negro votes are decisive, some by pluralities greater than Roosevelt's in 1944. This swelled his popular vote score. It was not enough to outbalance the Republican "upstate" vote in places like New York, Pennsylvania, and Michigan, which gave their electoral votes to Dewey, but it was sufficient in Ohio and Illinois, and possibly in California.

The tradition of the eleven Great Lakes and Plains states—the nation's biggest grocery basket—is Republican. Seven went for Dewey in 1944, and six for Willkie in 1940. Dewey, presuming on a revulsion against New Deal and postwar regimentation of the farmer, expected to sweep them all with the possible exception of Illinois and Minnesota. Instead, he took only five—Indiana, North and South Dakota, Nebraska, and Kansas. Iowa's swing behind Truman was, psychologically, the most crushing blow of all to the GOP. This was the very citadel of Republicanism, which had remained faithful since 1936. When Iowa defected to the Democrats in 1948, she took every other important farm and cattle state, except the aforementioned five, with her. It was a tribute to the efficacy of the grain-storage-bin issue and to a drastic mid-October break in farm prices. The farmers were riding a high crest of prosperity that year, but Truman frightened them into thinking that a Republican administration might take it away from them.

Another major factor was the contrast in campaign techniques and in the motivational appeals to the voters. The Truman campaign was positive, hard-hitting, and directed to the gut interests of the voters. He named names and places and gave chapter and verse (with whatever injury to the cause of accuracy) when he criticized something. And for every wrong and every fear, he had a palpable villain—the Eightieth Congress and, by extrapolation, Republican candidates and Republican office-holders in general. He gave the voters something to be "agin," which is the most powerful motivation of voter behavior.

By contrast, both Dewey's campaign and his personality were arid. He avoided direct controversy with his opponent. He was seldom specific or convincing when he elucidated the larger issues. Intellectually, his campaign was on a higher level than Truman's, just as it was in the matter of taste and decorum. By the same token it was overlaid with a palpable superciliousness. It was, said Clarence Buddington Kelland, national Republican committeeman from Arizona, "smug, arrogant, stupid. . . . It was a contemptuous campaign, contemptuous alike to our enemies and to our friends."

In fact, the demerits of the Dewey campaign technique may have bulked as large in the outcome as did the merits of the Truman technique. Jules Abels, in *Out of the Jaws of Victory*, pointed to what may have been a decisive and fatal factor in the Dewey operation in these words:

> The election was not thrown away by indifference or lack of effort. Preparation and more preparation had always been the distinguishing characteristic of Dewey and his team throughout his career. . . . The truth is that the type of campaign was the result not of careless, but of too careful and painstaking calculation. The Dewey campaign line was frozen into inertia not because it had been underthought, but because it had been overthought.

The consequence of this, as Abels and others have pointed out, was that when the first turbulence of a

Truman tide began to appear late in October, the Dewey crew, geared for smooth water only, were unable to trim sails in order to meet the rising seas.

Still another factor of importance was Truman's handling of the Russian blockade of Berlin. This had occurred in midsummer, and it had created an air of anxiety over the whole tenuous peace of Europe. The airlift that Truman had ordered seemed at first an act of desperation —which it probably was. But as the weeks wore on and tons of supplies continued to pour daily into Berlin, it became an act of defiance and of calling the Russian bluff. The country experienced a surge of pride, of which President Truman was the inevitable beneficiary. While foreign policy, per se, never became a flammable issue in the campaign, largely because of Dewey's forbearance, the dramatic success of the Berlin airlift greatly enhanced Truman's image as a leader.

Finally, in assessing the factors of the 1948 upset, there was the widespread miscalculation that the old New Deal dynamic had been buried in the grave with FDR. Dewey and his men believed that the concepts of the managerial revolution, so captivating to the Eastern elite in the postwar years, had captivated the rest of the country as well. In this new dogma the old political clichés, slogans, and alliances were written off as decadent, including particularly belief in the New Deal–forged coalition of labor, Negroes, city bosses, and Southern Bourbons. In its place was an aggressive, up-to-date, all-purpose conservatism of Republican hue with a base as wide as the continent.

They were wrong. Truman campaigned on an orthodox New Deal–Democratic platform. He held Dewey to a smaller proportion of the total vote (45.1 percent) than Dewey got running against Roosevelt in 1944 (45.8 per cent). If the figures are recast to lump the essentially

Democratic Wallace and Thurmond votes along with Truman's, the Democratic 1948 total becomes 54.9 percent, which is 1.6 percent above what FDR drew in 1944. In other words, it is clear that, instead of diminishing, the Democratic potential under Truman had grown.

Republican theorists in their postmortems attempted to explain Dewey's poor showing as attributable to Republican stay-at-homes who didn't bother to vote. Sam Lubell, in an expert analysis of the campaign for the *Saturday Evening Post* two months[5] after the election, came to a quite different conclusion:

> GOP victories in the industrial east were won less through new Republican adherents than by the apathy which kept much of the old FDR vote from the polls. Far from costing Dewey the election, the [Democratic] stay-at-homes may have saved him almost as crushing a defeat as Landon suffered in 1936.

At all events, Harry Truman was now President in his own right, his record was vindicated, and his leadership was open to no man's challenge. "You just have to take off your hat," the New York *Sun*, which rarely had said anything kind about him before, editorialized the day after election, "to a beaten man who refuses to stay licked! . . . The next few days will produce many long and labored explanations of what has happened. To us of the *Sun* there is no great mystery about it. Mr. Truman won because this is still a land which loves a scrapper, in which intestinal fortitude is still respected."

The President took all such accolades with becoming modesty. He set off for a rest at Key West—and within a week had summoned his aides to begin work on a new budget and State of the Union message.

[5]Issue of January 22, 1949.

Eisenhower in Office
ARTHUR LARSON

Generally speaking historians have been critical of the Eisenhower presidency. Liberal critics complain that not enough happened during these years, while conservatives berate the administration for not having returned to the policies of the 1920s. Actually, however, one might look at these years as a time of political rest between Democratic administrations. Arthur Larson, a former Eisenhower aide, in an obviously unobjective account, has tried to show the President's conception of his office, his major accomplishments, and has attempted to predict how history will view Eisenhower.

Reprinted by permission of Charles Scribner's Sons from *Eisenhower: The President Nobody Knew* by Arthur Larson. Copyright © 1968 Arthur Larson. (Title supplied by editor.)

President Eisenhower's distinctive "style" in the Presidency can be best understood in the light, once more, of three conscious principles with which he approached that office. These were: first, a profound—almost exaggerated—respect for the dignity of the office; second, a conviction that the principle of separation of powers required the President actually to impose restraints on himself because of the overwhelming power that the Presidency had acquired; and third, a belief that the incidental influence flowing from the Presidency itself should not be exploited to promote causes beyond those assigned to the President by the Constitution.

.   .   .

Because of the element of restraint running through all of these principles, it was tempting for Eisenhower's critics to try to apply to him the most ill-fitting label of all—"lack of leadership."

In September 1956, the President one afternoon treated me to a long dissertation on the subject of leadership. We were in the midst of the presidential campaign, and he had become irritated by Adlai Stevenson's repeated cracks about Eisenhower's weak leadership. Eisenhower's opinion of Stevenson by this time was at its lowest point. He recalled the first time he had ever heard of him. Stevenson was on a mission to Italy during the war. Eisenhower said the mission was a flop and "some of my friends there said—boy, we've got a guy here who's a real lemon." Stevenson's facility with words he recognized, but said that if that were a qualification for the Presidency "we ought to elect Ernest Hemingway."

The exposition on leadership triggered by Stevenson

culminated in Eisenhower's giving me his working definition of leadership, which contained two components: "Leadership is the ability to decide what is to be done, and then to get others to want to do it." As to both components, President Eisenhower's contribution to the presidential office was personal and in some respects unique.

With respect to the first, there is at last some indication that history will catch up with a fact that Eisenhower's close associates always took for granted: his capacity for prompt and definite decision-making was his most impressive quality. Murray Kempton, whose background is not known to include membership in any Eisenhower fan club, refers to him as "the President most superbly equipped for truly consequential decisions we may ever have had" ("The Underestimation of Dwight D. Eisenhower," *Esquire*, September 1967). If anyone has any doubt about this quality, he might consult Anthony Eden, for example, about the decision Eisenhower made that the Anglo-French-Israeli invasion of Suez would have to stop. Similarly crisp were the decisions to close out the Korean War, to abolish wartime price and wage controls, to land American troops in Lebanon, to send troops to Little Rock, and to turn the Congo crisis over to the United Nations.

· · ·

This decision-making ability was more than a matter of personal temperament. It was in a marked degree the product of confidence rooted in the most carefully organized staff and departmental system our government has yet seen. This administrative and organizational achievement is also coming to be recognized by responsible authorities, such as James McGregor Burns, as one of Eisenhower's most significant assets. At the time, and then in the early Kennedy period, there were those who ridiculed what they considered the excessive proliferation and formalization of staff work, attributed to an unwarranted carryover of methods from Eisenhower's Army background. But after the fiasco of the Bay of Pigs invasion, which in retrospect was carried out in a welter of misinformation and communications breakdowns that could never have occurred under the methodical Eisenhower procedures, there was less disposition to smile at the Eisenhower staff system.

The most conspicuous contrast between Eisenhower's administrative pattern and that of Kennedy and Johnson was in the use of the Cabinet, National Security Council, and Operations Coordinating Board. Under Eisenhower each of the three met faithfully every week. Kennedy promptly abolished the O.C.B., and convened the other two bodies only irregularly. Johnson also began by slighting the use of formal mechanisms—indeed, the N.S.C. was known to go without a meeting for six months at a time, during the most crucial phases of policy-making in the national security field, and the Cabinet met only thirteen times in 1965—but he later moved toward more systematic sessions, with the Cabinet meeting every two weeks.

•   •   •

The sheer educational function of these meetings was not the least of their values. Agendas were carefully planned. The post of Cabinet Secretary was created and was ably administered by Maxwell Rabb. A member was sometimes given an opportunity to make a formal half-hour presentation of some topic of importance in his field. These presentations were prepared with the utmost diligence. For example, on one occasion I was given a half-hour in Cabinet to present highlights of U.S.I.A. activities and needs. I used the most effective devices at the disposal of the world's largest communications machine, including smuggled-out film clips of heart-rending scenes from the Hungarian Revolution, films of dances in Southeast Asian villages depicting the evils of communism, anti-Communist comic books, and even little plastic phonographs, produced at a cost of fifty cents apiece, that we dropped by the thousands in 1957 into the Vietnamese back-country, where illiterate peasants could by turning a handle play little records containing messages from Diem. Needless to say, every member of the Cabinet had to have his turn at turning the handle. And so, powered by the members of the U.S. Cabinet, the scratchy voice of Diem filled the stately Cabinet Room with repeated appeals and assurances to his loyal people.

. . .

Some critics have extrapolated this Eisenhower performance into an indictment of general indecision and deficiency in leadership. Since I have been at some pains to emphasize Eisenhower's strength in decision-making and leadership in other connections, some reconciliation of these views is obviously needed.

My suggested explanation would return to my original distinction between domestic and foreign affairs. My examples of firm decision-making, effective leadership, and impressive results . . . have been and will be drawn largely from the realm of international relations, especially in keeping the peace. In this area Eisenhower knew exactly what he believed and where he was going. In the domestic area, however, he was admittedly inexperienced. Moreover, he started from a rather simplistic conservative base; on this, through exposure to the ideas of people like Secretary of Labor Mitchell, Secretary of Health, Education, and Welfare Marion Folsom, and

Under Secretary of HEW Nelson Rockefeller, and others, he erected the moderate liberalism of "Modern Republicanism." But this superstructure, of which the 1958 budget was partly symptomatic, was by no means as solid as the structure of convictions about world affairs that were entirely and intrinsically his.

• • •

The effectiveness of Eisenhower's methods, judged by the actual record of legislation achieved, becomes more apparent as the opportunity for making comparisons with subsequent Presidents increases. Of course, there is nothing in the Eisenhower record to compare with the spate of domestic legislation achieved during the honeymoon period of the Johnson administration, when the Democratic majority in both Houses was about two-to-one. But if the comparison is made with the Kennedy period, in which President Kennedy had surprising difficulty in getting cooperation from his recent colleagues, or with the later Johnson period, the Eisenhower achievement is more substantial than most people realize, given the fact that he had a Democratic Congress for three-fourths of his tenure. Let us take only the most difficult single legislative item confronting every President from year to year, that of foreign aid. President Eisenhower managed to get several foreign aid programs of $4 billion through Congress, but by 1967 the foreign aid appropriation had sunk to the all-time low of $2.295 billion. Even with allowance for a change in the content of "foreign aid," in proportion to the total national budget, which has more than doubled, the foreign aid figure has fallen to far below the Eisenhower level. Early in his administration Eisenhower got through Congress a $7-billion tax cut, and the most sweeping extension and liberalization of social security that had taken place up to that time.

Unemployment insurance legislation and workmen's compensation benefits were liberalized. The great federal highway program was initiated. Defense reorganization was achieved. The St. Lawrence Waterway was authorized. Successive Trade Agreements Acts were passed. If only the Republican 83rd Congress is considered, it is significant that out of eighty-three issues presented to Congress by the administration, Eisenhower won on seventy-four.

A significant but little-noticed footnote in this story is Eisenhower's record on using the veto and making it stick. From 1952 to 1959, through one Republican and two Democratic Congresses, President Eisenhower never had a veto overridden by the necessary two-thirds vote of each house of Congress. This remarkable record was finally broken in 1959, on a typical pork-barrel bill.

Eisenhower's concept of leadership, perfected during World War II, was the product of having to make not only generals but even Heads of State of the United States, England, France, and other allies work effectively in concert, armed only with such weapons as persuasion, patience, and firmness; armed also—it might be added—with a cool assurance in his own authority that would astonish some of his critics. Indeed, I remember being somewhat startled myself one day when he was recounting to me the tremendous arguments he used to have with Winston Churchill. The arguments usually stemmed from the fact that Churchill was a trial-and-error man, especially in wartime, said Eisenhower. Churchill always wanted to dash off here or there whenever an opportunity seemed to present itself—as against planning strategy in advance. "But it didn't really matter," concluded Eisenhower quietly, "because I was the boss."

• • •

President Eisenhower's standing in history will rest

mainly on this fact: in essentially the same stormy modern world that saw the Second World War under President Franklin D. Roosevelt, the Korean War under President Truman, the Bay of Pigs invasion under President Kennedy, and the Vietnam War and Dominican intervention under President Johnson, President Eisenhower closed out one war, the Korean War, and carried his country through eight difficult years without any war, large or small, and without any loss to Communist aggression.

As the years go by, the magnitude of this achievement will loom larger. The reason carries us back to this proposition: a President can only be judged relatively, and as the dreadful price of the failures of the Johnson foreign policy mounts higher, the comparative wisdom and skill of the Eisenhower years will stand out more brightly.

• • •

The principal answer, then, to the question, "What are the reasons for Eisenhower's success in keeping the peace?" is that he accurately sensed the new character of the international crisis-management task in a nuclear age. Several other contributing factors may be quickly listed. One is that Eisenhower, of all modern Presidents, was the most skillful in building and using the complex administrative structure of the Executive branch in such a way that the President had the fullest benefit of all its resources when making decisions. Another feature was his almost habitual inclination to insist that things be done through proper channels, by contrast with the rather disorganized decision-making process of some other modern Presidents. His insistence that threats to the peace be dealt with through the United Nations channels rather than through unilateral American action has been adduced as an unusually fortunate expression of that inclination.

Never losing sight of the prime objective of peace, Eisenhower managed to pursue two policies simultaneously that some people still think are incompatible: promoting better relations with the Russians and other Communists, and at the same time promoting the most effective defense arrangements against Communist aggression, principally through mutual security. Another key to his success was his advanced concept of national power—a complex blend of military strength and moral leadership, of national strength and international cooperation, through both alliances and the United Nations.

•   •   •

It is quite possible that we are going to witness a pendulum swing in the opinion of Eisenhower held by the sort of intellectuals who were his most consistent detractors for many years. The most significant indicator of this change is the article by Murray Kempton, the irreverent editor and columnist of the New York *Post,* in *Esquire* magazine for September 1967. The title of the article tells much of the story: "The Underestimation of Dwight D. Eisenhower." True, many of the Eisenhower qualities found by Murray Kempton to be underestimated are not exactly those aspired to by the 4-H Clubs or the Future Farmers of America. The picture that emerges is that of a man whose "cold intelligence," indeed whose "marvelous intelligence," was deliberately concealed behind a mask of assumed confusion, of which the ultimate expression was the garbled press conference. Moreover, in this portrait, Eisenhower was utterly unscrupulous, heartless in his relations with even his closest subordinates, and masterly in deception. But the most significant sentence of all is this:

> The Eisenhower who emerges here intermittently free
> from his habitual veils is the President most superbly
> equipped for truly consequential decision we may ever
> have had, a mind neither rash nor hesitant, free of the
> slightest concern for how things might look, indifferent
> to any sentiment, as calm when he was demonstrating
> the wisdom of leaving a bad situation alone as when he
> was moving to meet it on those occasions when he
> absolutely had to.

Murray Kempton concludes by vicariously confessing
the error of the original judgment of the intellectuals,
and in effect giving the signal for the new era in which
Eisenhower will be "in":

> He was the great tortoise upon whose back the world
> sat for eight years. We laughed at him; we talked wist-
> fully about moving; and all the while we never knew the
> cunning beneath the shell.

Murray Kempton's analysis, with its emphasis on Ma-
chiavellian deviousness, will shock many people, as it is
undoubtedly intended to, but at least it is more accurate
than the one it attempts to displace, that of bumbling
stupidity. By singling out Eisenhower's keen intelligence
and especially his superb capacity for making the big
decisions, Murray Kempton has given the pendulum a
hefty push in the right direction.

Some may think that I am here worrying too much
about the viewpoint of the intellectuals. There is a reason
for this. The great majority of people have always had a
good opinion of Eisenhower and his times. A Gallup poll
in January 1968, asking what living man Americans admired most in all the world, showed Eisenhower topping
the list. Moreover, with every year that passes, the Eisen-

hower years look relatively better, and the inclination to yearn for the "good old days of Eisenhower" becomes more and more prevalent. But if to this can be added the more mature long-range judgments of scholars, political philosophers, and professional historians, then Eisenhower's posture in history may well become an enviable one. Eisenhower himself has provided a good supply of source material for this reinvestigation in his two volumes on the White House years; indeed, Murray Kempton's unorthodox conclusions were apparently based upon a close though not pleasure-filled study of these volumes. I hope that the present book will add a few useful strokes to this emerging portrait. What is important is not so much a question of how "great" President Eisenhower was on some comparative scale, although, in my opinion, he unquestionably ranks among the great Presidents. What is important is that Eisenhower should be accurately understood for what he was and did in the Presidency. So far as Eisenhower is concerned, I am sure that he is not concerned about what adjective is applied to him. What he would most like to be said of him is that he achieved the highest objective of his or any other modern Presidency: in a nuclear world, teeming with violence on all sides, he successfully "waged peace" for the eight years of his incumbency.

McCarthyism as Mass Politics
MICHAEL ROGIN

*The early 1950s were years fraught with frustration and
Cold War tensions for the American people. Between
1950 and 1954 Wisconsin's Senator Joseph R. McCarthy
held the political spotlight and took advantage of these
fears. Earlier interpretations of McCarthyism tended to
stress psychological reasons for the movement. However,
recently scholars have begun to show that McCarthyism
was really part and parcel of American politics. Professor
Michael Rogin, a political scientist at the University of
California, Berkeley, was one of the first to bring this
fact to the surface.*

Reprinted from *The Intellectuals and McCarthy: The Radical
Specter* by Michael Rogin, by permission of The M.I.T. Press,
Cambridge, Massachusetts. Copyright © 1967 by The Massachusetts
Institute of Technology.

From 1950 through 1954, Joseph McCarthy disrupted the normal routine of American politics. But McCarthyism can best be understood as a product of that normal routine. McCarthy capitalized on popular concern over foreign policy, communism, and the Korean War, but the animus of McCarthyism had little to do with any less political or more developed *popular* anxieties. Instead it reflected the specific traumas of conservative Republican activists—internal Communist subversion, the New Deal, centralized government, left-wing intellectuals, and the corrupting influences of a cosmopolitan society. The resentments of these Republicans and the Senator's own talents were the driving forces behind the McCarthy movement.

Equally important, McCarthy gained the protection of politicians and other authorities uninvolved in or opposed to the politics motivating his ardent supporters. Leaders of the GOP saw in McCarthy a way back to national power after twenty years in the political wilderness. Aside from desiring political power, moderate Republicans feared that an attack on McCarthy would split their party. Eisenhower sought for long months to compromise with the Senator, as one would with any other politician. Senators, jealous of their prerogative were loath to interfere with a fellow senator. Newspapers, looking for good copy, publicized McCarthy's activities. When the political institutions that had fostered McCarthy turned against him, and when, with the end of the Korean War his political issue became less salient, McCarthy was reduced to insignificance.

Politics alone does not explain McCarthyism; but the relevant sociopsychology is that which underpins normal

American politics, not that of radicals and outsiders. Psychological insights are not relevant alone to the peculiar politics of the American Right. Equally important, the ease with which McCarthy harnessed himself to the everyday workings of mainstream politics illuminates the weaknesses of America's respectable politicians.

Attention to sociology and psychology must be concentrated within the political stratum, not among the populace as a whole. It is tempting to explain the hysteria with which McCarthy infected the country by the hysterical preoccupations of masses of people. But the masses did not levy an attack on their political leaders; the attack was made by a section of the political elite against another and was nurtured by the very elites under attack. The populace contributed to McCarthy's power primarily because it was worried about communism, Korea, and the cold war.

The analysis of McCarthyism presented here focuses on political issues, political activists, and the political structure. As an alternative to this interpretation of McCarthyism, the pluralists have suggested an analysis that goes further beneath the surface of American politics. To be sure, unlike La Follette and Hitler, McCarthy mobilized no cohesive, organized popular following. Nevertheless, for the pluralists the concept of mass politics captures both the flavor of McCarthy's appeals and the essence of his threat to American institutions.

·   ·   ·

The Context

The entry of the Senator from Wisconsin onto the political stage did not split apart a previously united Republican Party. The split in the GOP between the East and the western Middle West goes back decades before McCarthyism. In Populist and progressive days, the West North Central states were the center of liberal opposition to an eastern-dominated Republican Party. During the New Deal and World War II, the two wings of the Republican Party switched places. On "traditional economic issues" as well as on foreign policy, midwest Republicans had been more conservative than their eastern counterparts for a decade before McCarthyism. The midwest wing of the party had been more isolationist for perhaps half a century.

It was this wing that mobilized itself behind McCarthy. It supported him on the censure resolution in the Senate, and Republican businessmen in the Middle West were more sympathetic to McCarthyism than those in the East. McCarthy did not split apart an elite, the parts of which had been equally conservative before him. He rather capitalized on an existing liberal-conservative split within the existing Republican elite.

•　•　•

Democratic control of national politics added to Republican discontent. By 1952, the GOP had been out of power for twenty consecutive years. And Republicans were not accustomed to opposition; between 1856 and 1932 they failed to control the presidency for a total of only twenty years.

The international situation brought the frustrations of midwest conservatism to a head and at the same time seemed to offer a political issue and a way out. The new long-term importance of foreign policy reinforced an already powerfully moralistic political approach. Much as some progressives at the turn of the century had reacted with defensive moralism to the waves of immigrants, so conservatives now reacted to the Communist threat. There had not yet been time to become accustomed to the new situation.

Traditionally, the Middle West has been isolationist for both ethnic and geographic reasons. Many of the region's political leaders thought Roosevelt had forced the country into a war against Germany; now Truman seemed afraid to fight a much worse enemy. Communism represented to them the epitome of an alien world—athesim, immorality, destruction of the family, and socialism. But far from defeating this enemy or withdrawing from the outside world that it contaminated, the Democratic Party dealt in an ambiguous atmosphere of international involvement, limited war, and compromise with evil.

Communism in the abstract was threatening enough. The danger became concretized and symbolized by two traumatic events. The first of these was the "loss of China." The right wing insisted with a stridency born of inner doubt that only a failure to apply traditional American values and tactics could have caused this defeat. The loss of China was a loss of American potency; it could only cease to be frightening if those responsible were identified.

Following hard upon the loss of China came the Korean War. Wars in America often produce superpatriotism, and this in turn claims victims. Those suspected of opposing wars have often been the victims of 100 percent Americanism. But during the Korean War the superpatriots perceived the very prosecutors of the war as the ambivalent ones. This again was something new and reinforced right-wing Republican fears that the centers of power in the society were working against them. If Woodrow Wilson had not approved of all the excesses of the superpatriots during and following World War I, he at least approved of the war. In the Korean War, the powers that be seemed unenthusiastic; one had to seek support for superpatriotism elsewhere. This was fertile ground for McCarthy.

If China preoccupied conservative elites, the Korean War attracted the attention of the population as a whole. Here real fighting brought to a head amorphous cold war anxieties and intensified concern over communism. McCarthy's prominence coincides with the years of the Korean War. He made his famous Wheeling speech in February 1950, and as its impact appeared to be ending the Korean War began in June. Three years later a truce was signed, and a year after that the Senate censured McCarthy.

Less than 1 percent of a national sample interviewed in the early 1950's volunteered communism as something they worried about. Many more, however—34 percent—checked it off a checklist of things they had recently talked about. In addition, almost all families knew someone fighting in Korea. The poll data did not suggest a mass political uprising over the question of communism, but no more did it suggest the issue's political irrelevance.

•   •   •

The Ideology

. . . In their analysis of McCarthy's rhetoric, the pluralists have accepted the evaluation of McCarthyism presented by its proponents. Both the pluralists and the supporters of McCarthy agreed that McCarthyism was a democratic movement against the elite, that it was opposed to social pretension, that it represented a movement of morality in politics. If liberals have taken Populist rhetoric at face value and analyzed the movement in its own terms, the authors of *The New American Right* have done the same with McCarthyism. But I have argued that moralism was found as much on the Right as on the Left in pre-New Deal American politics and that appeals to the people have been a conservative weapon as well as a liberal one.

.   .   .

That McCarthy should be so widely viewed as a moral figure is no paradox to the pluralists. It is just in his cultivation of a political concern with good and evil that they find his relation to agrarian radicalism. But McCarthy attacked the traditional devils of the conservatives. Just as traditional conservatives had feared the intrusion of alien bureaucrats, alien social legislation, and alien agrarian radicals into their stable world, so McCarthy attacked communism. Godless radicals, intellectuals, and bureaucrats were targets of American conservatism many decades before McCarthyism. If he was more extreme than many conservatives, he was extreme within that tradition.

.   .   .

McCarthy's rhetoric was hardly principled; what principles there were had traditional conservative antecedents. Yet did not McCarthy attack traditional conservative institutions and defend the virtues of the plain people? How is this part of a traditional conservative approach?

In his Wheeling speech McCarthy attacked

> the traitorous actions of those men who have been treated so well by this Nation . . . who have had all the benefits that the wealthiest nation on earth has to offer —the finest homes, the finest college educations, and the finest jobs in Government we can give. . . . The bright

young men [in the State Department] who are born
with silver spoons in their mouths are the ones who
have been most traitorous. . . . [Acheson is a] pompous
diplomat in striped pants with a phony British accent.

Demonstrating his disdain for established institutions,
McCarthy appealed for classified information from State
Department employees. When Senator McClellan charged,
"Then you are advocating government by individual con-
science as against government by law," McCarthy replied,
"The issue is whether the people are entitled to the facts."

· · ·

But McCarthyism is alleged to be more than the exploits of a single man; it is said to reveal the stresses and
strains of the American social structure. Analysis of the
Senator and of the ideology he employed tells us little
about his reception. Did McCarthy's rhetoric in fact em-
bolden the masses to an attack on modern industrial
society? Did his "populist" rhetoric in fact attract ex-
radicals, or even ex-Democrats? Did the danger from
McCarthyism in fact flow from popular passions?

The Popular Following

In January 1954, a majority of the American population
approved of Senator McCarthy. For the next eleven
months, one third of the total population consistently
supported him; eliminate those with no opinion, and the
figure rises to 40 percent. (See table below.) This man,
terribly dangerous in the eyes of sophisticated observers
of American politics, had obtained the backing of millions of American people.

· · ·

McCARTHY'S POPULARITY IN THE GALLUP POLLS

Date	Favorable	Unfavorable	No Opinion
8/51	15%	22%	63%
4/53	19	22	59
6/53	35	30	35
8/53	34	42	24
1/54	50	29	21
3/54	46	36	18
4/54	38	46	16
5/54	35	49	16
6/54	34	45	21
8/54	36	51	13
11/54	35	46	19

Pluralist explanations focused on the "mass" character of McCarthy's appeal, challenging political leaders and cutting across party lines. But perhaps the single most important characteristic of supporters of McCarthy in the national opinion polls was their party affiliation; Democrats opposed McCarthy, and Republicans supported him. In April 1954, Democrats outnumbered Republicans more than two to one among those having an unfavorable opinion of McCarthy; 16 percent more Republicans than Democrats had a favorable opinion of the Senator. Totaling support for McCarthy in a series of Gallup Polls in the early 1950's reveals that 36 percent of the Democrats favored McCarthy while 44 percent opposed him. The comparable Republican figures were 61 percent for and 25 percent against. Democrats were 8 percentage points more against McCarthy than for him, Republicans 36 points more for him than against him. The total percentage point spread by party was 44 points. In these polls, as in the data reported by Polsby, no other single division of the population (by religion, class, education, and so forth) even approached the party split.

• • •

The polls provide us with considerable evidence about support for McCarthy, and reveal a broadly consistent pattern. When the influence of party is eliminated and often even when it is not, the lower socioeconomic groups, the more poorly educated, and the Catholics tended to support McCarthy, the big business and professional classes, the better educated, and the Protestants to oppose him. These differences cannot be dismissed as small or insignificant.

•   •   •

The data, in sum, do not suggest intense, active, mass involvement in a McCarthyite movement. Efforts to relate status frustrations and psychological malformations to McCarthyism have not proved very successful. Party and political issue cleavages structured McCarthy's support far more than pluralist hypotheses predicted. But the ignorant, the deprived, and the lower classes did support McCarthy, disproportionately.

•   •   •

What are we to conclude, then, about McCarthy's "mass" appeal? McCarthy's popular following apparently came from two distinct sources. There was first the traditional right wing of the midwestern Republican Party. Here was a group to whom McCarthy was a hero. He seemed to embody all their hopes and frustrations. These were the militants in the McCarthy movement. They worked hardest for him and were preoccupied with his general targets. To them, communism was not the whole story; their enemies were also the symbols of welfare capitalism and cosmopolitanism. These militants were mobilized by McCarthy's "mass" appeal. Yet this appeal had its greatest impact upon activists and elites, not upon the rank-and-file voters. And while McCarthy mobilized the Republican right wing, he did not change its traditional alliances. This was not a "new" American Right, but rather an old one with new enthusiasm and new power.

McCarthy's second source of popular support were those citizens mobilized because of communism and the Korean war. Concern over these issues throughout the society increased Republican strength, although this increase in popular support accrued not so much to McCarthy as to Eisenhower. McCarthy's strength here was not so much due to "mass," "populist," or "status" concerns as it was to the issues of communism, Korea, and the cold war. At the electoral level, there was little evidence that those allegedly more vulnerable to "mass" appeals were mobilized by McCarthy to change their traditional voting patterns.

•   •   •

The Elites

Conservative Republican activists provided McCarthy with the core of his enthusiastic support. In addition, groups ranging from Catholic Democratic workers to conservative southern senators contributed to McCarthy's power— the workers by verbal approval in the polls, the senators by their actions and silences in Washington. Having examined the contribution of the masses to McCarthyism, we turn now to the elites.

•   •   •

Most of those who mobilized behind McCarthy at the national level were conservative politicians and publicists, businessmen, and retired military leaders discontented with the New Deal, with bureaucracy, and with military policy. Of nineteen businessmen in the leadership of the Ten Million Americans mobilizing for McCarthy, only one had inherited wealth. These men had been part of the Republican right wing before McCarthy; they were joined by an occasional ex-agrarian radical like Burton Wheeler. Numbers of former Marxist intellectuals such as Louis Bundenz, James Burnham, and John Chamberlain became McCarthy publicists, but they lacked political influence or popular support. The political conservatism of the elite supporters of McCarthy ran the gamut of domestic and international policy.

* * *

Moderate Republicans were clearly less enthusiastic about McCarthy than the conservative wing of the party, yet without their support as well McCarthy would have been far less powerful. Eastern and moderate Republicans and their allies desired political power, and were also genuinely concerned about the Communist question. For a long time, they acquiesced in McCarthy's power. Viereck writes that McCarthy's targets were not the Communists, but those who had always stood for the rule of law and moderation, like Senator Watkins. By the time Watkins headed the committee which recommended McCarthy's censure, he was an anti-McCarthy pillar of strength. Earlier, however, he had been one of many Republican signers of a statement attacking the Truman administration and the Gillette committee investigation of McCarthy. The official Republican leadership did not sign this pro-McCarthy statement, but Watkins and other future McCarthy critics did.

* * *

The Senate in the McCarthy period was dominated by conservative Republicans and southern Democrats. About the former enough has already been said. The southern Democrats, embodying the institutional traditions of the

Senate, were unwilling to jeopardize the prerogatives of an individual senator or of the Senate as a whole. As McClellan of Arkansas remarked, "I do not want to do unto one of my colleagues what I would not want him to do unto me under the same circumstances." Southern senators were not pro McCarthy. But they were perhaps not unhappy to see their northern liberal colleagues and the Fair Deal administration embarrassed. (Reprisals from the populist masses hardly worried these safe-seat senators, particularly since southerners opposed this Catholic Republican in the polls.)

• • •

. . . institutional restraints and traditional allegiances may be alternatives to populist values, but they augmented McCarthy's power. The Senator capitalized on the routine politics of the political stratum—Senate traditions, executive-legislative rivalry, Republican party loyalty, anxiety to keep disputes out of the limelight. The general unwillingness of American politicians to assume responsibility for controversial actions became increasingly bizarre during the years of McCarthy's hegemony. This monumental insistence that politics continue as usual is surely a classic example of the banality of evil.

One would have hoped for a greater presidential appreciation of the dignity of the executive branch. One would have welcomed greater respect for the rule of law and for individual rights. Yet when Eisenhower finally fought for executive dignity and the rule of law, he had to resort to the instruments of publicity and open confrontation. Only with the publicity of the Army-McCarthy hearings did American politicians gain the confidence and integrity openly to oppose and then to ignore McCarthy.

Temporization and surrender having failed, the Eisenhower administration finally challenged McCarthy directly. Big businessmen who had heretofore supported the Senator began to back away, as he attacked their administration and an institution (the army) with which they identified. After the censure, the Senate "club" would have even less than usual to do with him. The respectable press, allegedly forced to publicize McCarthy's charges because they were news, stopped giving him coverage. Meanwhile, the Korean War had ended, and the tensions of the cold war eased. Observers agree that McCarthy's influence then reached a low point from which it never recovered. All McCarthy had left was the support of those in the populace basically hostile to American society. Undaunted, perhaps even encouraged by his attacks on the institutions in American life from which they were alienated these anomic "masses" continued to support the Wisconsin Senator. They had no more influence on his power than they had ever had. When McCarthy became a real antagonist of the institutions which conservatives respected—the Republican Party, the Senate, and the Army—he lost influence both among moderately conservative political leaders and among the population at large. As McCarthy became "radical," he lost his hold on American politics.

John Kennedy's Preparation for the Office of President
ARTHUR M. SCHLESINGER, JR.

John F. Kennedy's brief term as President has already provoked much controversy. As students delve further into his administration's policies, it appears that the young President had at least as much in common with past concepts as he did with future-oriented programs. Arthur Schlesinger, Jr., a prominent historian, served as Special Assistant to the President and is one of his staunchest defenders. In the following piece from his book A Thousand Days, *Schlesinger recounts how JFK began planning for his assumption of the Presidential office. The excerpt indicates the style and character the Kennedy administration would develop.*

Kennedy had a clear view of the kind of President he meant to be. Early in 1960 in a speech at the National Press Club he had sharply rejected a "restricted concept of the Presidency." The Chief Executive, Kennedy said, must be "the vital center of action in our whole scheme of government." The nature of the office demanded that "the President place himself in the very thick of the fight, that he care passionately about the fate of the people he leads, that he be willing to serve them at the risk of incurring their momentary displeasure . . . [that he] be prepared to exercise the fullest powers of his office—all that are specified and some that are not."

He was determined to be a strong President—and this meant for him, I believe, a President in the manner of Franklin Roosevelt. Kennedy was by no means an F.D.R. idolator. I think that he considered Roosevelt's policies, especially in foreign affairs, sometimes slapdash and sentimental. But he admired Roosevelt's ability to articulate the latent idealism of America, and he greatly envied Roosevelt's capacity to dominate a sprawling government filled with strong men eager to go into business on their own. He had mentioned to me a number of times the account of Roosevelt's fluid administrative methods in the last section of *The Coming of the New Deal*. The interregnum was now to provide a first test of Kennedy's own executive instincts and, in particular, of his skill in defending his personal authority against people striving, always for the best of motives, to contract his scope for choice.

·   ·   ·

Kennedy now had seventy-three days to go until inauguration. With all his resilience, the daily barnstorming in the general election added to the months of primary fights, had left him physically exhausted. In earlier times, a President-elect had four months to recover—and less to recover from. Palm Beach now promised him a badly needed respite.

• • •

The cabinet was only the beginning. There remained those vital levers of power in the policy-making jobs just below the cabinet, and these the new President had to control if he meant to command the executive branch. This was the domain of the Green Book and of Schedule C; here, presumably, 1200 places waited to be filled.

He had given Sargent Shriver the job of spying out the land and carrying through the occupation. Though people were sometimes deceived by Shriver's unruffled courtesy and easy amiability into dismissing him as something of a Boy Scout, the President-elect had confidence in his energy and imagination—a confidence Shriver had justified in the campaign and justified again now. He assembled a small group—Harris Wofford, the law school professor who had been with him during the campaign, Adam Yarmolinsky, a lawyer and foundation executive, Louis Martin, a Negro newspaperman who worked for the Democratic National Committee, Herbert Klotz, a New York businessman, and Thomas Farmer, a Washington lawyer. The Shriver staff immediately got on the telephone, and the great talent hunt began.

• • •

Kennedy, as usual, did not propose to give anyone exclusive authority. He therefore charged Shriver to work with Lawrence O'Brien, Ralph Dungan and Richard Donahue, who represented the political interest in appointments. In a sense, the Shriver group began with the positions and looked for people qualified to fill them, and the O'Brien group began with the people and looked for positions they were qualified to fill; one concentrated on recruitment and the other on placement. But the Shriver group understood the importance of finding people who would be loyal to the administration, and the O'Brien group understood the importance of finding people who would do a good job, so there was not too much friction between them. When disagreements arose, Yarmolinsky and Dungan were generally able to resolve them.

•   •   •

They worked night after night through November and December in offices provided by the Democratic National Committee, striving to make sure that all groups and regions were represented in their recommendations. They cast their net especially for women, for Negroes, for westerners. After a time, to be a Harvard graduate, a member of the Cambridge academic complex or an Irish Catholic was almost a handicap, surmountable only by offsetting evidence of spectacular excellence. (When McNamara's name first came up, there was concern until it was ascertained that he was a Protestant.) Politics mattered here a little more than in Palm Beach; but, if it was helpful to be a Democrat, it did not prove essential to have been a Kennedy Democrat. For a moment Ted Sorensen suggested a point system—so many points for having been with Kennedy before Wisconsin, so many for having been with Kennedy at Los Angeles, and so on—but the idea soon seemed irrelevant. As each cabinet member was appointed, a representative of the Shriver group provided him with a list of names carefully culled for his consideration. By mid-December, the first stage of the roundup was complete. Shriver now left for a holiday in the West Indies. Ralph Dungan took over the talent hunt, later continuing it from the White House.

Each department presented special circumstances. By the time Rusk was offered the State Department, for example, several crucial appointments in the foreign field —Stevenson, Bowles, Williams—had already been made. The next important place was the Under Secretary for Economic Affairs; and here the leading candidate was William C. Foster, a liberal-minded Republican businessman who had held important jobs in the Truman administration. But the prospect of a Republican appointment in addition to Dillon and McNamara seemed excessive, especially when a well-qualified Democrat was available. The well-qualified Democrat was George W. Ball, the Washington lawyer and long-time friend of Adlai Stevenson's who had been closely associated with Jean Monnet and the European Common Market. John Sharon carried word of Foster's impending designation to Stevenson, who called Senator Fulbright, then vacationing in Florida, and asked him to take the matter up with Kennedy. Fulbright went over to Palm Beach and suggested to the President-elect that giving Republicans so many top posts in State, Treasury and Defense was manifestly unfair to Democrats who had worked hard for his election. He added that this policy would create the impression that the Democratic party lacked men of sufficient stature. The argument proved effective. Kennedy withdrew the offer to Foster and appointed Ball; he later made Foster director of the Arms Control and Disarmament Agency.

The Ball argument also applied to the case of Averell Harriman. Kennedy had not known Harriman well, but he appreciated his staunch support before the convention and recognized that Harriman's record and experience in foreign affairs were unmatched in the nation. Still, both the President-elect and his brother remembered Harriman most as a political leader in New York, where he had not always been at his best, and they feared that, at sixty-nine and slightly deaf, he was too old for active service. When I once urged Harriman on Bobby, he said sympathetically, "Are you sure that giving Averell a job wouldn't be just an act of sentiment?" I said that I thought Harriman had one or two missions left under his belt. For some weeks after the election, Harriman heard nothing from Kennedy. In the meantime, the names of his less distinguished but more conservative contemporaries Lovett and McCloy were constantly in the newspapers as Kennedy advisers or possible Cabinet members. Harriman might well have wondered at this point whether he would not have done better to have stayed a Republican thirty-five years earlier instead of breaking with the New York Establishment and going over to Al Smith. But, if he felt this way, he gave no sign of it.

• • •

Harriman had many admirers on the New Frontier. In time Kennedy, though still a little skeptical, yielded to their enthusiasm and decided to appoint him as the State Department's roving ambassador. First, however, he asked Bill Walton to make Harriman promise to equip himself with a hearing aid. When Walton accomplished this delicate mission, the appointment went through.

Staffing the rest of the State Department involved complicated negotiations among Kennedy, Rusk, Bowles and the Shriver office. Kennedy wanted McGeorge Bundy somewhere on the top level of the State Department; for a moment in early December he had even wondered whether he might be a possible Secretary. He also thought that Walt W. Rostow, with his force and fertility of thought, should be counselor and chairman of the Policy Planning Council. But Rusk for various reasons resisted both Bundy and Rostow. From the institutional interests of the Department, this was a grievous error. Kennedy promptly decided to take them into the White House, Bundy as Special Assistant for National Security Affairs and Rostow as his deputy. The result was to give the White House an infusion of energy on foreign affairs with which the State Department would never in the next three years (even after Rostow finally got the policy planning job) quite catch up.

One reason for Rusk's opposition to Rostow was his desire to keep the post of counselor for his old colleague from Truman days George C. McGhee, who had served a decade before as Assistant Secretary for Near Eastern Affairs. The new Secretary had a temperamental preference for professionals both in Washington and in the field; and he was also rightly determined to rebuild the morale of the Foreign Service after the shocks of the Dulles-McCarthy era.

For its part, the Foreign Service was moving to take care of its own in the appointment of ambassadors and even of Assistant Secretaries. In late November, Loy Henderson, the dean of the career service and the retiring Deputy Under Secretary for Administration, suggested that the Department clear the appointment of seven senior Foreign Service officers as ambassadors to newly independent African states. Thomas Farmer of the Shriver staff intercepted the proposal and called it to the attention of Robert Kennedy. Africa, Farmer argued, was not a place for tired old men awaiting their pensions but for young officers with a career to make and even for people from outside the Foreign Service; it required an infusion of New Frontier spirit. Kennedy vigorously agreed, and, with the aid of Chester Bowles, the Henderson plan was killed. As for Assistant Secretaryships, the Shriver office did not accept the principle that they should necessarily go to professionals, noting that generals and admirals never dreamed of demanding to be made Assistant Secretaries in the Pentagon; and it darkly suspected that State was holding its Assistant Secretaryships down to the civil service salary level of GS-18 precisely in order to ward off outside appointments.

* * *

In the case of Defense, McNamara organized the personnel effort himself. He came to Washington early in December, set up an office in the Ford suite at the Shoreham Hotel and began to pursue a staff by round-the-clock telephoning all over the country. The President-elect and the Shriver office had suggested that he consider for Deputy Secretary Roswell Gilpatric, a New York lawyer and Democrat who had been Under Secretary of the Air Force under Thomas Finletter a decade before. After intensive inquiry, McNamara decided that Gilpatric, whom he had not yet met, was the man he wanted. He then began to track his quarry down, finally calling Gilpatric's country house on the eastern short of Maryland, waking his wife at six-fifteen in the morning and arranging to meet her husband later that day at the Baltimore airport. The two men sat in McNamara's automobile in a snowstorm discussing the terms of the appointment. Gilpatric was easy, resourceful and intelligent, and the partnership was immediately sealed.

* * *

And so, one after another, the departments began to acquire their new leaders. Robert Kennedy assembled a crack group from law schools and law offices to man the Department of Justice. Udall similarly worked out his own appointments for Interior. Hodges and Klotz produced the list for Commerce. Goldberg and Ribicoff consulted closely with Ralph Dungan in staffing Labor and Health, Education and Welfare. As the day of inauguration drew near, the Kennedy administration was beginning to take shape.

     •   •   •

While Kennedy was choosing the members of his administration, he was engaged in still another, and quite separate, effort to chart the main directions of policy. For this purpose, he set up a series of task forces in both domestic and foreign affairs.

The task force idea was hardly new in the Kennedy operation; Ted Sorensen had experimented with one variation or another in the pre-convention period. But the post-election task forces began with Stevenson's July proposal for a foreign policy report to be submitted early in the interregnum. A week after he told Stevenson to go ahead, Kennedy asked Stuart Symington to head a task force on the organization of the defense establishment; its members were Clark Clifford, Tom Finletter, Roswell Gilpatric, Fowler Hamilton and Marx Leva, all lawyers with defense experience. Up to this point, the Kennedy task forces seemed, in part at least, exercises in the propitiation of defeated rivals for the Democratic nomination. Then at the end of August he announced a committee to deal with national security policy; its chief members were Paul Nitze, David Bruce and Gilpatric, and it included no prominent politician. The Nitze and Stevenson assignments appeared to overlap, which somewhat irritated Stevenson. But Kennedy, in the mood of F.D.R., did not intend to confer on anyone exclusive rights to advise and perceived positive values in competition. So he placated Stevenson and looked forward to receiving both reports.

Before the election, Kennedy appointed four more task

forces—on natural resources, wheat, cotton and the use of agricultural surplus abroad. Meanwhile, Stevenson found himself more involved in the campaign than he had expected—he ended by delivering eighty-four speeches —and he therefore asked George Ball to work with him on his report. Eventually Ball prepared a first draft, discussed it with Fulbright, Bowles, Bruce and Finletter and brought it out to Libertyville the weekend before the election, where Stevenson put it into final shape. On November 14, John Sharon delivered the report to Kennedy in Palm Beach.

The report revolved in the main around Europe and reflected to a considerable degree Ball's preoccupations with NATO and with Atlantic trade policies. "The document has infirmities in emphasis, is uneven in treatment, and I apologize for its length," Stevenson wrote in a typically self-deprecatory cover letter. He thought there was too much detail on sharing the nuclear deterrent and not enough on disarmament and east-west negotiations, too much on strengthening the Atlantic Community and not enough on the problems of the underdeveloped world.

Yet, within its limits, it was an exceedingly able statement. Part I listed questions requiring immediate attention—the gold drain, the postponement of the discussions of the NATO deterrent, new initiatives in disarmament, assurances on Berlin, support of the Organization for Economic Cooperation and Development. Part II proposed long-term policies in the field of trade, economic development, NATO nuclear cooperation and arms control. Of particular interest was Ball's idea for a comprehensive economic bill which would combine new aid proposals with the delegation to the President of five-year authority to reduce tariffs by 50 percent across the board. Appendixes dealt with the problems of China, sub-Saharan Africa and the organization of the State Department. The memorandum concluded by recommending the formation of further task forces to deal with Latin America and Africa.

When Sharon handed Kennedy the document over the breakfast table at Palm Beach, he suggested that the President-elect might want to look first at the immediate recommendations. Kennedy promptly read Part I, throwing questions at Sharon as he turned the pages: How many presidential appointments would he have in State? Would Stevenson prepare a list of people whom he thought qualified for key. positions? How should the proposed peace or disarmament agency be set up? Were there Republicans who might be considered as head of this agency? ("He said," Sharon later reported to Stevenson, "that when one mentions the names of Rockefeller, Dillon and McCloy one has about exhausted the supply of 'good Republicans' and asked if we would come up with additional Republican names") What was the OECD doing—that is the kind of thing he had not been able to keep up with during the campaign? What about Cuba? How effective was the embargo? Would there be any chance of a 'rapprochement' with Castro after January 20 (Sharon noted that he asked this "rather rhetorically")? What about the problem of State Department allowances for ambassadors? When he finished Part I, Kennedy closed the volume and said, "Very good. Terrific. This is excellent. Just what I needed." Sharon then mentioned the recommendation for additional task forces, but Kennedy made no comment.

In the next few days, Ball and Sharon prepared answers to Kennedy's supplementary questions. In the meantime, the President-elect received the Nitze report on national security policy. This report provided an incisive analysis of the case for a more diversified defense posture. It then offered useful discussions of the relationship between defense policy and disarmament and of the balance-of-payments problem before concluding with some sketchy paragraphs on foreign policy. Actually the Stevenson and Nitze reports overlapped a good deal less than Stevenson may have feared or Nitze hoped. In any case, the two reports evidently convinced the President-elect that the task force approach would help in the interregnum. He told Sorensen to mobilize a broad range of domestic policy task forces, and on November 18 dictated a letter to Sharon proposing a list of further task forces for foreign policy.

He began with Latin America, saying that he wanted by early 1961 to have new proposals

> dramatic enough to catch the imagination of the people there. I would recommend appropriations called for by the authorization of last summer, $500 million [to carry out the Bogota Agreement] but that is hardly enough. What special steps could we take in the winter of 1961 or what recommendations could we make that would create an atmosphere of sympathy for Latin America? Who should chair the task force—what about Berle?

As for Africa:

> We should set up a similar task force. . . . What special proposals should we make in the winter of '61 in regard to raising the educational level, the fight against disease and improving the available food supply?

In addition:

> We should make a study of the State Department personnel in the field—how many speak the language; what steps can we take to improve that; the length of tenure

of the Department personnel in overseas assignments
—is it long enough; whether the Ambassador should be
given greater or lesser control over the various personnel and missions in his country—a related analysis
on the general competence and usefulness of the military aides in foreign service. We ought also to consider
how to get more Negroes into the Foreign Service.
We should study the whole USIA effort . . . How does
our effort in this field compare with the Communist
effort—Chinese as well as Russian—also Cairo's?
We should have a study of allowances for overseas personnel, not only in Foreign Service but for our other
overseas personnel. How do our allowances compare
with the British, French and Russian?
We should set up a task force on the distribution of our
agricultural surpluses abroad. . . . How much more
should be bilateral . . . multilateral? How can we put
more through the United Nations—maybe Hubert Humphrey could set up a task force on this.
We should prepare to set up an Arms Research Institute
and should get this in definite form so that we can send
it to the Congress early in the year. . . .
Each of these reports should not merely isolate the
problems and suggest generalized solutions, but should
incorporate particular suggestions which can be implemented by legislative action. These reports should be
completed by the end of December if possible.

He concluded by saying that he was sending copies of
this letter to Nitze, Bowles and Rostow. "I think it would
be helpful if you four could communicate and arrange
for the organization of these groups. I will rely on you,
John, to be in touch with everyone."

This letter expressed Kennedy's preliminary thoughts,
and in the end he did not send it (by accident, however,

a copy went to Bowles). On reflection he evidently decided that a four-headed directorate was too much. Instead, he called Sharon on November 23 and told him to set up task forces for Latin America, Africa, USIA and foreign economic policy. When Sharon asked him whether he wished these task forces to be coordinated with Nitze, Kennedy said emphatically, "No. There is no need to do that." He repeated this two days later, observing that, since Bowles had received a copy of the letter, he might head up one or two of the task forces, but "there is no need to work with Nitze." This was not that he liked Nitze less but that he liked a variety of advice more.

Almost immediately a new problem arose. Kennedy's senatorial staff was fighting an inevitable rearguard action against the horde of outsiders to whom their principal was suddenly yielding so much time and confidence. The staff regarded the Ball-Sharon operation with particular mistrust as a device to gain Stevenson a bridgehead in the midst of the Kennedy camp. Moreover, Sorensen undoubtedly felt that in the interests of order all the task force reports ought to clear through a single point. He therefore gave his own task force directive a broad interpretation and moved into foreign policy. As a result, when Sharon started phoning people for the Latin American and African task forces, he discovered that Sorensen and Goodwin had already signed them up. Fearing duplication and embarrassment, Ball and Sharon suspended their activity.

But, if Sorensen wanted to screen the task forces and their reports in the interests of order, Kennedy wanted the reports without screening in the interests of self-protection. When he learned of the situation, he said to Sharon, "I told Ted to turn all this over to you, that he was far too busy to take on this additional responsibility. I will see Ted this afternoon and clear this up with him.

You are the one who has charge of these task forces."
As soon as he had the word, Sorensen gracefully called
Sharon and arranged to turn over all the foreign policy
groups except three which were already at work—Latin
America, India and the overseas food program.

The task forces now shot forward in all directions. In
addition to the seven set up during the campaign, nineteen more were at work by mid-December—eleven in foreign policy and eight in domestic policy. Three further
domestic policy groups were added in January. Sharon
and Sorensen recruited what they regarded as the best
talent in the country—Roosa, Samuelson, Robert Triffin
and E. M. Bernstein on balance of payments; Galbraith,
Rostow, Robert Nathan, Max Millikan, Harlan Cleveland
on foreign economic policy; Berle and Lincoln Gordon
on Latin America; Samuelson, Seymour Harris and Walter Heller on the domestic economy; James M. Landis on
regulatory agencies; Paul Douglas on area redevelopment; Wilbur J. Cohen on social welfare; and many
others. The task force members volunteered their services; the expenses of the Ball-Sharon operation were met
by a grant from the Edgar Stern Foundation, while the
Sorensen operation was paid for by the Democratic National Committee. By inauguration twenty-four of the
twenty-nine groups had turned in their reports.

Kennedy did not read every word of every report, but
he looked at them all and studied some with care. Though
he sent most along to the cabinet or agency head who
would become responsible after January 20, he clearly
considered the task force effort as above all a service for
himself. Thus, when he appointed Rusk, he had Sorensen
pass on word to Sharon that "although he had designated
a Secretary of State, those working on the foreign policy
task forces were to understand that they had been com-
missioned by the President-elect and that their reports

and recommendations were to be channeled directly to him for consultation with the Secretary of State."

The documents varied in length and quality—the ones on Africa, foreign economic policy and regulatory agencies, for example, were small books; but, in sum, they represented an extraordinary canvass of vital issues by some of the nation's best specialists. The task force effort also equipped Kennedy with an instrument which he could use on special occasions during the transition; thus Ball and Sharon prepared the briefing papers which helped Kennedy to dazzle Eisenhower during their December meeting. It exposed him to people whom he might want in his administration and whom he had not met in the campaign (or had met perhaps only helping his opponents in the primaries); thus Ball and Gilpatric might not have come to his favorable attention if it had not been for the task forces. It encouraged his old staff to accept the necessity of enlarging his circle of advisers. It gave the men of the New Frontier an opportunity to work together in hammering out new policies. Out of the task force experience there came—for the President-elect and and for those close to him—a freshened sense of programs, of priorities and of people.

•   •   •

So the transition proceeded, with Kennedy presiding benignly over this diversity of activities and making sure that every thread was securely in his own hands. His second child, John, Jr., had been born at the end of November. The birth was difficult, and Jacqueline was making a slow recovery. This meant that she had to stay in Palm Beach, and it meant too that the President-elect spent as much time as he could there in the days between the election and the inauguration. The time passed placidly in Florida, punctuated by visitations from political dignitaries, press conferences (with Caroline teetering into the room in her mother's shoes), meetings with the new cabinet members and with the staff, swimming and golf.

The placidity was not complete. One Sunday morning in December, a man named Richard P. Pavlick parked his car in front of the Kennedy house to wait for the President-elect to drive to mass. He had loaded the car with seven sticks of dynamite, and his idea was to ram the Kennedy automobile and pull the switch that would set off the explosion. A letter later found on him said, "I believe that the Kennedys bought the Presidency and the Whitehouse and until he really became President it was my intention to remove him in the only way it was available to me." As Kennedy prepared to leave his house, Jacqueline and Caroline came to the door with him to say goodbye. Pavlick suddenly thought that he did not wish to kill him in front of his wife or children and decided instead to try again later. Though the Secret Service had received word from New Hampshire that Pavlick was uttering threats against the President-elect, they did not know until the following Wednesday that he had actually gone to Palm Beach. They immediately searched the town and the next day took him into custody.

On January 9, Kennedy came to Cambridge to address the Massachusetts Legislature and attend a meeting of the Harvard Board of Overseers. After luncheon he set up headquarters in my house on Irving Street. It was a gray, chilly day, but a good many spectators stood outside to catch a glimpse of the President-elect. He received a stream of visitors through the afternoon. McGeorge Bundy rode over on his bicycle to complete the arrangements which would bring him to the White House as Special Assistant for National Security Affairs. Abram Chayes agreed to go to Washington as Legal Adviser to the State Department. Jerome B. Wiesner discussed his assignment as Science Adviser. The task force on tax policy, with Stanley Surrey and Mortimer Caplin among its members, submitted its recommendations. In the middle of the afternoon, the President-elect decided he could wait no longer to select a chairman of the Atomic Energy Commission. Bundy promptly got Glenn Seaborg, Chancellor of the University of California, on the telephone, and Kennedy offered him the job.

At some point between interviews the President-elect turned to me, mentioned my conversation with Bobby in December and asked whether I was ready to work at the White House. I said, "I am not sure what I would be doing as Special Assistant, but, if you think I can help, I would like very much to come." He said, "Well, I am not sure what I will be doing as President either, but I am sure there will be enough at the White House to keep us both busy." I then asked whether this was firm enough in his mind for me to request leave from Harvard. He said, "Yes—but we won't say anything about this until Chester Bowles is confirmed. I don't want the Senate to think that I am bringing down the whole ADA."

He went south that evening and in the next few days began work on his inaugural address. Morning after morning, puffing a small cigar, a yellow, legal-sized pad of paper on his knees, he worked away, scribbling a few lines, crossing out others and then putting the sheets of paper on his already overflowing desk. Many people submitted suggestions, and Ted Sorensen gave his usual brilliant and loyal cooperation. Kennedy's hope was to strike a series of distinctive notes—to express the spirit of the postwar generation in politics, to summon America to new exertions and new initiatives, to summon the world to a new mood beyond the clichés of the cold war. (Walter Lippmann contributed to the last by suggesting, when he was shown a draft of the speech, that the references to the Soviet Union as the "enemy" should be replaced by "adversary"—a word which expressed Kennedy's intention more precisely and which he employed for the rest of his life.) As time passed, the speech took form. Then one day the President-elect stuffed the papers into his battered black briefcase and went north into the cold and snow.

On January 19 Kennedy held a final meeting with Eisenhower. They talked alone and then met with their advisers in the Cabinet Room. The discussion concentrated on points of crisis, and especially on the mounting difficulties in Laos. Eisenhower said that he had hoped that the South-East Asia Treaty Organization would take charge of the "controversy" but that the British and French did not want SEATO to act. Christian A. Herter, the retiring Secretary of State, added that he did not think that "the Soviet bloc" intended a major war in Southeast Asia but that they would continue to make trouble up to the brink. The United States, Herter recommended, must convince the communists of our intention to defend Laos, at the same time trying to persuade our allies to move with us in concert. If a political settlement could not be arranged in Laos, then this country must intervene. Eisenhower added that Laos was the key to all Southeast Asia. If the communists took Laos, they would bring "unbelievable pressure" on Thailand, Cambodia and South Vietnam. Laos, he said with solemnity, was so important that, if it reached the point where we could not persuade others to act with us, then he would be willing, "as a last desperate hope, to intervene unilaterally." He wondered for a moment why communist soldiers always seemed to have better morale than the soldiers "representing the democratic forces"; evidently there was something about "the communist philosophy" which gave their supporters "a certain inspiration and a certain dedication." Then he said that it would be fatal to permit the communists any part in a new Laotian regime, citing the experience of China and the Marshall mission.

Kennedy, listening quietly, finally asked how long it would take to put an American division into Laos. Secretary Gates replied: twelve to seventeen days from the United States, less if we used troops already in the Pacific. Gates went on to say that he was "exceedingly sanguine" about American capabilities for limited war; our forces were fully adequate to meet "any foreseeable test." Then he added that, while the United States was in excellent shape to meet one "limited war situation," it could not of course meet two limited war "situations" going on at the same time.

Secretary of the Treasury Anderson spoke about the balance-of-payments crisis. The erosion of the gold position, he said, was continuing unabated; measures had to be found to reverse the present trend.

The *tour d'horizon* reached Cuba. On November 18 Kennedy learned for the first time from Allen Dulles and Richard Bissell of CIA that on March 17, 1960, the Eisenhower administration had decided to equip and drill Cuban exiles for possible action against the Castro regime. The outgoing President now said that it was "the policy of this government" to aid anti-Castro guerrilla forces "to the utmost." At present, "we are helping train anti-Castro forces in Guatemala." Eisenhower recommended that "this effort be continued and accelerated."

Twenty-four hours later, as he took the presidential oath in the freezing cold of Capitol Plaza, these became John F. Kennedy's problems.

Tragic Figure
ERIC F. GOLDMAN

Lyndon Johnson came to the Presidency under the most tragic of circumstances. Replacing the slain John Kennedy, Johnson immediately began to implement the programs his predecessor had been working on, and by 1968 the Johnson administration could boast a much better legislative record then the previous administration. Yet LBJ was a most unpopular leader, and in the end this unpopularity forced him from the national political scene. Eric Goldman played a role in the administration and here gives his views as to why the President became a "tragic figure."

Excerpted from *The Tragedy of Lyndon Johnson* by Eric F. Goldman. Copyright © 1968, 1969 by Eric F. Goldman. Reprinted by permission of Alfred A. Knopf, Inc.

The rest of 1966, then 1967, and into 1968—the Johnson Presidency was more of the same, only more so.

The Vietnam War slogged on, increasingly taking mastery over Lyndon Johnson and most phases of his Administration. President Johnson became more and more the war chief, not the domestic leader. The key antipoverty program kept running into serious difficulties, as any such drive inevitably would. Even this effort, once so central to LBJ's interests and emotions, was finding no strong friend in the Oval Office.

·　·　·

Month by month President Johnson's control over Congress weakened. The attrition he had predicted was in full operation; of equal importance, President Johnson the war leader was much less in a position to halt the conservative swing. Even before the disastrous congressional election of 1966, the second, 1966 session of the Eighty-ninth Congress had proved a caricature of the majestic drive of social legislation in 1965. The Administration won approval for a few significant bills, including the Truth-in-Packaging Act, the measure creating a Transportation Department in the Cabinet, the first auto safety regulations, and authorization for a pioneering demonstration-cities program. Generally, it asked for little and got less.

The House and Senate created by the election of 1966 —the Ninetieth Congress—fully lived up to expectations. President Johnson showed a flash of his old wizardry in bringing a semblance of home rule to Washington, D.C., now two-thirds Negro. Throughout the post-World War II period, Presidents had tried to get such legislation past the Southerners and their G.O.P. allies in the House of Representatives. This time LBJ turned the trick by acting under the powers given to him by the Federal Reorganization Act of 1949, a move which does not require congressional approval but can be vetoed. He devised a form of home rule so additionally baited with delicacies for various congressional blocs that he split the opposition coalition and prevented the House from voting it down. The Administration also managed to squeeze through Congress the Public Television Act, Truth-in-Lending, the actual appropriation for the demonstration-cities program, a law banning discrimination in 80 percent of the nation's housing, and restrictions on interstate traffic in firearms. But during the Ninetieth Congress the White House was asking for still less and less and getting a steadily lowered percentage.

The two "must" items in the 1968 Administration program were a 10 percent tax surcharge and a crime-control bill; these were obtained only at a heavy price. The Crime Control Act gave much-needed aid to local law enforcement agencies, but it also authorized wiretapping on an alarmingly broad basis and included a provision designed to counteract Supreme Court decisions strengthening the rights of defendants in criminal cases. President Johnson achieved his tax surcharge only by bowing publicly to Congressman Wilbur Mills's demand for a $6 billion slash in federal expenditures, a blow at the whole Great Society edifice constructed in 1965.

The assaults on Lyndon Johnson mounted, unprecedented in their extent, their personal venom and the variety of people engaging in them. These days were not 1964 and 1965; in March 1968 LBJ's general approval rating in the Gallup poll plummeted to 36 percent—the lowest since Harry Truman's nadir of 32 percent. The only type of event that seemed to help President Johnson in the public opinion surveys was a hint of peace. He grew more and more bitter, especially at critics of the Vietnam War. He devoured memos given him by aides describing the name-calling directed at other war Presidents. Increasingly he was seeing himself as the lonely, traduced figure limned against history, resolutely doing right, grimly awaiting the verdict of the future.

As early as August 1966, at lunch with his old friend Merriman Smith, the senior White House correspondent of United Press International, President Johnson warned not to take it for granted that he would run again. He pointedly extolled the delights of life at the ranch and his eagerness to teach young people at the University of Texas. Beginning in late 1966, and then more and more frequently, his conversation included phrases like "in the time left to me" and "there is so much to do and so little time." He toured his ranch, paused at a great tree, remarked disconsolately, "This is the tree I expect to be buried under. When my grandchildren see this tree, I want them to think of me as the man who saved Asia and Vietnam, and who did something for the Negroes of this country." To a visitor at the White House, he told of his yearning to be "like an animal in the forest, to go to sleep under a tree, eat when I feel like it, read a bit, and after a while, do whatever I want to do." In January 1968 President Johnson put the blunt question to Horace Busby: "What do you think I ought to do?" He showed no surprise or annoyance at Busby's answer that he thought the President should withdraw.

On March 31, 1968, I and the millions of others sat at our television sets for a speech of President Johnson's that he had labeled as especially important. I had not seen LBJ on television for quite a while and I was shocked. My mind went back over the changes in his appearance and manner during his five years in the White

House. There were the days immediately after the assassination—the rangy, rugged figure, every antenna alert, trailed by edgy aides, looking around him with those hard, piercing eyes, always as if he were sniffing out friend and foe, always as if he were remembering that a smile or a handshake might be needed here or there. Although becoming the President in manner and appearance, he still seemed a bit the Texas senator playing another role, a touch flamboyant in dress, a trifle overzealous in being friendly, a little awkward in the aura of the Oval Office.

•   •   •

President Johnson talked for thirty-five minutes, then paused—he had not lost his pleasure in surprises—looked over to Lady Bird Johnson who was seated nearby, and said, "I shall not seek, and I will not accept, the nomination of my party for another term as your President."

He gave his reason. "For 37 years in the service of our nation, first as a Congressman, as a Senator and as Vice-President, and now as your President, I have put the unity of the people first. . . . In these times, as in times before, it is true that a house divided against itself . . . is a house that cannot stand.

"There is division in the American house now. There is divisiveness among us all tonight. And holding the trust that is mine, as President of all the people, I cannot disregard the peril. . . . [this brings to] the progress of the American people and the hope and the prospect of peace for all peoples." President Johnson did not mention another reason that was in every viewer's mind: almost certainly he could not have won the election of 1968.

•   •   •

The question of a President's just place in history is

complicated not only by shifts in opinion as time passes but by the inherent difficulties of the assessment process. Arthur Schlesinger, Sr., included among the men to whom he sent his 1962 questionnaire a sometime historian, President John Kennedy. The President was interested and started to fill out the ballot. Then he stopped. "How the hell can you tell?" he remarked. "Only the President himself can know what his real pressures and his real alternatives are. If you don't know that, how can you judge performance?" On other occasions, he commented that some of his predecessors were given credit for doing things to which they had no practical alternative. Historian-President John Kennedy's ultimate test seemed to be concrete achievements. It was an intriguing commentary on the problem of judging Presidents from a Chief Executive who, at least in domestic affairs during his short tenure, was far more notable as an opinion-builder than as an achiever of specific legislation.

Of course if Lyndon Johnson represented posterity, two of the basic questions he would ask of his Administration would be, Did the President serve as a President of national unity? Did he help bring the South back into the Union? No doubt his answer to both would be an affirmative so ringing it could be heard down any corridor of time. It should be noted that while President Johnson stated that he was withdrawing because of serious division in the United States, he did not blame himself for the split. The full context of the renunciation speech makes it plain that he was talking about the division brought about by other people, and a short while later he came close to declaring publicly that he had played no part in creating the rancorous atmosphere. It may be doubted that posterity will go along with this judgment.

The future will probably be much more ready to agree

with President Johnson's self-assessment on the question about the South. Unquestionably, in 1968 that region was closer to the mainstream of American life than it had been for decades. In considerable measure this resulted from long-running trends. Yet the fact that it was a Southern President who put through the tough civil rights laws made an enormous amount of difference. So too did Lyndon Johnson's skillful exploitation of this fact, the general thrust of his domestic policies, and his persistent, patient message to the South—delivered publicly and still more often privately—to let up on "nigra, nigra" and concentrate on economic and social advancement.

Central to any long-range judgment of the Johnson Administration is the President's decision to commit large-scale American combat forces in the Vietnam War. I happen to be among those who became convinced that the action was a grave mistake, unnecessary for the national security, inconsistent with a mature American foreign policy, disruptive of our world leadership, destructive of urgently needed domestic programs, and dubious in terms both of the American tradition and of Judeo-Christian morality. If this assessment—which seems to approximate that of much of educated America in late 1968—holds, the Vietnam War will certainly prove a heavy drag on the LBJ reputation.

Just how heavy is quite a different matter. Other Presidents called great or near-great today made moves in foreign policy which are now generally considered serious errors—whether Theodore Roosevelt's imperialist gasconading in Latin America and Asia, Woodrow Wilson's Sunday-schoolish peacemaking after World War I or John Kennedy's bloody fiasco at the Bay of Pigs. But in the passage of time, the specific was submerged in the general memory of the man. If President Johnson or his successor brings the Vietnam War to an end without much further damage, in time a kindly haze may obscure the pointless clomp of American soldiers across a defenseless civilization, even napalm and what amounts to an American defeat.

This is more possible because the future might emphasize a consideration which President Johnson stressed in private and intimated in public. In a sense, he inherited the Vietnam commitment. Three previous Chief Executives—of different parties and foreign policy attitudes— had increased the American noncombat involvement in the area. At least two of these Presidents believed that preventing South Vietnam from falling under Communist rule was important to the national security of the United States. None faced a situation in which he had to decide whether the area was important enough to enter the fighting war. Lyndon Johnson was the Chief Executive who had to make that choice. Another generation may decide that he made an error prepared for by his predecessors and one which any one of them might have committed.

And always there is the possibility which many anti-LBJ commentators of the 1960's simply refused to entertain. The Vietnam intervention might *not* have been a mistake; President Johnson may have a point when he says, Let the future decide. He intervened militarily in South Vietnam because he believed that move was the only alternative to a major threat to the security of the United States. Without America in the fighting, South Vietnam would have come under Communist control, he was convinced; this would be followed by a gradual fall of most of Asia to Communism, the domination of that continent by a hostile and potentially powerful China and—because China had not been warned off—by ultimate war between it and the United States. If a President

other than Lyndon Johnson should accept a compromise
Vietnam peace which was followed by such a chain of
developments, Lyndon Johnson would be more than for-
given: he would emerge a figure of Churchillian stature,
a wise, courageous voice crying out in a crowd of timid
and myopic men.

The President's place in the long sweep of American
domestic affairs can be assessed with much more assurance. Three times in the twentieth century the United
States has faced the harsh facts of an industrializing,
urbanizing civilization—at the beginning of the century,
under Theodore Roosevelt and Woodrow Wilson; after
the crash of 1929, under Franklin Roosevelt; and then,
slowly, in the period following World War II.

The 1930's were *sui generis*. The urgency was unique;
so too was the public mood. The situations in the early
1900's and after World War II were much more alike.
In both instances, there was little sense that the country
was falling apart. National opinion, jabbed by a zealous
left and troubled by the arguments of a dogged right,
was slowly forming around the proposition that the general population was being given too little access to economic and social opportunity. More laws were needed;
the President ought to lead Congress in getting them.

At the start of the century Theodore Roosevelt bounded
into the White House, caught up the strands of dissi-
dence, wove them into an attractive pattern. America of
the early 1900's did not easily dismiss an agitator who
bore one of the nation's most aristocratic names, who
could charm a Sunday school class or lead a regiment,
turn out historical essays or lasso a steer, and who, in
addition, happened to be President of the United States.
"Teddy," the journalist William Allen White observed,
"was reform in a derby, the gayest, cockiest, most fashionable derby you ever saw." TR moved few bills through

Congress but he prepared the way for Woodrow Wilson who, without derby or gaiety, had the roused public opinion, the votes in Congress, and the Covenanter certitudes to grind the bills through the House and the Senate.

After World War II, the process began all over again. New needs—whether money for schools or action on urban transportation or justice for Negroes—were pressing. The opinion kept building, the opposition kept fighting, and another generation of leaders prepared the way for another wave of action. Harry Truman, his expletives and vetoes poised, fought off a Congress that yearned to turn back. Dwight Eisenhower, before he drifted into his second somnolent term, led the Republican party into some accommodation with the day. John Kennedy appeared, a second Theodore Roosevelt, associating social change with vigor and glamour and the mischievous cocked eye, legislating little but educating many. Then Lyndon Johnson, the cloakroom operator, re-enacted the presbyter-professor Woodrow Wilson. He too seized the moment to execute the decade's needs—seized it so firmly and wrung it so hard that he built a monument to himself in that 1965 Congress which wrote into law almost everything which the public had decided was long past due.

•   •   •

Probably—but all this is in the murky realm of speculation. There remains a hard, clear fact. Lyndon Johnson entered the White House unhailed, and functioned in it unloved. Only once did warmth and a degree of affection go out to him—when he told the country he was leaving the Presidency.

What went wrong? Obviously LBJ was an able, hardworking President, eager to serve the interests of the American people, more than eager to win their camaraderie. He tried desperately hard, and he delivered in important respects. In the anti-LBJ atmosphere of the 1960's, it is only fair to call the roll. Lyndon Johnson did take over the Presidency at a moment of national emotional disarray and conduct a skillful transition. He did win the election in his own name and win it by a huge majority. He did put through Congress a powerhouse program of legislation, almost all of which was widely applauded. He did run an Administration which functioned without major corruption and in many key posts, was manned by officials of unusually high caliber. Time after time, Americans have judged their Chief Executives primarily by one criterion: What happened to bread-and-butter living during the Administrations? LBJ presided over an America that—without a single break of as much as a month—was the most generally prosperous nation in all of man's five thousand years of recorded history.

What went so wrong? White House aides kept telling President Johnson that the whole source of the public's disaffection was his courageous stand on Vietnam. Well before I resigned, I became accustomed to the litany. Any war creates frustration and resentments, and discontent is always directed at the leader. Abraham Lincoln himself was assailed with unbridled vehemence. Modern limited wars, with their especially frustrating quality, exacerbate these public feelings.

All this was consoling to the President, but three stubborn facts remained. There was that "image crisis" of 1965 when, at the height of LBJ's success and before foreign policy issues were central, the widespread distaste was plain. Moreover, American wars have not usually rendered Chief Executives unpopular in their own time. On the contrary, as Commander in Chief the President has generally proved a rallying point for support and enthusiasm. Finally, important elements in the disaffection appeared to have little to do with Vietnam. Many Americans were snappish about Lyndon Johnson not so much because they were positive he was wrong on Vietnam but because they believed he was the kind of man who was quite capable of making a bad mistake in foreign or any other kind of policy, and having made it, of not admitting it or moving to correct it.

During the campaign of 1964, when the evidence indicated both that President Johnson would win easily and that the trend was as much anti-Goldwater as pro-Johnson, the President would remark querulously to visitors, "Why don't people like me?" One guest, too old to be concerned about preferment by the White House and enough of a Washington character to get away with irreverence, answered the question. He said, "Because, Mr. President, you are not a very likable man." Bald as it is, this was a major part of Lyndon Johnson's problem with the American people. The fact that he was not a very likable man could not be concealed from the public despite all the arduous efforts of his friends and aides, myself included, who wanted so much to believe otherwise and who did their damnedest to present him in a way that would convince themselves and the country.

• • •

Always fighting off the devils of insecurity, Lyndon Johnson was vain, not proud; boomerish, not confident; for the most part, grandiose, not grand, in conceiving his programs, and grandiloquent, not eloquent, in expressing them. Gnawed by his inner needs, he turned his marriage with a woman he deeply loved into a near-tyranny; a congressional career shot through with instincts for the national good into a feral pursuit of personal domination; a Presidency marked by a broad streak of idealism into what so often appeared to be an exercise in self-interest.

Self-interest—here is the only-too-well-recognized part of the LBJ story. As a student of history, I have read a great deal about men in political or nonpolitical life who are said to have been motivated not by dedication to ideas, passion for ideals, emotional responses to human situations but merely by self-aggrandizement. I have never really believed the analyses. I think over the array of people I have known well, many of whom are not particularly noble, and they have never seemed totally dominated by self-interest. Neither was Lyndon Johnson—and perhaps Lyndon Johnson especially was not.

But President Johnson, lashed by his insecurity, fought his better angels harder than any man I have ever known. It was a hostile world out there, far removed from Mother and Texas and his trusted buddies; you had to keep handling it. Most of the time he appeared afraid to rely on anything except the doctrine that life and politics and government are simply a conflict and confluence between the self-interest of various people and groups. He seemed driven to function as Machiavelli in a Stetson, part of which posture was to keep assuring everyone that rugged he-men in Stetsons would never be Machiavellis. So lacking in confidence, so defensive and wary, those eyes always searching around the room or across the country, he was determined that nobody or no circumstance would get the better of him by playing to his strong personal ideals and emotions. This attitude led to increasing justification for, and ever more extended practice of, his natural bent toward exorbitant secretiveness, labyrinthine maneuverings, a sanctimonious glossing over of reality, the plain withholding of truth which had no need of being withheld and the plain distortion of truth which, at least in part, was much better stated and done with.

The American public delights in ferreting out the shortcomings of its Chief Executives. All the time the men were in the Oval Office, a nation of President-watchers knew that Franklin Roosevelt was an incorrigible political gamesman; that Harry Truman could sound like the village calliope; that Dwight Eisenhower often tried to grin away massive problems; that John Kennedy had some of the frailties as well as the assets of the charmer. But if the American public is endlessly critical, it has also shown itself remarkably indulgent, provided that the virtues of the President appear to outweigh his defects. In this balance, the critical weight is the judgment that at bottom the President is a "good man," fundamentally decent, putting the welfare of the nation first in all of his really important considerations. Most Americans have believed this to be true of every President from the thirties through 1963. It was Lyndon Johnson's basic difficulty that he did not leave such an impression.

•   •   •

In foreign policy, the pervasive suspicion meant that LBJ was given little benefit of the doubt. Worried citizens, facing World War I, World War II or the Korean War, were inclined to hesitate before opposing the President. He was a good man doing his best, with greater knowledge of the situation than themselves; the odds were that he was right. Few worried citizens hesitated to oppose Lyndon Johnson's Vietnam policy, and once in opposition, their attacks came with special virulence. During my White House period, I was naturally in communication with endless critics of the war. With a handful of exceptions, all assumed—usually having granted somewhat grudgingly that Lyndon Johnson really cared whether men were dying—that his moves for peace would be shaped by his reading of his own political interests.

•   •   •

Among all age groups, the idealism which had helped sweep along the FDR program, and which LBJ kept trying to touch, was turning to a far more demanding program. That talk of quality in American life, in addition to material quantity, had substance. The emerging reformism sought not simply better pay for teachers and more school buildings but a drastically altered educational atmosphere and curriculum; not simply Medicare for the grandparents but aid for the aged fitted into a whole social welfare structure that found a way of asserting human dignity. A new era, a new pattern of social and political forces, a new agenda—President Johnson, acting upon the kind of consensus domestic policy that would merely codify and expand the 1930's, was about as contemporary as padded shoulders, a night at the radio and Clark Gable.

Again in the mood of the New Deal period, the President assumed that foreign policy was something you had, like measles, and got over with as quickly as possible. Suddenly forced to confront the world, he grasped into the past and laid hold of an attic doctrine which included even apostrophes to the flag and international deeds of derring-do. At the farthest stretch of his modernity, he reached thinking that was basically of a Cold War type. In the 1960's, a considerable and influential part of the public simply would not go along with such foreign policy.

They assumed that international affairs were a constant high priority subject. Contemptuous of talk of the flag and derring-do, they were alarmed by what they were sure were outmoded Cold War attitudes of crusading against Communism and of joining with foreign regimes which sought to use military power to stop social change. Out of a sense of guilt over America's past role in world affairs, a sympathy with the aspirations of underdeveloped nations, and fear of nuclear holocaust, they favored accommodation, compromise, political and economic rather than military moves. A Chicago manufacturer caught perfectly the disjunction between President Johnson and this opinion when he wrote me: "The President may be right in going into Vietnam. I can't make up my mind. What really worries me is the kind of thinking that led to his decision." The letter added: "Perhaps it's because I am 37 and he is 57."

The Chicago manufacturer was a Metroamerican. Constantly growing in influence in determining national opinion, Metroamerica was increasingly the focal point of the abrasion between President Johnson and his public. There the uneasiness with him as a human being was greatest; the dissatisfaction with his domestic and foreign policies, the strongest. There, too, was the chief gathering place and the projectory for a disaffection that joined the criticisms of the man and of his programs and added a third —one concerning "style"—which really had little to do with the other two but increased the virulence of both of them.

Some of the attitudes and fashions of Metroamerica were hardly ennobling. They represented little more than the pennyante snobbery of parochialism, like the Texas lady—I wish I could discover her name, she belongs in a history of the period—who listened to Lyndon Johnson deliver a speech shortly after he entered the White House and commented, "It's good to have a President who speaks without an accent." Many of Metroamerica's standards, parochial or not, were a good deal more praised than practiced. But attitudes and fashions Metroamerica had, and they were applied to Lyndon Johnson with all the rigidity and venom of any newly emerging class.

It is a truism to state that by the 1960's mass communications had largely obliterated local differences in the United States. The statement is fundamentally accurate but in one important respect it is off base. The Metroamerican—whether he lived in New York, Chicago, San Francisco or Houston—tended to take his style of life from the successful classes of the Northeast: to him, everything else was darkest boorishness. Lyndon Johnson used to say in the Senate days, "No Southerner can be elected President." He would have been right if he had said, No Southerner, and particularly no middle-aged Texan from a middle-class background, could win the Presidency in the 1960's and maintain peace with Metroamerica. Mention almost any of the personal habits of Lyndon Johnson—the big white Continental or the sentimentalities—and you bring up something that made Metroamerica snicker.

And always there remained the Kennedys. After his election victory in 1964, President Johnson may have eliminated virtually all references to President Kennedy in his public remarks. He could not eliminate the fact that his predecessor was legend and that the legend was a restive, bitter, yearning element in the whole life of the generation, especially in Metroamerica. Lyndon Johnson had become President by virtue of the death of John Kennedy, and that death continued a major determinant of his Presidency. Not only had the urge to be different from JFK affected what LBJ did and did not do day after day; every difficulty of President Johnson with public opinion was magnified by the Kennedy legend, which made John Kennedy precisely the opposite of all the things that Americans, and especially Metroamericans, thought were wrong with Lyndon Johnson. And throughout the Johnson Administration the JFK legend gradually, but more and more completely, blended with the day-by-day activities of Senator Robert F. Kennedy.

Everything LBJ did, everywhere he turned, there was

RFK, pointing up another element in President Johnson's problem with his public. Robert Kennedy was the looks, the voice, the long stabbing finger of the martyred President. He was youthfulness, the North, celebrities, the new-mode family, Hickory Hill always full of interesting people, canoeing into high rapids and then sitting quoting Aeschylus, the Metroamerican's unabashed ambition and the Metroamerican's savor for the throw-away manner. He was post-New Deal politics, talking the quality of American civilization, moving increasingly toward outright opposition to the Vietnam War, centering his domestic legislative program on the cities, probing for a voting coalition based not on the old economic lines but on the new sense of alienation bringing together Negroes, young people, intellectuals and suburbanites who had acquired money at the price of malaise.

Sixty-six days after President Johnson's speech of withdrawal, on the night Senator Kennedy scored an important win in his long-shot campaign for the Democratic presidential nomination, more crazed bullets had been fired in Los Angeles. An RFK legend had immediately started forming, an idealization of the younger brother that joined perfectly with the JFK legend. Robert Kennedy, so many were so sure, would certainly have been elected President, ended the war, lifted the Negro, given purpose to youth and to suburbia, brought about an America cleansed and reinvigorated.

The Johnson years were clamped in grim parenthesis of happenstance. Lyndon Johnson came into the White House to the caissons for John Kennedy and he left it to the dirges for Robert Kennedy. He entered and he departed with a Kennedy uppermost in the national thinking and emotions, and perhaps he had not been much elsewhere during his five years in the White House.

In the final months of his Presidency, Lyndon Johnson

kept shifting in mood. At times he was bitter and petulant at his repudiation by the nation; at times philosophical, almost serene, confidently awaiting the verdict of the future.

Never was he the mere lame duck. Still stalking, endlessly stalking the Oval Office, he kept doing things, seeking to shore up his domestic achievements and to bring his foreign policy one step further along what he considered a proper path. Strange, complex man in strange, complex circumstances—too astute not to know how seriously things had gone wrong, too limited by background and by self to grasp what had really happened.

No one who worked in Lyndon Johnson's White House can fail to have been moved by the dedication, the abilities and the force he brought to the Presidency of the United States. It was just as difficult not to recall the lines from one of his copybook poems, John Greenleaf Whittier's *Maud Muller:* "For of all sad words of tongue or pen, The saddest are these: 'It might have been!'" The story of Lyndon Johnson's Presidency is a story of tragedy in the ancient haunting sense of the word, the strong man overwhelmed by forces, from within and without.

Hurtled into the leadership of the United States and of the free world in the fiercely demanding 1960's, he was not ready for them. Seriously flawed in personal characteristics, his virtues could not transform him into an engaging public figure. Functioning in the shadow of a relentless legend, he was beset by a host of attitudes which that legend continuously fed.

Lyndon Johnson could win votes, enact laws, maneuver mountains. He could not acquire that something beyond, which cannot be won, enacted or maneuvered but must be freely given. He could not command that respect, affection and rapport which alone permit an American

President genuinely to lead. In his periods of triumph and of downsweep, in peace as in war, he stood the tragic figure of an extraordinarily gifted President who was the wrong man from the wrong place at the wrong time under the wrong circumstances.

The Inevitability of Richard M. Nixon
THEODORE H. WHITE

Richard M. Nixon waited a long time to become President. Serving for eight years as Vice President, then losing the 1960 election, and finally failing in a comeback attempt in California politics, it seemed that he was politically through by the mid 1960s. However, by 1968 it was obvious that Nixon had regained his strength, so much so in fact that he won the election. Theodore White, who has written a series of books on the Presidential elections of the 1960s has analyzed how the candidate Nixon was able to secure the nomination. In White's estimation much of the explanation lies in the smoothness of the operation as well as in the use of the media.

From *The Making of the President 1968* by Theodore H. White. Copyright © 1969 by Theodore H. White. Reprinted by permission of the author and Atheneum Publishers.

All through the spring months, Richard Nixon moved on a calendar of his own.

Students mobilized in February and March; Romney withdrew; Kennedy entered; Rockefeller dropped out, then entered again; ambition refreshed itself in Ronald Reagan; the assassinations happened, the first an act of racial barbarism, the second totally incomprehensible; men died by the thousands in Vietnam; riots stained the nation at home.

But Nixon persisted, undeviatingly, in the course he had set himself in the beginning; and so we must turn back to January to pick up the unfolding of his primary strategy first, next his media strategy, then his delegate hunt and organization, and finally once more to the man himself.

The nation's turmoil of spirit seemed best reflected in the open war in the Democratic Party; yet the placid quality of the Republican contender's campaign reflected his different reading of the turmoil—that millions of Americans yearned for quiet. It was in these spring months that I was talking to Ray Price, the soft-spoken writer who so deeply influences Nixon's thinking on the liberal side, and he explained the thrust of his leader's thinking. "We're in a period when people want a change, but they're all caught in this terrible complex of fears, almost unstructured fears, amorphous fears. They live in a welter of frustrations, and this is a year for the outs, for the people who associate themselves with stability. But it's got to be a dynamic stability, not a status-quo stability, and that's what we're trying to communicate in our general posture."

To communicate a promise of stability and a sense of

dynamism at the same time is one of the most delicate of all political feats. In his later election campaign Richard Nixon rested his thrust on stability rather than on dynamism and, thus, refusing the dynamics of either the left or the right, almost lost the election. But this was the theory and philosophy of his inner court, and the yet unwritten script of his administration-to-be. "Nixon," said Price at another time, "is neither a conservative nor a liberal, he is a centrist." And it was, retrospectively, as a centrist that he faced the succession of tactical problems which presented themselves in his takeover of the Republican Party in 1968.

The situation was clear as early as January of the year: The country was torn, the consensus of Lyndon Johnson had dissolved, the administration had lost the confidence of the American people, the apparently hopeless war went on. The situation insisted on alternative national leadership. Historically and practically, the alternative had to be a candidate of the Republican Party. But the Republican Party was also split. How, then, to capture the Republican Party? More specifically—how was Nixon to capture that Party without tearing it apart as Goldwater and Rockefeller had done in 1964? No one could claim greater credit from the Party's non-commissioned officers than Richard M. Nixon. Had it been a vote within an army, the Party regulars would have chosen Richard Nixon as their corps commander. Yet he was a corps commander who had not won a victory on his own since 1950, eighteen years before.

Cherishing Nixon as they did, the Republican leaders cherished victory more. The object of politics is to gain power; and in this year of opportunity they could not afford to squander the chance on a permanent loser. Thus, the first tactical problem of the Nixon camp was to erase, as he stated it, "the loser's image." This meant fighting in open primaries, an outdoor sport, the first celebration of whose rites would be, as always, in New Hampshire. Only after Nixon had proved himself in New Hampshire, in Wisconsin, in Nebraska, in Oregon, would his delegate apparatus have the leverage to pry open the hidden loyalties that remained his among the major delegate-brokers of the Republican Party. All the primaries would be important; a single loss would spoil all plans; but none would be more important than the opener, in New Hampshire, on March 12th.

. . .

Then it is over in New Hampshire: a clear, smashing victory. Nixon receives 80,667 votes in New Hampshire's Republican primary, more votes than any candidate in any Presidential primary in that state's history. His margin over his write-in opponent, Nelson Rockefeller, is seven to one. In the Democratic primary he receives four times as many write-ins as Robert F. Kennedy. The total vote is the largest ever in any New Hampshire Presidential primary; and Nixon's share is larger than all other Democratic, Republican and write-in candidates put together.

With such superlatives as these, the Nixon organization is in business; the delegate round-up can now go forward with a Nixon the winner, not a Nixon the loser.

And from here on one could ignore Mr. Nixon on the outdoor primary trail and concentrate on the campaign as programmed indoors; for from the very first day of Mr. Nixon in New Hampshire, the public Nixon was also operating as the programmed Nixon.

As programmed indoors, the Nixon campaign, from primary to election day, was a new perception of American politics, a new appreciation of the environment of communications.

Half a dozen names form the constellation of Richard Nixon's communications group—Leonard Garment, Frank Shakespeare, William Safire, Herbert Klein, Harry Treleaven, H. R. Haldeman. These men, collectively, had greater importance and greater impact than any other communications group in any Presidential campaign; but the governing philosophy can perhaps best be traced to H. R. Haldeman.

• • •

To the campaign of 1968 he brought a perception based on his sad memories of the Nixon campaigns of 1960 and 1962, as later sophisticated by his experience in mass-marketing as an advertising executive. The scene of American politics, he felt, had totally changed and the traditional marketing of candidates had become obsolete. Thus, in his much-quoted basic memorandum to Nixon at the end of 1967, he laid down the following theses: Americans no longer gather in the streets to hear candidates; they gather at their television sets or where media assemble their attention. A candidate cannot storm the nation; at most he can see and let his voice be heard by no more than a million or two people in a Presidential year ("The reach of the individual campaigner," says Haldeman, "doesn't add up to diddly-squat in votes"). One minute or thirty seconds on the evening news shows of Messrs. Cronkite or Huntley/Brinkley will reach more people than ten months of barnstorming. One important favorable Washington column is worth more than two dozen press releases or position papers. News magazines like *Time* or *Newsweek*, picture magazines like *Life* or *Look* are media giants worth a hundred outdoor rallies. Therefore the candidate must not waste time storming the country, personally pleading for votes—no matter what he does, he can appear in newsprint or on television only once a day. The inner strength and vitality of the candidate must not be wasted; if you do more than one thing a day, you make a mistake. If you test a man's physical strength too far, you push him beyond the realm of good judgment; both candidate and the following press must be given time to stop, rest, reflect and write. The importance of old-style outdoor campaigning now lies less in what the candidate *tells* the people than in what he *learns* from them—with the important secondary value that outdoor exertions do provide the vital raw-stuff for television cameras. To his basic memorandum, Haldeman could always add some particularly poignant memories of 1960: "We started Nixon off in 1960 sick and under medication and then we ran his tail off." He meant not to do it again.

The Haldeman memorandum—with its obvious new insights and disturbing implications—framed the Nixon campaign from January of 1968 down almost to its last weekend in California in November of 1968. It was to be a campaign based on the great media of public influence; through them, Nixon would reach the people.

•　•　•

The smoothness that marked the Nixon delegate operation of 1968 came partly from experience, but even more from the fact that the Republican Party was waiting for him.

From 1967 on, no matter how high or low Romney or Reagan or Rockefeller rose or fell in the various national polls of all Americans, one polling result remained consistent: in polls limited only to Republican voters, Nixon outran any rival. And in every survey of Republican committee and county leaders, the delegates-prospective and delegate-brokers of 1968, Nixon continually ran far ahead of any other Republican rival. He was of the fiber and bone of the Party. For sixteen years, from 1952 on, though every Presidential and off-year election except 1962, he had campaigned for Senators, Congressmen, Governors, appearing in rain, snow, sun, storm, at fund-raisers, testimonials, Party gatherings. Only his image as a loser restrained Republican leaders from committing to him at once, for self-interest always restrains emotions. Once New Hampshire had ruptured the loser image, it was only necessary for Nixon's captains to shake the trees—and delegates would fall into their baskets; and the regional apparatus of Nixon was ready.

• • •

By the end of 1967, at their Washington offices, Sears and Ellsworth could already rack up rough charts of convention strength. New England was questionable territory; Governor John Volpe of Massachusetts toyed with the idea of making himself a regional favorite son and, in no uncertain terms, made known he could easily be deterred by offer of the Vice-Presidency—either from Nixon, Romney, Rockefeller or Reagan, it mattered not. The solid bloc of industrial states stretching across the Midwest was similarly confused—Pennsylvania, Ohio, New York, New Jersey, Minnesota, all chancy. Illinois looked better for Nixon, but its politicians, like those in the other big states, waited to see Nixon run in the primaries. The South was up for grabs. No one had the lock on that bloc of votes, as Goldwater had had so early in 1964; the Southern leaders, like the Midwesterners, waited on the primaries. But almost all the Rocky Mountain states were safe; so were the Border states, already solid for Nixon. California would be yielded to Ronald Reagan without a fight. And, as early as December of 1967, Nixon had passed the word from New York to Washington: no muscle tactics. If the nomination came his way, it must come in goodwill, not as it came to

Goldwater in 1964, who locked up his delegates early, arm-twisting his way to a majority and then tearing the Party apart at the convention. Thus, the directive—go easy; scout; be ready; a nomination won by an intra-Party fight would be useless in the November election.

• • •

At Atlanta, Mr. Nixon went on to meet with the Southern leaders—Senator Strom Thurmond of South Carolina, Senator John Tower of Texas, and other considerable individuals of the Republican Party of the South. Since so much has been made of this Georgia meeting and of its later binding imperatives on the Miami convention as well as the present course of the administration of the United States, one should note now what the principal figure recalled some months later: the meeting was not presided over by Strom Thurmond but by Peter O'Donnell, Texas Republican State Chairman. At issue were two things: first, the convention votes of Southern delegates at Miami, and, second, the philosophy of a Nixon administration.

On civil rights, which was the chief concern of the Southern Republicans, Mr. Nixon agreed that the Supreme Court phrase "all deliberate speed" needed reinterpretation; he agreed also that a factor in his thinking about new Supreme Court Justices was that liberal-interpretationists had tipped the balance too far against the strict-construction interpreters of the Constitution; and he averred, also, that the compulsory busing of school students from one district to another for the purpose of racial balance was wrong. On schools, however, he insisted that no Federal funds would be given to a school district which practiced clear segregation; but, on the other hand, he agreed that no Federal funds should be withheld from school districts as a penalty for tardiness in response to a bureaucratic decision in Washington which ordained the precise proportions of white or black children by a Federal directive that could not be questioned in the provinces.

More specifically, as he "wrapped up" the campaign on June 1st, Mr. Nixon noted that Strom Thurmond seemed most interested in national-defense policy; and he gave reassurance to Senator Thurmond that he, too, believed in strong defense. The Southerners, in general, wanted to be "in" on decisions, not to be treated like pariahs on the national scene as Negroes had previously been treated. On this, too, Nixon gave reassurance. No particular veto on Vice-President or Cabinet members was requested, although Mr. Nixon assured them they would be in on consultations. To their desire that he campaign heavily throughout the South, Nixon could not give entire assurance—Deep South states like Mississippi and Alabama he felt were lost, but he *would* stump the Border South. The Southerners wanted some clearance on Federal patronage; they agreed that a new administration ought, indeed, to include large personalities from the South; and some would have to be Democrats, since the Democrats are still the Establishment in the South. But the Southerners wanted no appointments that would nip the growth of the Southern Republican Party; they did not insist on veto, only on consultation.

All in all, Mr. Nixon could please and reassure the Southern chairmen; and when he left, his nomination was secure. There would later be the threat of Nelson Rockefeller; but the Rockefeller threat was one jaw of a trap which could be effective only if the other jaw, Ronald Reagan, could operate. With the understanding at Atlanta, the Reagan move was blunted and the convention could safely be turned over to Richard Kleindienst, who now had a clear field for his talents.

•   •   •

The concept that governed both convention tactics and election strategy was simple: the nomination must be won without splitting the Party, the election must be won without splitting the nation. Inherent in this concept was a strategy of blandness; and in the strategy, a flaw—for unless he could expand his base from his minority-party Republican loyalists, Mr. Nixon would emerge ultimately as a minority President. Yet, without passion or dynamism, he could not expand the base. Artistically, the flaw translated itself as boredom. Another synonym, however, for boredom is "unexciting," and millions of Americans in their year of stress wanted precisely that—an "unexciting" Presidency, a calm and soothing regime which would not prod them with the increasing perplexities of America and the world, nor with the dramatics that seemed, increasingly, to be substituting for politics in their country.

The very smoothness of the Nixon campaign machinery promoted this sense of non-excitement. By Key Biscayne in June, the organization that had finally emerged to cap the Nixon drive reflected a good deal of the campaign. It was exciting chiefly to *aficionados* of political technique as an almost perfect model of what a campaign should be—at once spankingly efficient in all substantive functions, yet simultaneously tailored to the personality of the candidate as well.

· · ·

Whatever judgment history will make on Richard Nixon must wait for years, and will rest on his record in the White House; that judgment must concern itself with the drama of government and policy. But already in 1968 one could see that, though there was to be little drama in Richard Nixon's campaign, there was a drama in the man, in his turning-about in himself; yet it was a drama too dense for easy analysis.

•   •   •

There should, and must, be a statute of limitations in politics; and thus, just as I had in 1960, when I came to cherish John F. Kennedy, tucked away his early denunciation of Communist conspirators in the China division of the State Department, so, as I approached the campaign of 1968, I tried to tuck away the records, files and utterances of Richard Nixon of the 1950's.

Yet they could not be so easily tucked away. The Nixon of 1968 was so different from the Nixon of 1960 that the whole personality required re-exploration. Something had transformed his thinking; it was important to try to read all over again the quality of his mind.

•   •   •

. . . by the late spring of 1968 my reportorial observation on Nixon had deeply changed from that of 1960—chiefly because he had changed too. There was in all he said, even in discussing the most hostile personalities, a total absence of bitterness, of the rancor and venom that had once colored his remarks. I had learned, as I had not known before, how diligent and untiring a worker he was—and how phenomenally driven to get to the bottom of things. There remained to bother me several other maters: the peculiar fatalism of the man, the Kismet with which he looked forward to the happening of events; the ability of the man to stand up to the strain and heat of violent decision; and the nature of his dreams, which, in a President, are the most important qualities of all.

THE SOCIAL SCENE

The Age of Television
KURT LANG and
GLADYS LANG

*Television as a medium of news and entertainment
emerged in the 1950s. It is obvious that television has
had a tremendous impact on post-World War II American society, but its precise influence is impossible to
ascertain. Kurt and Gladys Lang, both sociologists, are
interested in the role of television in politics. In the following excerpt they recall some of the highlights of television political coverage in the 1950s, as well as point out
some of the ramifications of the use of television in
politics.*

The era of radio seems to have passed so quickly that its impact on political life had hardly been considered when the "new age of television" arrived. Most of us remember the major milestones of television "firsts," in which the dramatic potential of that medium for disseminating public events was initially revealed. The first generation of children who cannot remember life without a television set are just coming of voting age in 1968. Politics without video is inconceivable to them.

The discussions of mass media experts in the early 1950's, when nationwide coverage first became a reality, centered on the "front-row seat" that television gave every viewer. Enthusiasts believed that television, because it enlarged the viewer's social world beyond belief, enabled him to become intimately acquainted with persons and places to which he would never, without television, have access. It transformed the mass society into a mass neighborhood. Television's personalities entered the daily lives of people and involved them in interactions that have been called "para-social." The characters in TV serials and hosts of other programs became significant social personalities with whom interactions were sustained. Public participation, via video, in the political life of the country would have a similar para-social character.

What were the major events that first aroused our interest in political television? In 1950, a Senate subcommittee's investigations into organized crime were televised. Witness after witness from gangland was paraded before the TV camera and subjected to questioning by Senator Kefauver and his chief counsel, Rudolph Halley. The committee's investigations brought to the national consciousness the prevalence of crime. One investigation of the public response to the hearings indicated a high degree of emotional arousal and indignation, but when it came to doing something to remedy the situation, this study indicated that only a small minority of persons were sufficiently motivated to take even modest political action, such as writing to their congressman. Could it therefore be said that the presence of the television cameras had no effect? Crime and corruption became one of the major issues in the 1952 elections, and Kefauver, thanks to television, emerged as its chief opponent to become a leading contender for the Democratic nomination and, in 1956, ultimately to be nominated for Vice President. His chief counsel was elected president of the New York City Council, winning against the Democratic machine.

In 1951, television's role in another event made us question the allegedly automatic reportorial accuracy of video reporting. On April 11, in the midst of the Korean War, President Harry S Truman's summary dismissal of General Douglas MacArthur, a World War II hero and commander-in-chief of the American forces engaged in battle, stirred up a national furor. The White House communiqué relieving MacArthur of all his commands clearly stated the reason for dismissal: the general, through his public statements, had repeatedly invaded the field of policy-making, the prerogative of the President. The statement concluded with deep regret that "General MacArthur is unable to give his wholehearted support to the policies of the United States government and of the United Nations in matters pertaining to his official duties." In other words, he was dismissed for insubordination and not for technical incompetence.

MacArthur's departure from Japan, a week after his dismissal, and his homeward journey after fourteen years of continuous service abroad were more like a triumphal march than a voluntary acceptance of the President's supreme authority. A reporter and a historian, in describing the mood of the country, said it was doubtful "if there has ever been in this country so violent and spontaneous a discharge of political passion as that provoked by the President's dismissal of the General and by the General's dramatic return from his voluntary patriotic exile."

All this had little to do with television. But from the moment MacArthur reached the continental United States, television cameras accompanied him on every public appearance from his first landing in San Francisco, where he received a hero's welcome, to his stops in other cities, large and small. The press reports, including television newsreels, of his reception gave an impression of mass hysteria and an active outpouring of political outrage. The authors were then residing in Chicago, and MacArthur Day as celebrated there seemed to offer a unique opportunity for a systematic study of crowd behavior and of the role of the media of mass communication, particularly television, in this kind of event.

Our main goal was stymied. The air of curiosity and casualness exhibited by most members of the crowd was a surprise to every observer reporting from the scene. But those watching the televised welcome saw pretty much what they had expected to see. What intrigued us was: why should "reality" as experienced over television have diverged so much from the "reality" of personal participation in the event? Those who participated in the study could no longer believe that reportorial accuracy was intrinsic in the technical capabilities of television.

• • •

With our interest once aroused by MacArthur Day, it was natural that we should turn our attention to the presidential campaign as it was shaping up for 1952. Not only were both political conventions to receive national political coverage for the first time, but this promised to be the first campaign in which both parties would make a major investment in television.

The 1952 Republican convention turned into a two-way contest, with Eisenhower gaining a narrow victory over Senator Taft. The convention "proved," in the words of ABC commentator Elmer Davis, that "it was no longer possible to commit grand larceny in broad daylight"—in other words, in front of the glaring eyes of the TV cameras. "Larceny" referred to the dispute over the seating of contested delegations from three Southern states; the resolution of the dispute turned out to be crucial for the outcome of the nomination, because the successful challenge of credentials enabled Eisenhower to get enough additional delegates to be assured the nomination. But whether and how television affected the public response and, through it, the decision of the convention are quite other questions.

A more deliberate effort to use television to solicit a public reaction occurred during the campaign and aroused our curiosity about the "television personality." It made us wonder in particular about the supposedly terrifying capacity of the television camera to reveal the truth and to expose disingenuousness of every sort. Thus, Adlai Stevenson, who clearly could not resist a joke, especially on himself, insisted after the 1952 election that he had "clearly won the bosom-beating and public-stripping contest of last fall." The issue he raised is a serious one, however. It concerned the successful defense by Richard M. Nixon, in front of the television cameras, of the $18,235 expense fund donated by seventy-six of his California supporters.

•   •   •

Nixon's half-hour program was produced by an advertising agency. For the first fifteen minutes he sat behind a desk and spoke directly to the audience. In simple and measured words, he told about his personal ordeal in having his honesty and integrity questioned when he had a big mortgage on his house and his wife was wearing a cloth coat, not a fur coat. During the second fifteen minutes he moved out from behind his desk and stood talking to the audience; the camera, at appropriate moments, revealed Mrs. Nixon looking at her husband as he addressed the television audience. The broadcast concluded with an unprecedented appeal to the public to wire and write the Republican National Committee, as the chief authority over his campaign, whether or not he should be dropped from the ticket.

. . .

In transferring true and tried propaganda techniques to a medium whose effects were so immediate, there might result what Walter Lippmann called "mob law by modern electronics." Many of us shared his misgivings over the new partnership between television and public life and, like him, were disturbed while watching Nixon's fight for his political life. Wrote Lippmann:

> The charges against Senator Nixon were so serious that for five days General Eisenhower reserved his own judgment on whether to clear him or condemn him. Why? Because the evidence, the law, and the moral principles at issue are none of them simple or obvious. . . . They have to do with matters which can then be decided only by some sort of judicial process. How, then, can a television audience be asked or allowed to judge the matter before General Eisenhower finished his inquiry and reached his conclusion? . . . What the

television audience should have been given was not Senator Nixon's personal defense. That should have been made first before General Eisenhower. What the television audience should have been given was General Eisenhower's decision, backed by a full and objective account of the facts and of the points of law and of morals which are involved.

The whole question of the television personality in politics was raised by still other events. The televised Army-McCarthy hearings, in which the Wisconsin senator attempted to bulldoze with reckless charges several members of the defense establishment, held the country's attention in 1954. These hearings certainly coincided with the turn in the senator's fortunes, and television is often cited as a major cause of McCarthy's downfall and his censure by the Senate. In front of the pitiless TV cameras, it was alleged, McCarthy revealed himself to the public not as a patriot but as the demagogue he actually was.

We know of no evidence to support this simple an explanation. McCarthy's standing in the polls began to slip only after the Senate moved to take action against him. Hence, whatever role television played in the destruction of the myth of McCarthy's invincibility was certainly something different than a mass reaction to his antics before the cameras. Had not the Nixon episode shown that important issues could be sidestepped without this redounding to the detriment of the candidate? After the hearings, powerful political forces in the Senate and on Capitol Hill were finally stirred to action. McCarthy's public performance was among the actions they used to discredit him. The Nixon speech, by contrast, was not only a smoother performance, but as campaign oratory it was less open to challenge.

The Army-McCarthy hearings also marked the first time that one of McCarthy's charges met an immediate challenge from an opposing counsel. This happened during an interchange with lawyer Joseph Welch that had all markings of a courtroom drama. The "instant reply" was subsequently built into the televised debates of 1960, in which Richard M. Nixon was paired against John F. Kennedy. Our study of this confrontation, shows again how responses to a television personality are determined by political convictions. If this is so, we can infer that the dramatic impact of Nixon's "Checkers" speech on millions of viewers—we made no study of our own of this incident—was less a product of what he said than a reflection of Eisenhower's great appeal to voters. Many persons, Republicans and Democrats alike, did not want to see the general embarrassed politically and hence were ready to exonerate Nixon as long as he offered them a rationale for doing so.

A final issue concerns the implications of television, as a medium of political communication, for the functioning of the institutions of government. The televised presidential press conference has become an established institution. It appears that, as a result, the interchange between the President and reporters may be less free than it was before. On the other hand, pressure for televised debates between contenders for major political offices is building. There are demands for modifications of the "equal time" provision to enable the networks to accommodate these debates without undue loss of revenue.

The latest of the innovations in communications technology concerns the quick dissemination of presidential election returns to the public while polling in some areas of the country is still in progress. Again our interest lies mainly in how political perceptions concerning the electoral process may be influenced by the new techniques of mass communication, all of which together make possible a freer and more unimpeded flow of political information to the public.

How to Use Television in Politics
JOE McGINNISS

Television campaigning became crucial in the 1968 Presidential election. Each candidate relied heavily on this method of reaching the voters, but none did it more effectively than Richard M. Nixon. Joe McGinniss observed Nixon's use of the media and has written a stimulating and thought-provoking account of what he witnessed. If one believes this young political commentator, the President was packaged and sold to the American people by the television industry. The implications of this argument are self-explanatory.

Excerpted from *The Selling of the President 1968* by Joe McGinniss. Copyright © 1969 by JoeMac, Incorporated. Reprinted by permission of Trident Press, division of Simon & Schuster, Inc. (Title supplied by editor.)

"I am not going to barricade myself into a television studio and make this an antiseptic campaign," Richard Nixon said at a press conference a few days after his nomination.

Then he went to Chicago to open his fall campaign. The whole day was built around a television show. Even when ten thousand people stood in front of his hotel and screamed for him to greet them, he stayed locked up in his room, resting for the show.

Chicago was the site of the first ten programs that Nixon would do in states ranging from Massachusetts to Texas. The idea was to have him in the middle of a group of people, answering questions live. Shakespeare and Treleaven had developed the idea through the primaries and now had it sharpened to a point. Each show would run one hour. It would be live to provide suspense; there would be a studio audience to cheer Nixon's answers and make it seem to home viewers that enthusiasm for his candidacy was all but uncontrollable; and there would be an effort to achieve a conversational tone that would penetrate Nixon's stuffiness and drive out the displeasure he often seemed to feel when surrounded by other human beings instead of Bureau of the Budget reports.

One of the valuable things about this idea, from a political standpoint, was that each show would be seen only by the people who lived in that particular state or region. This meant it made no difference if Nixon's statements —for they were not really answers—were exactly the same, phrase for phrase, gesture for gesture, from state to state. Only the press would be bored and the press had been written off already. So Nixon could get through the campaign with a dozen or so carefully worded responses that would cover all the problems of America in 1968.

· · ·

Roger Ailes, the executive producer of the Mike Douglas Show, was hired to produce the one-hour programs. Ailes was twenty-eight years old. He had started as a prop boy on the Douglas show in 1965 and was running it within three years. He was good. When he left, Douglas' ratings collapsed. But not everyone he passed on his way up remained his friend. Not even Douglas.

· · ·

The set, now that it was finished, was impressive. There was a round blue-carpeted platform, six feet in diameter and eight inches high. Richard Nixon would stand on this and face the panel, which would be seated in a semicircle around him. Bleachers for the audience ranged out behind the panel chairs. Later, Roger Ailes would think to call the whole effect, "the arena concept" and bill Nixon as "the man in the arena." He got this from a Theodore Roosevelt quote which hung, framed, from a wall of his office in Philadelphia. It said something about how one man in the arena was worth ten, or a hundred, or a thousand carping critics.

At nine o'clock Central Daylight Time, Richard Nixon, freshly powdered, left his dressing room, walked down a corridor deserted save for secret service, and went through a carefully guarded doorway that opened onto the rear of the set.

· · ·

Then the director hit a button and Bud Wilkinson appeared on the screen. And what a placid, composed, substantial, reassuring figure he was: introducing his close personal friend, a man whose intelligence and judgment had won the respect of the world's leaders and the admiration of millions of his countrymen, this very same man who had been seen entering Jerusalem moments ago on tape: Richard Nixon.

And the carefully cued audience (for Jack Rourke, the warmup man, had done his job well) stood to render an ovation. Richard Nixon, grinning, waving, *thrusting*, walked to the blue riser to receive the tribute.

It was warmly given. Genuine. For Nixon suddenly represented a true alternative: peace, prosperity, an end to discord, a return to the stable values that had come under such rude and unwarranted attack. Nixon was fortification, reaffirmation of much that needed to be re-affirmed. They needed him now, these Republicans, much more than they had in 1960. Then they were smug; and they did not especially like him. They toyed with him, as a small boy would poke a frog with a stick. They made him suffer needlessly, and, in the end, their apathy had dragged a nation down. Now, on this night, this first night of his campaign to restore decency and honor to American life, they wanted to let him know they cared. To let him know 1960 would not happen again.

. . .

There was a rush of sympathy; a desire—a need, even—to root. Richard Nixon was suddenly human: facing a new and dangerous situation, alone, armed only with his wits. In image terms, he had won before he began. All the old concepts had been destroyed. He had achieved a new level of communication. The stronger his state-ment, the stronger the surge of warmth inside the viewer. *Received impressions.* Yes, this was a man who could lead; infinitely preferable to the gray and bumbling

Johnson; the inscrutable, unsuccessful Rusk. A man who —yes, they remembered, even through the electronic haze—had stood up to Khrushchev in the kitchen. And, it was obvious now, who would stand up to Jerry Rubin in the street.

His statements flowed like warm milk, bathed the audience, restored faith in the Founding Fathers, rekindled the memory of a vigorous Eisenhower, of ten, of fifteen years before. *"The American Revolution has been won,"* he had said in his acceptance speech at Miami, *"the American Dream has come true."*

Morris Liebman, the Jewish attorney, asked the first question: "Would you comment on the accusation which was made from time to time that your views have shifted and that they are based on expediences?"

Richard Nixon squinted and smiled. "I suppose what you are referring to is: Is there a new Nixon or is there an old Nixon? I suppose I could counter by saying: Which Humphrey shall we listen to today?"

There was great applause for this. When it faded, Richard Nixon said, "I do want to say this: There certainly is a new Nixon. I realize, too, that as a man gets older he learns something. If I haven't learned something I am not worth anything in public life.

"We live in a new world. Half the nations in the world were born since World War Two. Half the people living in the world today were born since World War Two. The problems are different and I think I have had the good sense—I trust the intelligence—to travel the world since I left the office of Vice President and to bring my views up to date to deal with the new world.

"I think my principles are consistent. I believe very deeply in the American system. I believe very deeply in what is needed to defend that system at home and abroad. I think I have some ideas as to how we can promote peace, ideas that are different from what they were eight years ago, not because I have changed but because the problems have changed.

"My answer is, yes, there is a new Nixon, if you are talking in terms of new ideas for the new world and the America we live in. In terms of what I believe in the American view and the American dream, I think I am just what I was eight years ago."

Applause swept the studio. Bud Wilkinson joined in.

The farmer asked a question about farming; the Polish-Hungarian delivered an address concerning the problems of the people of eastern Europe. His remarks led to no question at all, but no matter: Richard Nixon expressed concern for the plight of eastern Europeans everywhere, including northern Illinois.

Then Warner Saunders, the Negro, and a very acceptable, very polite one he seemed to be, asked, "What does law and order mean to you?"

"I am quite aware," Richard Nixon said, "of the fact that the black community, when they hear it, think of power being used in a way that is destructive to them, and yet I think we have to also remember that the black community as well as the white community has an interest in order and in law, providing that law is with justice. To me law and order must be combined with justice. Now that's what I want for America. I want the kind of law and order which deserves respect."

John McCarter, the businessman, asked about Spiro Agnew. Nixon said, "Of all the men who I considered, Spiro Agnew had the intelligence, the courage and the principle to take on the great responsibilities of a campaigner and responsibilities of Vice President. And who also had the judgment so that if anything happened, the President of the United States could sit in that chair and make decisions that need to be made that would make the difference between war and peace and that I would have confidence in him." Then he called Agnew "a man of compassion."

McCarter came back later wanting to know if Nixon thought the Chicago police had been too harsh on demonstrators in the streets.

"It would be easy," Nixon said, "to criticize Mayor Daley and by implication Vice President Humphrey. But it wouldn't be right for me to lob in criticism. I am not going to get into it. It is best for political figures not to be making partisan comments from the sidelines."

The show went on like that. At the end the audience charged from the bleachers, as instructed. They swarmed around Richard Nixon so that the last thing the viewer at home saw was Nixon in the middle of this big crowd of people, who all thought he was great.

•   •   •

Three days later, Roger Ailes composed a memorandum that contained the details of his reaction to the show. He sent it to Shakespeare and Garment:

> After completing the first one-hour program, I thought I would put a few general comments down on paper. After you have had a chance to look them over, I'd like to discuss them briefly with you so we can steadily improve the programs up to the time he becomes President. I viewed the complete tape the morning after the show.
> Mr. Nixon is strong now on television and has good control of the situation.
>
> I. The Look:
>   A. He looks good on his feet and shooting "in the round" gives dimension to him.

B. Standing adds to his "feel" of confidence and the viewers' "feel" of his confidence.

C. He still uses his arms a little too "predictably" and a little too often, but at this point it is better not to inhibit him.

D. He seems to be comfortable on his feet and even appears graceful and relaxed, i.c., hands on his hips or arms folded occasionally.

E. His eye contact is good with the panelists, but he should play a little more to the home audience via the head-on camera. I would like to talk to him about this.

F. We are still working on lightening up his eyes a bit, but this is not a major problem. This will be somewhat tougher in smaller studios, but don't worry, he will never look bad:

1. I may lower the front two key spots a bit.

2. I may try slightly whiter makeup on upper eyelids.

3. I may lower the riser he stands on a couple of inches.

G. The "arena" effect is excellent and he plays to all areas well. The look has "guts."

H. Color lights are hot and he has a tendency to perspire, especially along the upper lip.

1. Whenever he is going to tape a show, the studio air conditioning should be turned up full at least four hours prior to broadcast, and camera rehearsal should be limited as much as possible in this time period to keep the lights off and the heat down. If camera rehearsal is necessary, the air conditioner should be turned on sooner and the studio sealed off. Keep all studio doors (especially the large leading doors) closed.

I. An effort should be made to keep him in the sun

occasionally to maintain a fairly constant level of healthy tan.

J. Generally, he has a very "Presidential" look and style—he smiles easily (and looks good doing it). He should continue to make lighter comments once in a while for pacing.

II. The Questions and Answers:

A. First, his opening remarks are good. He should, perhaps, be prepared with an optional cut in his closing remarks in case we get into time trouble getting off the air. I don't want to take a chance of missing the shots of the audience crowding around him at the end. Bud can specifically tell him exactly how much time he has to close.

B. In the panel briefing we should tell the panelists not to ask two-part questions. This slows down the overall pace of the show and makes it difficult for the viewer to remember and thus follow. Instead, the panelists should be instructed that they can continue a dialogue with Mr. Nixon—ask two questions in a row to get the answers.

C. Some of the answers are still too long and over half tended to be the same length.

•   •   •

—On one answer from Warner Saunders, he gave an unqualified "yes" and that was good. Whenever possible he should be that definite.

D. He still needs some memorable phrases to use in wrapping up certain points. I feel that I might be able to help in this area, but don't know if you want me to or if he would take suggestions from me on this. Maybe I could have a session with Price and Buchanan.

III. Staging:

A. The microphone cord needs to be dressed and looped to the side.

B. Bud Wilkinson felt there should be more women on the panel since over half the voters are women. Maybe combine a category, i.e., woman reporter or negro woman.

C. The panel was too large at eight. Maximum should be seven, six is still preferable to give more interaction.

D. Bud should be able to interject more often with some prepared lighter or pacing questions.

E. The family should be in the audience at every show. Should I talk with them, Whitaker, or will you?

F. Political VIPs should be in the audience for every show. Nixon handles these introductions extremely well and they are good for reaction shots.

G. I am adding extenders to the zoom lens on all cameras to allow closer shooting for reactions.

IV. General:

A. The show got off to a slow start. Perhaps the opening could be made more exciting by:

    1. adding music or applause earlier.

B. The excitement of the film made the quietness of the dissolve to the studio more apparent.

C. Bud should be introduced with applause.

D. When film is not available it might be good to have David Douglas Duncan shoot a series of interesting stills which could be put on film and synchronized to the Connie Francis record. I'd like to try this—it might give us a classy "standard" opening to use.

E. To give the director as much advantage as possible—the fewer last-minute changes, the better. In Chicago we luckily had excellent facilities and a fast crew plus plenty of rehearsal time. In the California show, because of studio priorities, our rehearsal time is cut in half.

F. I will work with the director on the art of using the reaction shot for better overall program value.

G. In general, I usually feel "down" immediately after taping a show. I was more pleased after viewing the tape than I was that night after the show.

Violence
HUGH DAVIS GRAHAM and
TED ROBERT GURR

Violence in the United States, or in the world for that matter, is not new. What is new is the concern of the government and citizens generally about its nature, causes, and consequences. In part, this interest has been fostered by the killings of John Kennedy, Martin Luther King, and Robert Kennedy as well as by the various upheavals in the nation's cities throughout the 1960s. Hugh Davis Graham, a historian, and Ted Robert Gurr, a political scientist, codirected a research study for the National Commission on the Causes and Prevention of Violence. Some of their findings are presented here.

Excerpted from "Conclusion," *Violence in America: Historical and Comparative Perspectives,* edited by Hugh Davis Graham and Ted Robert Gurr. Reprinted from the Signet Books edition published by The New American Library, 1969. (Title supplied by editor.)

Our current eruption of violence must appear paradoxical to a generation of Americans who witnessed the successful emergence from depression to unparalleled affluence of a nation they regarded as the world's moral leader in defense of freedom. Only a decade ago America's historians were celebrating the emergence of a unique society, sustained by a burgeoning prosperity and solidly grounded on a broad political consensus. We were told —and the implications were reassuring—that our uniqueness was derived from at least half a dozen historical sources which, mutually reinforcing one another, had joined to propel us toward a manifestly benevolent destiny. We were a nation of immigrants, culturally enriched by the variety of mankind. Sons of the frontier, our national character has grown to reflect the democratic individualism and pragmatic ingenuity that had conquered the wilderness. Our new nation was born in anticolonial revolution and in its crucible was forged a democratic republic of unparalleled vitality and longevity. Lacking a feudal past, our political spectrum was so truncated about the consensual liberal center that, unlike Europe, divisive radicalism of the left or right had found no sizable constituency. Finally, we had both created and survived the great transformation from agrarian frontier to industrial metropolis, to become the richest nation of all time.

It was a justly proud legacy, one which seemed to make sense in the relatively tranquil 1950's. But with the 1960's came shock and frustration. It was a decade against itself: the students of affluence were marching in the streets; middle-class matrons were besieging the Pentagon; and Negro Americans were responding to victories in civil rights and to their collectively unprecedented prosperity with a paradoxical venting of outrage. In a fundamental sense, history—the ancient human encounter with poverty, defeat, and guilt as well as with affluence, victory, and innocence—had finally caught up with America. Or at least it had caught up with white America.

Historical analysis of our national experience and character would suggest that the seeds of our contemporary discontent were to a large extent deeply embedded in those same ostensibly benevolent forces which contributed to our uniqueness. First, we are a nation of immigrants, but one in which the original dominant immigrant group, the so-called Anglo-Saxons, effectively preempted the crucial levers of economic and political power in government, commerce, and the professions. This elite group has tenaciously resisted the upward strivings of successive "ethnic" immigrant waves. The resultant competitive hierarchy of immigrants has always been highly conducive to violence, but this violence has taken different forms. The Anglo-Americans have used their access to the levers of power to maintain their dominance, using legal force surrounded by an aura of legitimacy for such ends as economic exploitation; the restriction of immigration by a national-origin quota system which clearly branded later immigrants as culturally undesirable; the confinement of the original Indian immigrants largely to barren reservations; and the restriction of blacks to a degraded caste. But the system was also conducive to violence among the latter groups themselves— when, for instance, Irish-Americans rioted against Afro-American "scabs." Given America's unprecedented ethnic pluralism, simply being born American conferred no automatic and equal citizenship in the eyes of the larger society. In the face of such reservations, ethnic minorities had constantly to affirm their Americanism through a kind of patriotic ritual which intensified the ethnic competition for status. As a fragment culture based on bourgeois-liberal values, as Hartz has observed, yet one populated by an unprecedented variety of immigrant stock, America's tightened consensus on what properly constituted "Americanism" prompted status rivalries among the ethnic minorities which, when combined with economic rivalries, invited severe and abiding conflict.

•   •   •

The second major formative historical experience was America's uniquely prolonged encounter with the frontier. While the frontier experience indubitably strengthened the mettle of the American character, it witnessed the brutal and brutalizing ousting of the Indians and the forceful incorporation of Mexican and other original inhabitants, as Frantz has so graphically portrayed. Further, it concomitantly created an environment in which, owing to the paucity of law enforcement agencies, a tradition of vigilante "justice" was legitimized. The longevity of the Ku Klux Klan and the vitality both of contemporary urban rioting and of the stiffening resistance to it owe much to this tradition. As Brown has observed, vigilantism has persisted as a socially malleable instrument long after the disappearance of the frontier environment that gave it birth, and it has proved quite congenial to an urban setting.

Similarly, the revolutionary doctrine that our Declaration of Independence proudly proclaims stands as a tempting model of legitimate violence to be emulated by contemporary groups, such as militant Negroes and radical students who confront a system of both public and private government that they regard as contemptuous of their consent. Entranced by the resurgence of revolution in the underdeveloped world and of international university unrest, radical students and blacks naturally seize upon historically sacrosanct doctrine of the inherent right of revolution and self-determination to justify their rebellion. That their analogies are fatefully problematical in no way dilutes the majesty of our own proud Declaration.

The fourth historic legacy, our consensual political philosophy of Lockean-Jeffersonian liberalism, was premised upon a pervasive fear of governmental power and has reinforced the tendency to define freedom negatively as freedom *from*. As a consequence, conservatives have been able paradoxically to invoke the doctrines of Jefferson in resistance to legislative reforms, and the Sumnerian imperative that "stateways cannot change folkways" has historically enjoyed a wide and not altogether unjustified allegiance in the public eye (witness the debacle of the first Reconstruction, and the dilemma of our contemporary second attempt). Its implicit corollary has been that forceful and, if necessary, violent local and state resistance to unpopular federal stateways is a legitimate response; both Calhoun and Wallace could confidently repair to a strict construction of the same document invoked by Lincoln and the Warren court.

A fifth historic source both of our modern society and our current plight is our industrial revolution and the great internal migration from the countryside to the city. Yet the process occurred with such astonishing rapidity that it produced widespread socioeconomic dislocation in an environment in which the internal controls of the American social structure were loose and the external controls were weak. Urban historian Richard Wade has observed that—

> The cities inherited no system of police control adequate to the numbers or to the rapid increase of the

urban centers. The modern police force is the creation of the 20th century; the establishment of genuinely professional systems is historically a very recent thing.

Throughout the 18th and 19th century, the force was small, untrained, poorly paid, and part of the political system. In case of any sizeable disorder, it was hopelessly inadequate; and rioters sometimes routed the constabulary in the first confrontation.

Organized labor's protracted and bloody battles for recognition and power occurred during these years of minimal control and maximal social upheaval. The violence of workers' confrontations with their employers, Taft and Ross concluded, was partly the result of a lack of consensus on the legitimacy of workers' protests, partly the result of the lack of means of social control. Workers used force to press their grievances, employers organized violent resistance, and repeatedly state or federal troops had to be summoned to restore order.

The final distinctive characteristic—in many ways perhaps our most distinctive—has been our unmatched prosperity; we have been, in the words of David Potter, most characteristically a "people of plenty." Ranked celestially with life and liberty in the sacrosanct Lockean trilogy, property has generated a quest and prompted a devotion in the American character that has matched our devotion to equality and, in a fundamental sense, has transformed it from the radical leveling of the European democratic tradition into a typically American insistence upon equality of opportunity. In an acquisitive society of individuals with unequal talents and groups with unequal advantages, this had resulted in an unequal distribution of the rapid accumulation of abundance that, especially since World War II, has promised widespread participation in the affluent society to a degree unprecedented in history.

• • •

Is man violent by nature or by circumstance? In the Hobbesian view, the inescapable legacy of human nature is a "life of man solitary, poor, nasty, brutish, and short." This ancient pessimistic view is given recent credence by the ethologists, whose study of animals in their natural habitats had led them to conclude that the aggressive drive in animals is innate, ranking with the instinctive trilogy of hunger, sex, and fear or flight. But most psychologists and social scientists do not regard aggression as fundamentally spontaneous or instinctive, nor does the weight of their evidence support such a view. Rather they regard most aggression, including violence, as sometimes an emotional response to socially induced frustrations, and sometimes a dispassionate, learned response evoked by specific situations. This assumption underlies almost all the studies in this volume: nature provides us only with the capacity for violence; it is social circumstances that determines whether and how we exercise that capacity.

• • •

The experience of the United States is consistent with this general pattern. For all our rhetoric, we have never been a very law-abiding nation, and illegal violence has sometimes been abundantly rewarded. Hence there have developed broad normative sanctions for the expression or acting out of discontent, somewhat limited inhibitions, and—owing to Jeffersonian liberalism's legacy of fear of central public authority—very circumscribed physical controls. Public sympathy has often been with the lawbreaker—sometimes with the nightrider who punished the transgressor of community mores, sometimes with the integrationists who refused to obey racial segregation laws. Lack of full respect for law and support for violence in one's own interest have both contributed to the justifications for private violence, justifications that in turn have helped make the United States historically and at present a tumultuous society.

On the other hand, the United States also has characteristics that in other countries appear to minimize intense revolutionary conspiracies and internal wars. Thus far in our history the American political system has maintained a relatively high degree of legitimacy in the eyes of most of its citizens. American political and economic institutions are generally strong. They are not pervasive enough to provide adequate opportunities for some regional and minority groups to satisfy their expectations, but sufficiently pervasive and egalitarian that the most ambitious and talented men—if not women—can pursue the "American dream" with some chance of success. These are conditions that minimize the prospects of revolutionary movements: a majoritarian consensus on the legitimacy of government, and provision of opportunity for men of talent who, if intensely alienated, might otherwise provide revolutionary cadres. But if such a system is open to the majority yet partly closed to a minority, or legitimate for the majority but illegitimate for a minority, the minority is likely to create chronic tumult even though it cannot organize effective revolutionary movements.

•   •   •

Does violence succeed? The inheritors of the doctrines of Frantz Fanon and "Ché" Guevara assert that if those who use it are sufficiently dedicated, revolution can always be accomplished. Many vehement advocates of civil order and strategists of counterinsurgency hold essentially the same faith: that sufficient use of public violence will deter private violence. This fundamental agreement of "left" and "right" on the effectiveness of force for modifying others' behavior is striking. But to what extent is it supported by theory and by historical evidence?

The two most fundamental human responses to the use of force are to flee or to fight. This assertion rests on rather good psychological and ethological evidence about human and animal aggression. Force threatens and angers men, especially if they believe it to be illegitimate or unjust. Threatened, they will defend themselves if they can, flee if they cannot. Angered, they have an innate disposition to retaliate in kind. Thus men who fear assault attempt to arm themselves, and two-thirds or more of white Americans think that black looters and arsonists should be shot. Governments facing violent protest often regard compromise as evidence of weakness and devote additional resources to counterforce. Yet if a government responds to the threat or use of violence with greater force, its effects in many circumstances are identical with the effects that dictated its actions: its opponents will if they can resort to greater force.

· · ·

Governmental uses of force are likely to be successful in quelling specific outbreaks of private violence except in those rare circumstances when the balance of force favors its opponents, or the military defects. But the historical evidence also suggests that governmental violence often succeeds only in the short run. The government of Imperial Russia quelled the revolution of 1905, but in doing so intensified the hostilities of its opponents, who mounted a successful revolution 12 years later, after the government was weakened by a protracted and unsuccessful war. The North "won" the Civil War, but in its very triumph created hostilities that contributed to one of the greatest and most successful waves of vigilante violence in our history. The 17,000 Klansmen of the South today are neither peaceable nor content with the outcome of the "War of Northern Aggression." State or federal troops have been dispatched to quell violent or near-violent labor conflict in more than 160 recorded instances in American history; they were immediately successful in almost every case yet did not significantly deter subsequent labor violence.

The long-range effectiveness of governmental force in maintaining civil peace seems to depend on three conditions . . . public belief that governmental use of force is legitimate, consistent use of that force, and remedial action for the grievances that give rise to private violence. The decline of violent working-class protest in 19th century England was predicated on an almost universal popular acceptance of the legitimacy of the government, accompanied by the development of an effective police system—whose popular acceptance was enhanced by its minimal reliance on violence—and by gradual resolution of working class grievances. The Cuban case was quite the opposite: the governmental response to private violence was terroristic, inconsistent public violence that alienated most Cubans from the Batista regime, with no significant attempts to reduce the grievances, mostly political, that gave rise to rebellion.

• • •

If revolutionary victory is unlikely in the modern state, and uncertain of resolving the grievances that give rise to revolutionary movements, are there any circumstances in which less intensive private violence is successful? We said above that the legitimacy of governmental force is one of the determinants of its effectiveness. The same principle applies to private violence: It can succeed when it is widely regarded as legitimate. The vigilante movements of the American frontier had widespread public support as a means for establishing order in the absence of adequate law enforcement agencies, and were generally successful. The Ku Klux Klan of the Reconstruction era similarly had the sympathy of most white Southerners and was largely effective in reestablishing and maintaining the prewar social and political status quo. The chronicles of American labor violence, however, suggest that violence was almost always ineffective for the workers involved. In a very few instances there was popular and state governmental support for the grievances of workers that had led to violent confrontations with employers, and in several of these cases state authority was used to impose solutions that favored the workers. But in the great majority of cases the public and officials did not accept the legitimacy of labor demands, and the more violent was conflict, the more disastrous were the consequences for the workers who took part. Union organizations involved in violent conflict seldom gained recognition, their supporters were harassed and often lost their jobs, and tens of thousands of workers and their families were forcibly deported from their homes and communities.

The same principle applies, with two qualifications, to peaceful public protest. If demonstrations are regarded as a legitimate way to express grievances, and if the grievances themselves are widely held to be justified, protest is likely to have positive effects. One of the qualifications is that if public opinion is neutral on an issue, protest demonstrations can have favorable effects. This appears to have been an initial consequence of the civil-rights demonstrations of the early 1960's in the North. If public opinion is negative, however, demonstrations are likely to exacerbate popular hostility. During World War I, for example, pacifist demonstrators were repeatedly attacked, beaten, and in some cases lynched, with widespread public approval and sometimes official sanction. Contemporary civil-rights demonstrations and activities in the South and in some northern cities have attracted similar responses.

The second qualification is that when violence occurs during protest activities, it is rather likely to alienate groups that are not fundamentally in sympathy with the protesters. We mentioned above the unfavorable consequences of labor violence for unions and their members, despite the fact that violence was more often initiated by employers than by workers. In the long run, federally enforced recognition and bargaining procedures were established, but this occurred only after labor violence had passed its climacteric, and moreover in circumstances in which no union leaders advocated violence. In England, comparably, basic political reforms were implemented not in direct response to Chartist protest, but long after its violent phase had passed.

The evidence supports one basic principle: Force and violence can be successful techniques of social control and persuasion when they have extensive popular support. If they do not, their advocacy and use are ultimately self-destructive, either as techniques of government or of opposition. This historical and contemporary evidence of the United States suggests that popular support tends to sanction violence in support of the status quo: the use of public violence to maintain public order, the use of private violence to maintain popular conceptions of social order when government cannot or will not. If these assertions are true—and not much evidence contradicts them—the prolonged use of force or violence to advance the interests of any segmental group may impede and quite possibly preclude reform. This conclusion should not be taken as an ethical judgement, despite its apparent correspondence with the "establishmentarian" viewpoint. It represents a fundamental trait of American and probably all mankind's character, one which is ignored by advocates of any political orientation at the risk of broken hopes, institutions, and lives.

To draw this conclusion is not to indict public force or all private violence as absolute social evils. In brief and obvious defense of public force, reforms cannot be made if order is wholly lacking, and reforms will not be made if those who have the means to make them feel their security constantly in jeopardy. And as for private violence, though it may bring out the worst in both its practitioners and its victims, it need not do so. Collective violence is after all a symptom of social malaise. It can be so regarded and the malaise treated as such, provided public-spirited men diagnose it correctly and have the will and means to work for a cure rather than to retaliate out of anger. Americans may be quick to self-righteous anger, but they also have retained some of the English genius for accommodation. Grudgingly and with much tumult, the dominant groups in American society have moved over enough to give the immigrant, the worker, the suffragette better—not the best—seats at the American feast of freedom and plenty. Many of them think the feast is bounteous enough for the dissatisfied students, the poor, the Indians, the blacks. Whether there is a place for the young militants who think the feast has gone rotten, no historical or comparative evidence we know of can answer, because absolute, revolutionary alienation from society has been very rare in the American past and no less rare in other pluralistic and abundant nations.

. . .

The effort to eliminate the conditions that lead to collective violence may tax the resources of a society, but it poses less serious problems than increased resort to force. American labor violence has been mitigated in the past 25 years partly by growing prosperity, but more consequentially because employers now have almost universally recognized unions and will negotiate wage issues and other grievances with them rather than retaliate against them. The movement toward recognition and negotiation was strongly reinforced when workers in most occupations were guaranteed the right to organize and bargain collectively in the National Labor Relations Act of 1935.

. . .

Intensely discontented men are not will-less pawns in a game of social chess. They also have alternatives, of which violence is usually the last, the most desperate, and in most circumstances least likely of success. Peaceful protest, conducted publicly and through conventional political channels, is a traditional American option. As one of the world's most pluralistic societies, we have repeatedly albeit reluctantly accommodated ourselves to discontented groups using interest and pressure-group tactics within the political process as a means of leverage for change. But it also is an American characteristic to resist demonstrative demands, however legal and peaceful, if they seem to challenge our basic beliefs and personal positions. Public protest in the United States is a slow and unwieldly instrument of social change that sometimes inspires more obdurate resistance than favorable change.

Another kind of group response to intense stresses and discontents is called "defensive adaptation" by Bernard Siegel. It is essentially an inward-turning, nonviolent response motivated by a desire to build and maintain a group's cultural integrity in the face of hostile pressures. The defensive group is characterized by centralization of authority; attempts to set the group apart by emphasizing symbols of group identity; and minimization of members' contacts with other groups. It is an especially common reaction among ethnic and religious groups whose members see their social environments as permanently hostile, depreciating, and powerful. Such adaptations are apparent, for example, among some Pueblo Indians, Black Muslims, and Amish, and many minority groups in other nations. This kind of defensive withdrawal may lead to violence when outside groups press too closely in on the defensive group, but it is typically a response that minimizes violent conflict. Although the defensive group provides its members some, essentially social and psychological, satisfactions, it seldom can provide them with substantial economic benefits or political means by which they can promote their causes vis-à-vis hostile external groups.

A third general kind of response is the development of discontented groups of positive, socially integrative means for the satisfaction of their members' unsatisfied expectations. This response has characterized most discontented groups throughout Western history. In England, social protest was institutionalized through the trade unions, cooperative societies, and other self-help activities. In continental Europe, the discontent of the urban workers and petit bourgeoisie led to the organization of fraternal societies, unions, and political parties, which provided some intrinsic satisfactions for their members and which could channel demands more or less effectively to employers and into the political system. In the United States the chronic local uprisings of the late-18th, the 19th, and the early-20th century—such as the Shay, Whiskey, Dorr, and Green Corn Rebellions—have been largely superseded by organized, conventional political manifestations of local and regional interests. Labor violence similarly declined in the United States and England once trade unions were organized and recognized.

The contemporary efforts of black Americans to develop effective community organizations, and their demands for greater control of community affairs, seem to be squarely in this tradition. So are demands of student protesters for greater participation in university affairs, attempts of white urban citizens to create new neighborhood organizations, and the impulse of middle-class Americans to move to the suburbs where they can exercise greater control over the local government.

The initial effects of the organization of functional and community groups for self-help may be increased conflict, especially if the economic and political establishments attempt to subvert their efforts. But if these new organizations receive public and private cooperation and sufficient resources to carry out their activities, the prospects for violence are likely to be reduced. The social costs of this kind of group response seem much less than those of public and private violence. The human benefits are likely to be far greater than those attained through private violence or defensive withdrawal.

.   .   .

Out of Sight and Ignored
NICK KOTZ

Violence is usually thought of as having to do with physical force. But another subtle form of violence does exist in our society—the want and deprivation of the poor. Aided by the actions of the federal government, the decade of the 1960s saw the problems of poverty and hunger surface, causing a national disgrace in some quarters. Pulitzer prize-winning reporter Nick Kotz has written about hunger in America and has found fault with the way in which the nation as a whole has acted in attempting to deal with the problem.

Excerpted from the book *Let Them Eat Promises* by Nick Kotz. © 1969 by Nick Kotz. Published by Prentice-Hall, Inc., Englewood Cliffs, New Jersey.

In this country, thousands of young children feel pain. Some do not call it "hunger" because they have never known the feeling of a full stomach. Countless Americans are physically and mentally maimed for life, their entire destiny and contribution to society sharply limited by what they eat in the first four years of life or even by what their mothers ate during pregnancy. Hungry children cannot concentrate and do not learn at school; they develop lifetime attitudes about a hostile world. Malnourished men, already handicapped by limited education, are too listless to work. Modern science now has demonstrated clearly that the effects of malnutrition are far more significant than was ever imagined. We are now beginning to learn the costs of hunger—both to our national economy and to the individuals who suffer its effects.

Yet, after hunger and malnutrition among some ten million Americans became a clear political issue, South Carolina's Strom Thurmond and likeminded allies in the United States Senate almost succeeded in curbing a national study of the problem. "There has been hunger since the time of Jesus Christ and there always will be," stated Thurmond.

No one could argue with the first part of the senator's statement. The problem of hunger has been part of the human condition since the beginning, and various solutions, over the centuries, have been integral to the progress of civilization. Hunger has eliminated entire cultures from this planet, has changed the course of history for others. Little more than a hundred years ago, for example, a potato famine in Ireland brought scores of Irish to this country. Other severe food shortages contributed to the waves of immigrants seeking food and freedom in a nation that was rich in both. As we approach the twenty-first century, science has advanced to the point where men have traveled to the moon and returned safely, yet two-thirds of this world's people still suffer from malnutrition. Entire populations are stunted in physical development because they lack adequate diets. In America, however, the problems of hunger are not even remotely the same as those faced by underdeveloped nations where the population increase is outpacing ancient, outmoded agricultural methods, where the capacity to feed everyone does not exist.

This new American tragedy is that hunger and malnutrition, excruciating human misery and disease, should exist for millions—in the richest nation with the highest individual standard of living known to mankind. This is not the America of frozen colonial winters and men chewing on leather; of American soldiers scavenging for food as they fought their neighbors over questions of Union; of apple-selling Depression days when the poor died quietly and unknown while the very rich died in spectacular leaps from tall buildings that had been constructed of paper. This is the story of hunger in the America of the $900 billion gross national product, of the $200 billion federal budget, of 1.2 cars and 1.3 television sets per family, of eight million pleasure boats, of block-long supermarkets with entire meals frozen to be prepared instantly in automated kitchens. This is the America that pays farmers $3 billion annually not to plant food because it has developed an ingenious ability to produce far more than paying customers can eat, the America that spends millions on dieting because the affluent consumer can afford to eat too well. For the first time, this is the America fully equipped with the ability, the technology, and the wealth to fulfill its most sacred promises—life, liberty, and the pursuit of happiness.

Yet this nation in the late 1960s looked hunger in the

eyes but could not see it, glimpsed the truth about hunger but called only for more study of the problem, discounted hunger as a result of either laziness or ignorance, and finally—even after it reluctantly accepted the problem—could not arrange its national priorities to feed more than a fraction of the malnourished and hungry poor in 1970.

The nation should not have needed a survey to know that many millions of Americans suffer from inadequate nutrition, not because they are ignorant about proper diet, but because they are poor. More than one million Americans live in families with no income at all. Another five million Americans have less total income than the amount the Agriculture Department estimates is needed to maintain a barely minimum diet. Another nine million have such low income that maintaining an adequate diet would require spending from 50 to 100 percent of their meager funds on food alone. How can any of these 15 million poor Americans afford proper nutrition?

The answer is that millions cannot, and the government now is admitting it.

· · ·

During the recession of the late 1950s, hunger *had* been a problem, raising questions about woefully insufficient food aid to the jobless, but it never gained momentum as a political issue. During the 1960 Presidential campaign, John F. Kennedy had said that 17 million Americans go to bed hungry at night, but pressured by opponent Nixon to clarify that statement, Kennedy explained that he was quoting statistics on potential malnutrition.

Moved by the poverty he saw during the West Virginia primary, President Kennedy, on his first day in office, doubled the existing commodity aid program, and during the following years the quantity of food aid was expanded greatly. Compared to existing programs, these reforms were impressive; compared to the need, they were minimal. The fact that millions of Americans had too little to eat still made no strong impression on government or the public, and there still was no national commitment.

How could mass hunger among the American poor be ignored for so long? Why did the food aid reformers succeed in drawing attention to the subject in 1967 when others before them had failed?

To answer these questions, to follow the hunger story to its source, trace the history of certain American institutions. Travel to the plantation country of the Deep South to learn how its peculiar political, social, and economic institutions really operate for the cotton planter and for the black cotton worker; visit the company coal town in Appalachia to glimpse the effect of its institutions on the lives of miner, management, and absentee owner; walk in the rich fruit and vegetable valleys of Texas and California to see how life is shaped for the grower and for the Mexican-American picker. Follow agricultural laborers along the migrant stream to see how they fit into the institutions of Connecticut at tobacco picking time and of Iowa during the vegetable harvest; study the American Indian from Colonial days to his present home on a United States government reservation. And finally, to understand fully how poor people fit into a *new* set of American institutions, go along with all these forgotten Americans as they move into the bulging urban ghettoes.

* * *

As the Poverty Subcommittee and Citizens' Board of Inquiry traveled the nation, they saw countless examples of food and welfare benefits withheld or granted to suit the needs of local institutions. Food and welfare aid, in minimal amounts, were available for the docile poor who "stayed in line," but these benefits could be withheld from anyone who challenged or threatened the institutions by demanding full participation in society. In Greenwood, Mississippi, food aid benefits were cut off to punish Negroes leading a voter registration drive. In company coal towns of Kentucky, mothers who petitioned that the schools supply their children school lunches found that their schools responded by cutting their children out of the Neighborhood Youth Corps program. Indians in Oklahoma and Mexican-Americans in northern New Mexico learned that new poverty aid went only to those who blindly accepted corrupt local leadership.

Food aid programs in agricultural regions throughout the nation were turned on or off to suit the convenience and labor needs of the growers and planters. Coal companies in Appalachia, cotton planters in the Deep South, and vegetable-fruit growers in the Southwest all tried to keep their cheap labor in virtual bonded indebtedness by advancing them survival funds which they could never repay. The U.S. Department of Labor cooperated fully in the system of migrant labor, by which human beings are shipped and housed like cattle. In a more traditional kind of politics, surplus commodities were distributed in Des Moines and Chicago at the whim of the party bosses. The relationship between the poor and such institutions as local government, business, agriculture, or influential community organizations rarely was examined or understood.

Until the mid-1960s affluent America had never looked closely at the intimate details of extreme poverty. Entire groups of human beings were seen only dimly on the American landscape, as millions of Negroes, Mexican-Americans, Indians, Anglo-Saxon Appalachians, and scattered white men everywhere struggled with problems of poverty that the rest of the country did not comprehend.

• • •

Throughout our history, certain of our citizens have been systematically and legally excluded from the economic and social benefits which are provided to make life better for middle and upper America. The rural black and brown and white Americans whose sweat produced the cotton and the vegetables were the last to receive any of the legislative benefits of child labor regulations, minimum wage laws, unemployment compensation, collective bargaining rights, and social security. Many of these rights are still denied them today. Add to this the oppressive racial and ethnic discrimination that has been sanctioned throughout our history and, in the case of the American Indian, has been government-administered right down to 1969, when babies are dying from lack of food on Navajo reservations. The nation's concept of these "other Americans" was an abstract, distant one at best and never extended as far as an examination of diet and medical health. Even when the entire nation was stricken with the Depression of the 1930s, America responded mainly to meet the temporary economic needs of its middle class.

From the 1950s onward the civil rights movement drew increasing attention to the life of the black poor in the South. As the more obvious legal rights were won—at least on paper—the movement turned to the basic conditions of life throughout this country; and the War on Poverty, with its massive failures and overpromised programs, contributed to our learning process. But billion-dollar programs do not automatically solve problems of poverty, and the poor continued to complain, as riots swept the streets.

Throughout the 1960s, the nation expected instant success from its antipoverty efforts. If children continued to drop out of school despite Head Start, if job training courses did not produce instant mechanics, if the poor failed to hold jobs provided them by the magnanimity of private industry, then critics assumed this was proof of their conclusions about the worthlessness of the poor, about their laziness and indifference. It was only after the programs were well under way that the human victims of poverty finally came into view, and the program planners began to realize that generations-rooted poverty does not give way to simple solutions—especially when it is promoted and still supported by the basic local institutions.

A better school may help a child, but not if the child is sick, hungry, and sleepless from a night spent in the turbulent environment of overcrowded housing. A man may desire eagerly to participate in a job training program, but will fail if he lacks basic educational skills or the energy needed to perform the job. Job training will lead only to disillusionment if there is not a job available at the end of the course. If men still suffer and are not helped, it makes little difference that the government pours billions into programs.

The War on Poverty at least was a beginning. Out of the civil rights movement came dignity and self-determination. The Economic Opportunity Act, in its Community Action Program, tried to carry forward these all-American attitudes with a requirement of "maximum feasible participation of the poor"—a concept which met with resistance from political bosses in the cities, segregationist politicians in the South, self-righteous liberals, and well-entrenched philanthropic leaders. For whatever their reasons, most leaders of the established institutions firmly opposed giving the poor a real voice in determining their own future.

But there were important exceptions to this pattern of resistance, and the exceptions included other influential American institutions. Harvard University gave Dr. Robert Coles the freedom to roam the country and help the distressed; the Midwest department store fortune of the Marshall Field family backed Leslie Dunbar's commitment to raising Negro political power in the South; Walter Reuther committed the strength of his labor union to Richard Boone's efforts to develop indigenous leadership in the slums; the prestige and money of the NAACP Legal Defense Fund supported the energetic work of a young lawyer named Marian Wright. Finally, Robert Kennedy, assisted by the able Bill Smith and Peter Edelman, was buttressed by the power of the U.S. Senate, even though other powerful senators opposed his campaign. Each of these individuals worked within the framework of established American society, even as they dissented so that "these conditions will change, those children will live." Demonstrating intelligence, compassion, and courage in initiating the crusade against hunger, each saw the need for change and acted on it.

In the past, poor people spoke, if at all, to the government or the public only through welfare workers, precinct leaders, or plantation bosses. Purposefully or inadvertently, the story was lost in translation. But with new channels open to them, the poor could give vivid accounts of exploitation, discrimination, faulty government programs. They talked about the problems of poverty in terms of inadequate housing and clothing, of missing medical care, and of hostile or indifferent government officials. Now for the first time the poor began to speak for themselves in a voice louder than a whisper.

The voice said, "We are hungry."

Student Unrest in the 1960s
ALLEN YARNELL

Today in the United States it is fashionable to speak of a student culture, or counter-culture, that is thriving wherever youth is present. Both terms are imprecise and few, if any, of those who use them know exactly what they are talking about. What is known, however, is that at the beginning of the 1960s students began to assert themselves in a way that was very different from times past in America. Universities today are thought of as being breeding places for revolution. Berkeley, Columbia,

San Francisco State, Jackson State, and Kent State have become synonymous with student unrest and opposition to the established rules of order. Consideration of the real causes for the tragic campus confrontations has been avoided by much of society, and in this essay an attempt will be made to get at some of those causes.

Traditionally, college students in this country have been thought of as still-growing children being educated in order to enter the business or professional world. During the 1950s campuses in the United States were very quiet, with the exception of football celebrations or panty raids, and professors often criticized their students for lethargy. Perhaps the quietude was a function of the Eisenhower years generally, for those were years of taking stock in America—a middle class-oriented breathing spell—after which more social action would come. The election of John F. Kennedy in 1960 *seemed* to herald the coming of the new times.

Kennedy time and again made known his view that youth was wanted and needed in the government. College students identified with this young, vigorous President far more than they ever had with Dwight Eisenhower. Certainly, the nation's young people reacted in an overwhelmingly favorable manner to the Peace Corps, a program designed specifically to bring youth into government. The killing of John Kennedy in November 1963 had a tremendous impact on students. Here was a man who had held out some hope to the youth of the country. Where was that youth to turn now?

While Kennedy had inspired some college-age people to a form of activism, the civil rights movement provided a dramatic opportunity for social action for many students who were seeking to bring about change within the system. Blacks and whites entered the struggle for real equality in America. The college generation of the early 1960s was showing that it was quite different from what had preceded it. If nothing else, there was a moral commitment to equal rights and people were willing to work for it. At the same time some students began to realize that their position in society was one in which power was denied to them. As students became active in government and the "movement," they began to argue that they should have more control or power in their own areas, namely the colleges and universities. Critics of this mode of thought often point to the "radical" outlook of the now famous Port Huron statement, issued by the Students for a Democratic Society in 1962, as a main factor in stirring up student unrest. These critics fail to realize, however, that the seeds of discontent had been planted by society itself. The SDS merely responded to and took advantage of the situation. Students had been urged to take an active part in the system, and when they finally did, aiming their efforts at the campuses, the schools proved to be unresponsive. This was both frustrating and ironic, for the very people entrusted to educating this group were, by and large, oblivious to its needs.

The first major instance of student unrest in the 1960s took place on the campus of the University of California, Berkeley, in 1964. The issue was over free speech on campus, and although the disturbance received national media coverage, most Americans were not overly concerned by this one campus revolt. After 1964, however, another ingredient was added to the simmering pot of student discontent—Vietnam. Students by the thousands registered their criticism of the war and the way in which Lyndon Johnson escalated it after implying in 1964 that it would not become a major conflict. A great double cross had taken place. Many students believed that Barry Goldwater's foreign policy strategy was being put into effect by the man who had defeated him.

It is safe to say that by 1965–1966 increasing numbers of students were very much alienated by the system. The war continued, becoming more and more unpopular, with the Johnson administration seemingly paying no attention to student criticism. And students were becoming more and more disturbed at the impersonality that had become part of the college experience. At large universities quips like "go see the computer" became part of the jargon of registration. Added to that was the feeling that sitting in a lecture with two hundred other students and taking notes as if one were an automaton was something less than the best form of education. Students wanted to change *their* institutions of higher learning. Abolishing ROTC programs, changing traditional curriculum, and ridding the campus of war-related activities became some of the goals students fought for. And in the late 1960s black students made their specific demands felt, with much support from the student community generally, by literally forcing universities and colleges to provide courses in Afro-American studies. Many felt that real power was within the grasp of the college student.

The Columbia University disturbances in New York City during April and May of 1968 seemed to bring many of the problems causing student unrest to a head. (Columbia is discussed in some detail by Roger Kahn in the next section.) Students, angry about a university administration that seemed far removed from them, irritated over defense work being done on the campus, and specifically resentful over the university's intention of building a new gymnasium where a park existed, had a confrontation with the school's officials. Students attempting to hold buildings were beaten and arrested by New York City police in what has now become the famous middle-of-the-night raid. When the open hostilities had subsided (and Columbia's president, Grayson Kirk, had wisely decided to resign) the university was left in a sad state. The battles between students, police, and school personnel had resulted in anger, frustration, and distrust. By and large, the citizens of New York City looked with contempt and rage at those Columbia students who had tried to gain control. Many thought that these troublemakers had to be put in their place and, subsequently, the real reasons for the unrest were ignored by the city's residents.

Why is it that throughout the 1960s and into the 1970s so much of the adult population has tended to disregard or has failed to take student demands seriously? The answer, I think, stems from a stereotyped image that people have of students. The American student is thought to be lacking in mature judgment and incapable of making important decisions. This image is reinforced by the goodly proportion of college students who receive their allowances for four years or more from their parents. Parents often think of the campus as a place for big dances and athletic events, and incidentally as a place that will prepare their offspring for the real world. At just about any parents' weekend the school is spruced up, and event after event (there is always a major sports event of some sort) is scheduled to show fathers and mothers what today's colleges are all about. It is no wonder that adults are surprised and bewildered when disturbances take place. On their visits to the campus they have not been presented with a real situation. Rather, a great public relations effort has been put forth by both students and administrators to make certain that people will come away with the feeling that everything is going very well on their campus.

Also involved in the student stereotype is the visual image. Adults see college youth in jeans, wearing no shoes, with long hair and beards, and quite often react negatively to what they see. Parents see the campuses as swarming with hippies who want to destroy the system, when actually—almost by definition—a hippie would exclude himself from a campus. The hippie movement is a dropout movement. Genuine hippies are not university students, nor do they want to be. Instead they are seeking a better life by attempting to break away from the established society's way of doing things. Older people must be made aware of the distinctions in the thinking of today's youth. The nonuniversity population must be educated so that it can fully understand the problems that face the student. It is imperative that communication links be formed so these groups can better comprehend each others' actions.

Thus far, this essay has attempted to survey some of the causes and misunderstandings involved in student unrest. In terms of actual confrontations through 1968, Berkeley and Columbia were the most serious. However, in May 1970 the country was shocked by the shooting of students on two campuses, Kent State in Ohio and Jackson State in Mississippi. Kent State, where four young people were killed by Ohio National Guardsmen, received much more coverage by the media than predominantly black Jackson State where two were killed. What led to these tragic events? To be sure, on both campuses there were events unique to the situation. Generally, however, the incidents can be related to the United States' actions in Southeast Asia. At the end of April, American troops were sent into Cambodia, temporarily, to destroy enemy sanctuaries and installations. American students were stunned by this move and quickly joined ranks in expressing vehement opposition. As campus disturbances spread, so too did anger and hostility on the part of those who could not understand what the nation's youth was so upset about. At Kent State, when it was felt that matters were out of hand, the National Guard was sent in to quiet things down. Students and Guardsmen, many of them the same age, faced each other; the outcome of that confrontation was written in blood, the blood of students. Kent State, with its four slain, stands as an example of what can happen when government is insensitive to what students are saying. And the shootings at Jackson State, where law enforcement officials fired into a dormitory because sniper fire had allegedly come from it, also shows what can happen when student concerns are taken lightly.

The resentment over the United States' movements in Cambodia was so strong that the Nixon administration, almost immediately, began to put an end to the operation. Students on hundreds of campuses had demonstrated their presence and for once they were listened to. The deaths at Kent State and Jackson State illustrate dramatically that student unrest is a serious matter, which must be dealt with as such.

In 1971 things had apparently cooled down on the campuses. In California, for example, Governor Ronald Reagan shifted his attacks from the universities to the welfare system. Professors seemed greatly relieved because they could teach without disruption and could get back to the normal routine of educating. But does that mean that student unrest is over? The answer is an emphatic No. While riots have ended, at least as this essay is being written, the underlying causes are still present. The war goes on and continues to provide a reason for students to remain critical of the system. And in the United States, the most affluent nation in the world, corporations report that it is increasingly difficult to find first-rate college graduates to work for them.

Because students have grown up during a time of prosperity and affluence, they are less interested in the goal of material wealth than the students of earlier periods. There seems to be a feeling that the good life, from a material point of view, will always be there. This idea persists today, even though college graduates with every conceivable major cannot find employment. And for those who do graduate and take a position, student values still remain crucial. These people think about affecting society in a positive way. As students they came to believe they had a role to fulfill in bringing about change. As adults in the business world they can continue that work and help bridge the gap between the generations.

The Gathering Storm: The Vice President Who Had to Go to the Country

ROGER KAHN

In April and May of 1968 Columbia University became a battleground between students, administrators, and police. The crisis was precipitated by the desire of the school administration to build a new gymnasium. Why should this seemingly harmless act have been so important? Roger Kahn, a first-rate journalist, supplies the answer as he describes the forces that led to the trouble. Implicit in his analysis is a feeling for the frustration of the Columbia student.

Reprinted from *The Battle for Morningside Heights*, with omissions, by permission of William Morrow and Company, Inc. Copyright © 1970 by Roger Kahn.

In what has become a famous quotation from the left, Tom Hayden is supposed to have said of Columbia, "The one thing we knew we could count on was the continuing stupidity of Kirk and Truman." The judgment is harsh and incomplete. What the SDS could really count on was the irrationality, not of men but of a structure.

To make their revolutionary impact on campus, the radicals required prerequisites. The student body would best be disorganized. Unified students, with a real voice in running a university, tend to trust the democratic processes and shun radical action. The university authorities and faculty ideally would be involved in planning the Vietnam War. It would be difficult to focus Vietnam protest against, say, the peaceful faculty of Haverford. The university administration should be insensitive to the Negro drive for equal status. Arrogance toward blacks, and the underprivileged generally, is a model of an elitism. It can be called fascistic in debate.

Columbia met every prerequisite surpassingly. Its students were disorganized, its faculty did help with war planning and its administrators were insensitive to the poor people living near the campus. Beyond that, it was a weird autocracy. The president ruled without the advice and consent of a university senate. The faculty was passive. The trustees, under venerable law, could not be professors: educators were excluded from the management of Columbia. It would be difficult to find a purer kernel of irrationality among the great institutions of the American society.

According to Tomec Smith, past president of the Columbia University Student Council, the CUSC was organized shortly after World War II, when war veterans on campus wanted "to have some say" in their lives. "They were able to make a deal," Smith says. "The university agreed to consult them on matters pertaining to student life.

"A little while later, the university raised tuition. The students were informed.

"'All right,' they said. 'That pertains to us. We want to consult. Let's see your books.'

"As far as I know the council was not consulted for the next fifteen years."

A powerless council was tolerable during the Silent Fifties, when the torpor of Eisenhower's White House infused the country. But with the sixties, sleepers awoke. Now the student body became receptive to groups that, unlike their council, got things done. As politics grew strident, new political action organizations formed. CORE reached Columbia in 1963. An Independent Committee on Vietnam followed soon afterward.

Columbia's alliance with the American military, firm under Butler, the president who dismissed a pacifist, was reinforced under Eisenhower. Then, as the military needed more and more intellect, Columbia and her faculty profited nicely. The university was awarded $16 million in defense contracts during 1967. Although this does not approach M.I.T. ($92 million), it is better than the defense business of all but four other American universities. But Columbia, the ally of the military, had to pay a price.

Among the twenty-nine instructional departments at the college, one is openly devoted to war. The Department of Naval Science and Tactics, currently under Commander Julius M. Larson, U.S.N., teaches amphibious warfare, weapons analysis and seven other courses in bellicosity. Students who complete a four-year program win commissions in the naval reserve. Following tradition, the 1965 awards to outstanding N.R.O.T.C. students were to be handed out on College Walk in May.

The radical, or at least anti-war, movement at Columbia surfaced on a rainy spring afternoon in 1965. Because it rained May 7, the ceremonies were moved into the rotunda of Low. Vietnam was worsening, and, protesting "campus militarism," a mixed group of students staged a rally in front of Ferris Booth, the student activities center, 200 yards southwest of Low. Despite the rain, the rally drew 200 people.

Three representatives of the Independent Committee on Vietnam and two whites from CORE spoke. When the rally was over, about 150 of the demonstrators marched through the rain toward Low. Fifteen campus police, in gray uniforms, waited in an uncertain line. When the students charged, the outnumbered police stepped aside. The students swept up the thirty steps of Low, but there they stopped. The glass library doors were locked. Locked glass doors were sufficient to stop Columbia radicals in '65. The group was standing, indecisive, when twenty-three patrolmen from the 26th Precinct appeared at the bottom of the steps.

The city police formed a double file and marched up the steps toward the demonstrators. The blue of cops and the plaids of students merged. Some students shouted. A policeman threw a punch. The scuffling grew rougher. A policeman slammed someone into a glass door, which shattered. Inside Low, Grayson Kirk was watching the fight. He ordered the Naval R.O.T.C. ceremony stopped, and with this announcement, police and rioters dispersed. For only the second time since the riotous commencement of 1811, student protest had interrupted an important university function.

Kirk first wanted to discipline the protesters. They could be placed on probation, suspended or even expelled. But when hundreds of students and faculty petitioned for an investigation, Kirk settled for a fact-finding commission. In the immutable manner of commissions, this one proposed the creation of another commission. The second group was to investigate "the quality and nature of student life" at Columbia.

As SDS grew at Columbia, the Independent Committee on Vietnam waned. Many of the same people were in each, and SDS had a broader appeal. The developing SDS met often, talked long, planned avidly and, in the autumn of 1966, organized a peaceful protest march when recruiters from the CIA came to Columbia. But mostly in 1966, SDS, like the clock as the hour approaches, was collecting its energy to strike.

CIA was a rather diffuse issue; the Columbia connection appeared shadowy and undramatic. Immediacy was more than ever the key: relating outside problems urgently to the campus. Looking elsewhere, SDS found a stronger case in Columbia's intercourse with a comparatively obscure body called the Institute for Defense Analyses.

The IDA was established by the Department of Defense and by the Joint Chiefs of Staff in 1955 to obtain organized research from university sources on the technology of making modern war. Clemenceau's remark that "war is too important to leave to the generals" is obsolete. Modern warfare is now too *complicated* for generals. Preparing is a business for physicists and chemists; it has been since weaponry exploded into the atomic bomb. Today's generals are tacticians and executives, administering programs conceived by Ph.Ds. IDA contractors plan weapons, such as the ABM, evaluate weapons systems and devise stratagems for global war. This highly secret agency is housed in a faceless modern building, 400 Army Navy Drive, in Arlington, Virginia, which it shares with a bank. To one side stands the interminable Pentagon. To another are the crowded airlanes approaching Washington National Airport.

The IDA runs on an annual budget of about $15 million and exists principally but not exclusively on government contracts. Technically, it is a private corporation. Five universities, M.I.T., Case Institute, Stanford, Tulane and California Institute of Technology, served as the original institutional sponsors. Seven others came later. Columbia joined in 1959. What finally made the IDA immediate to Morningside Heights was that President Grayson Kirk became an IDA trustee and a Columbia trustee, William A. M. Burden, became IDA board chairman.

In 1967, the SDS leaked information to *The Daily Spectator*. The SDS charged accurately that a number of Columbia professors possessed IDA contracts. The radicals also asserted that the IDA had "a facility" on the Columbia campus. Norman Christeller, the general manager of the IDA, is still furious about the second charge. Christeller smokes a pipe and wears spectacles, and works in shirtsleeves. He is an excutive, rather than a scientist, and his manner is forceful and informal. As we were sitting in his Arlington office, with shuttle planes shrill beside the window, he was a man with paternal pride in IDA. The *Spectator* had lied about his baby.

"I want to point out," Christeller said, "that a *Spectator* reporter telephoned and asked point-blank if we maintained a facility at Columbia. We did and I described it to him."

Behind the spectacles, Christeller's mild eyes showed anger. "The facility is a small safe, two feet across by three feet deep by one foot high. It's used to keep classified papers. I explained this to the *Spectator* reporter. Then he wrote there was a secret IDA facility at Columbia, without stating what it was, so that it looked as if we had a building up there, a major installation, possibly performing secret work. The reporter never wrote that all we had was this small safe."

Norman Christeller emphasizes the non-defense work, which forms a certain portion of the IDA program. "For example," he says, "we studied the feasibility of the supersonic transport plane, looking at it from a number of angles, including the U.S. balance of payments. Our study was not encouraging." He argues that war planning can turn out to be anti-war. "A projection of nuclear casualty rates makes a brilliant case for permanent peace."

"But before you do any study, you have to get it funded."

"That's right."

"Well, could you fund a study on the long-term effects of the Vietnam War on the American economy?"

Christeller shakes his head. "I wish we could."

Someone prominent in the defense complex points to the IDA as a force for moderation. "You have thinkers there, men of sense and moderation. A helluva lot of their work is putting a check on the hawk-nuts in the Pentagon." Others suggest that attacking IDA is just one more irrationality. To assault the IDA is to assault armorers. Why attack the men who forged the breastplates that cloaked the heart of warlike Gothic kings? It is not they, but kings, who make the wars.

These are fair areas for debate, but the SDS needed a disruptive issue. By planting a story in *Spectator* and getting an overstated account as a bonus, the SDS was successfully using the liberal press to oversimplify a complex issue. Columbia stood with the war lords. That was that. The pace on campus was quickening every spring. Kirk needed help. He soon would shuffle his staff, demoting Jacques Barzun, promoting David Truman from

Dean of Columbia College to Executive Vice President. But not Barzun, not Truman, nor anyone else in administration recognized the severity of the gathering storm.

In late April, 1967, four U.S. marines set up tables in the lobby of John Jay Hall, an undergraduate dormitory at the southeast corner of the main campus. The marines were there to recruit.

Ted Kaptchuk, Columbia '68, chairman of the SDS, was preparing leaflets urging a powerful protest. While the marines were inside John Jay, a few hundred pickets would surround the building. The marines would then be trapped. The pickets would keep them trapped until the university administration agreed to terminate campus recruiting for "war-related" groups: Army, CIA, Air Force, Dow Chemical.

Kaptchuk won limited student support, but at the same time a group of about fifty other students decided that SDS activity on campus had gone too far. They prepared a counter-strategy.

On schedule, the marines moved into the lobby of John Jay Hall. Then fifty conservative students formed a protective cordon. When the radicals closed in, they could not reach the marines. The SDS people set up a picket line and chanted, "Marines must go."

The conservatives, the so-called jocks, set up a counter-chant. "SDS must go. SDS must go." The four marines, splendid in dress uniforms, looked edgy.

It was a hot afternoon. Radicals and conservatives closed on a narrow patch of lawn in front of John Jay. The crowd milled rather than scuffled at first.

"War-lover!"

"Go cut your hair!"

"Jocks must go."

"You guys only believe in free speech for yourselves."

And then a crusher. "Ah, fuck you."

"What did you say?"

"I said, fuck you, Mac."

The crowd was so heavy and so boisterous under the hot sun that no one could say for certain who was shouting what. The last expletive is significant because immediately afterward, a stocky, well-built radical and a blond jock in white shirt began punching one another. There were four other fist fights. Then a Columbia official announced that the marine recruiters were leaving for the day. "Recruiting will be stopped," he said. "It will be resumed tomorrow."

On the following day eight hundred students peacefully picketed in the Van Am Quadrangle, before John Jay, Livingston and Hamilton. About five hundred marched in support of the marines. There was no further violence; the marines finished their business, attracting few volunteers, and left. The day was done, but the question of campus demonstrations had risen clearly as the moon. Then Kirk, demanding a solution, ordered: No further demonstrations inside buildings. His thinking proceeded straight from the philosophies of King Canute.

The SDS did not have to contrive a second issue with impact beyond the campus. A second one was offered by Columbia, one of the largest and most aggressive landlords on earth.

Only the Roman Catholic Church owns more property within Manhattan than Columbia. Including the land underneath Rockefeller Center, Columbia's off-campus real estate exceeds $70 million. In addition, Columbia holds mortgages worth about $80 million. According to published figures, Columbia assets at the end of 1967 were $425 million. "Land and buildings being used," that is, the campus, had a book value of $130 million. Arithmetic demonstrates that more than half the university assets—$280 million—were land, buildings, mortgages. No

other American university has a comparable commitment
to real estate. Harvard, with an endowment of more than
a billion dollars, does not own one parcel of investment
real estate. Almost sixty percent of Harvard's money
rests, or grows, in common stocks.

Columbia came into its fortune because Manhattan real
estate appreciated. The historical pattern has continued.
Columbia, the multiversity, is first a real estate holding
company. At least five of Columbia's trustees are prominent in real estate and building finance. Three collabo-
rated in erecting an office building in the Wall Street area,
with a timely opening loan from Columbia. There is no
evidence of anything illegal, just the time-honored business practice of people using contacts to find financing,
tenants and profit. The men who run Columbia, the trustees, think like realtors. Their attitude, and the attitude
of administrators, is often that of the realtor; above all,
what is going to happen to property values.

In late 1966, Percy Uris, a chairman of the Trustees
Finance Committee, assembled an entire block (Front
Street, South Street, Gouverneur Lane and Wall Street)
in the financial district of Manhattan. Columbia (Percy
Uris, trustee) then leased the land to Uris Buildings Corporation (Percy Uris, chairman) at an annual rent of
$400,000 until the year 2009. Uris Buildings planned to
erect an office building, but to help obtain financing, it
needed a committed tenant. An early committed tenant
was the First National City Bank (Alan Temple, Columbia trustee, vice-president). Financing was eased by a
$22 million loan to Uris Buildings from the Irving Trust
Company (William Petersen, Columbia trustee, president).
One real estate deal. Three Columbia trustees. Of such
is the kingdom of academe.

In the cyclic nature of Manhattan development, the
West Side began a decline after World War II. Despite

excellent transportation and commanding views, the region twenty-five blocks north of the theater district slumped. "The only time I go west of Fifth," says the East Sider in one recent story, "is when I'm going to Europe. I take a taxi straight to a Hudson River pier."

When West Side real estate values declined, Columbia's institutional approach was not, what can we do to help the city that harbors us? Instead it was a furious determination to help Columbia.

In the days after World II, a Puerto Rican immigration to New York began. The Latins jammed into Eastern Airlines coaches—federal subsidy kept the fare low—and settled in pockets on the West Side. Old residents were moving to the suburbs. Now venerable brownstones became slum roominghouses. One four-story building on West 75th Street, once a two-family home, came to house eighty people and a brothel. Puerto Ricans in New York found menial jobs or none, but apparently Manhattan poverty was more bearable than whatever had been left. They remained. On summer nights on the West Side, once-quiet streets resounded with dull drums and moaning songs.

A few years after the Puerto Rican influx, Negroes began overflowing Harlem. Birth rates in Harlem were high —so were death rates—and there was also a tide of mankind rolling up from the dirt farms of the South. When Harlem overflowed, the current ran west.

During the fifties, the Puerto Rican population of Morningside Heights nearly doubled. It rose from 1,650 to 3,014. The black increase was almost seven hundred percent, 470 to 3,133. Stated differently, whites were ninety-one percent of the Morningside Heights population in 1950. Ten years later, they were seventy-three percent. What was happening to American cities everywhere was happening in miniature around Columbia. As one instructor remarked in a letter, "What a wonderful opportunity for Columbia to research something more important than new weapons systems. What a chance to research how the American city could survive integration."

But the trustees and executives of Columbia, the real estate holding company, had a prior and overriding commitment. They had to protect real assets. Their method was to drive off the underprivileged.

According to one researcher, "The Columbia exclusionary process that developed is a kind of cultured racism. We are not talking about men with a redneck hatred for niggers and spics. What is involved is a 'distaste.' "

Columbia's earliest effort to preserve its neighborhood dates from 1947. In that year Morningside Heights, Incorporated, was organized. Dominated by Columbia, MHI also included Union Theological Seminary, St. Luke's Hospital, the Jewish Theological Seminary and Riverside Church. Its announced purpose was "to promote the improvement" of the neighborhood as "an attractive residential, educational and cultural area." It was also to prevent squabbling among members about who bought what parcel of land. David Rockefeller was the first president.

MHI is an example of private enterprise falling flat. The ultimate problem was conflict of interest: public good versus private gain. "Whoever owns the land has the leverage," says Warren Goodell, an important Columbia vice-president. Playing for leverage and saving a community are inimicable, and in the end Columbia grabbed land.

When MHI built a middle-income development in the early 1950's, many indigenous residents, put out of their homes, were bitter. *Fortune* Magazine reported that "the whole community has experienced a psychological and physical turning [against MHI and Columbia]." By 1959,

MHI decided that its job was just too large. The directors signed a report attesting to neighborhood change and asked for an urban renewal plan. That would have brought city officials and federal funds into the area.

Why did Columbia and MHI wait too long to call for help? The answer seems to be that to Columbia trustees, MHI was part of an enormous private plan for private gain. After decay depressed realty values, the West Side of Manhattan was to be turned into an upper income area. Property values would then increase like an algebraic progression. Columbia's endowment would sextuple. So, incidentally, could the fortunes of trustees with investments and careers in Manhattan real estate. The master scheme would proceed between cultural redoubts: Columbia on the north and Lincoln Center on the south.

Grayson Kirk and the multiversity trustees wanted a Columbia complex running from 110th Street to 123rd, and from the handsome buildings of Riverside Drive to the cliffs of Morningside Park. The projected plan would double space for classes, offices and laboratories. Faculty and student housing would be constructed. The new Columbia tract, three-quarters of a square mile in all, would be the largest urban intellectual hegemony in history. At the time of the riots, Columbia trustees were considering schemes to press clear up to 135th Street and the river.

At the south end Lincoln Center, an uneven mix of white stone and glass, stands completed. The center includes a glorious opera house, an acoustic enigma of a concert hall, theaters, the Juilliard School of Music, a bandshell. Around it one finds more than a dozen new apartment buildings, charging rentals of $100 a room. They have replaced old buildings where $100 was the rent for two or three *floors*.

Between Columbia's projected southern border at 110th Street and Lincoln Center lies an area approaching four

square miles. Much of it is rundown and ready for renewal. The potential developers' profits could reach billions.

One cannot draw absolute lines. One cannot say here,
this is how much Columbia wanted a better neighborhood for a university park, and here, this is how much
Columbia trustees wanted a West Side boom for private
profit. What one can say is that the lines of interest inter-
sected. The policy that emerged was inhuman.

In all, Columbia had acquired only twenty-seven off-
campus buildings in the Heights by 1934. Twenty-two
buildings were added in the next twenty years. Then
Columbia expansionists went wild: eighteen new buildings between 1955 and 1959; fifty-three new buildings between 1960 and 1964; sixty-two more in the years before
the strike. In nonarithmetic, human terms, the story becomes an assault of Columbia, the immense institution,
on underprivileged human beings, living in Manhattan's
SROs.

The SRO, a single-room-occupancy building, is the foul
essence of the New York slum. It was once an apartment
house. Now it has been broken into single rooms. Each
is equipped with a sprinkler to prevent death by fire.
Few other precautions are taken.

One social worker, Joan H. Shapiro, pictures SRO life
like this:

> Physical idleness and passivity, enforced by debilitation
> and limited life chances, create a vacuum. The future,
> over which one had no control and for which one
> could not plan, held no promise of change. The passage
> of days was marked rhythmically in two-week cycles
> by "check days"; when welfare checks arrived, the rent
> and money owed to the manager of the building was
> withheld, and the rest given to the tenant. Over the

remaining thirteen days, tenants eked out an existence on an average of $19.80 for food and personal items for one person. Sporadic violence was the only form of excitement.

.   .   .

One recent day a tenant in a Manhattan SRO went out and bought a rifle. Later, high on narcotics, he began shooting birds. Or he thought he was shooting birds. Actually his rifle was pointed, from his sixth-floor window, down and across the street. On the opposite sidewalk, a man fell over, a bullet through his chest. He gurgled briefly, bled and died. He had been a hard-working man, the superintendent of several buildings. The killer told the police over and over again, "I was just trying to kill some pigeons."

The cruelty of the SRO is profitable. Occupying the same space, eight derelicts pay more rent than a single family. New York officials have plans for outlawing the SROs. Even now children are barred. But hundreds of SROs continue to rot on the West Side of Manhattan. There is no more frightful testament to a failure of the American society.

Columbia did not approach SROs as a civic helper. Stanley Salmen, coordinator of university planning from 1956 to 1967, articulated the attitude. "Some SROs are well run, but about half are pits of degradation, a disgrace to the city and *impossible neighbors to institutions attracting students from all over the world.*" Salmen uttered the limit of Columbia compassion. SROs were first a logistics problem. They had to be cleared quickly, or to be captured.

During the last decade, Columbia removed 6,800 SRO tenants from its environs. For the victims, Columbia created a new division, called, ironically, the Office of Neighborhood Services. Bertram Weinert, the first director, was fired. He failed to remove tenants quickly enough. Weinert's successor, Ronald Golden, "placed more emphasis on meeting deadlines."

In clearing the buildings, Columbia employees varied technique to meet the obstacle. A number of middle-class apartments "had to be" demolished to allow Columbia expansion. Here the university reduced services: dumbwaiters were sealed so that garbage would be carried by hand; heat was withheld in winter. Marie Runyon of 178 Morningside Drive, who has fought Columbia eviction for ten years, reports, "We do get plenty of heat in summer. When the thermometer hits ninety, they send heat." Only six tenants are left in Miss Runyon's apartment building. It has all the geniality of a ruin.

People like Miss Runyon understand law and lawyers. Harassed beyond a certain point, they take Columbia to court. Occupants of SROs are afraid of the law. Many have criminal records. A representative case of Columbia's neighborhood services took place at an SRO calling itself the Oxford Hotel.

A tenant of the Oxford, a woman named Yvelle Walker, tried to pay her rent after Columbia had purchased the building.

"Keep the rent," said a Columbia agent. "Columbia is going to use this place for offices. Everyone has to get out." He offered her $25 to move. Miss Walker, within her rights and the law, refused.

A week later, Columbia refused the rent again. "Just hurry," the agent said, "and find a place to move."

That night, the lock in the door to Miss Walker's room was plugged with a sticky substance, possibly wax. She could not get into her own room. She spent the night with friends. She left the Oxford Hotel soon afterward.

Another tenant of the Oxford, Bernard Moore, charges that a Columbia agent persuaded the police to harass him. Once, after attending a meeting of the Riverside

Democratic Club, Moore returned to his room and found that it had been searched. Soon he moved out. The last tenants in the Oxford fled in 1967. It now houses the Goddard Institute for Space Studies.

Neglect is as effective as harassment, and Columbia perfected neglect in its stewardship of 609 West 115th Street, an SRO known as Conhar Hall, A building inspector found sixty-three violations in Conhar Hall during October, 1966. Conhar Hall tenants were without heat or hot water. The elevator was not functioning. Windows were broken. Garbage went uncollected. Doors had no locks. Toilets leaked. Roaches crawled. Rats prowled. Several months later, Conhar Hall was ready for demolition. All of its tenants had gone.

Columbia's treatment of other SRO tenants followed a three-stage pattern. First buildings were neglected. Then the occupants were harassed with door pluggings and police pressure. Finally, if this failed, rent checks were refused and eviction proceedings begun. There has probably never been a more efficient removal of people by a university, nor one as kindless, The numbers are cold testimony: within four recent years, nine SROs were demolished. Three were converted to university use. More than a thousand people literally were put into the street.

Columbia, the multiversity, wanted land, buildings, power. That policy overrode all others. The academic compassion of the sociology instructor was only incidental; the sociologist's employer had created grief.

Seen in the light of this history, Columbia's unbuilt gymnasium is more than a mixed facility for black and white. It is an outpost to the barony, keeping the blacks in place, nine floors below, and discouraging crossings from the neighborhood of Harlem to the neighborhood of Morningside Heights.

The gymnasium issue was as real as prejudice.

Environment and the
Quality of Political Life
GRANT McCONNELL

*Another form of violence in America has been man's
abuse of the environment. Historically, as political scientist and conservationist Grant McConnell explains, there
has been a movement to save our national resources since
the turn of the century. However, the drive of the 1960s
and 1970 is different from that of the Progressive period.
McConnell believes that advances in American technology
have led to changes in thinking in terms of conservation.
His observations on the role of a national culture are
especially interesting.*

Excerpted from "Environment and the Quality of Political Life,"
Congress and the Environment, by Grant McConnell, edited by
Richard A. Cooley and Geoffrey Wandesford-Smith. Copyright ©
1970 by the University of Washington Press.

Recently one of the scholarly journals carried the observation that the conservation movement "has come of age." In its implicit recognition of the growing effectiveness of conservation, this is a statement in which all of us must take much interest. This paper glances back over some of the history of conservation and looks at some of the reasons why it is possible to say that conservation has come of age.

．　　．　　．

I

What has been the nature of the conservation movement in recent years, and in what ways has it changed? Consider what the situation was in 1954. The drive for the Upper Colorado Storage Project was in high gear, and the fate of Dinosaur National Monument and with it the sanctity of the entire National Park System was all but sealed. Conservation representatives were valiantly testifying before hostile senators from Utah and other Rocky Mountain states. Senator Watkins, for example, attempted with all the advantages of his official position to break the dignity and courage of David Brower, who was dramatically demonstrating the technical possibility of an alternative plan that would leave Echo Park untouched. One of the facts that Senator Watkins extracted was that the Sierra Club was an organization of a mere eight thousand members. In the Northwest, the Olympic Park had just been subjected to another of its periodic attacks. And in the Northwest, also just a year later, it became apparent that the North Cascades were marked for the sort of "intensive management" by the Forest Service that could only spell destruction of their unique values of wilderness and beauty. A handful of people met in a living room in Auburn, Washington, to discuss the problem; it was a very glum occasion.

Contrast this situation with that of the first decade of this century. The conservation movement was apparently the strongest political force in the country. It was led by an unusually gifted politician, Gifford Pinchot, a man who not only had a very firm idea of what he was about but also had the ear of a very sympathetic President. He was largely responsible for the act establishing the Forest Service and for creating the administrative doctrine by which the agency has been run since. In 1908 he and his chief held a conference of the governors of the United States, justices of the Supreme Court, members of Congress and representatives of some sixty-eight national societies, and other distinguished individuals. The subject was conservation—conservation of forests, minerals, soils, and water. There was a spate of similar conferences around the country, and "conservation" must have been a word of greater currency then than any other of its length in the English language. And it was in 1908 that the term, "conservation movement," was invented—once again the work of Pinchot and his associates.

*   *   *

In the years between 1905 and 1910, Gifford Pinchot put forth mighty efforts to make conservation a popular cause. Not only did he invent a name, coin slogans, and hold meetings—he wrote and spoke endlessly. To him we can be grateful for the fact that nobody today will admit he opposes conservation—to do that would be equivalent to spitting on the flag or decrying motherhood. It is a great advantage. But we should not lose sight of the fact that in hard political terms, he got his real results by virtue of his close personal association with Theodore Roosevelt. When Roosevelt left office and took off for his

African safari, the influence of Pinchot quickly faded, and, with it, that of the conservation movement he had invented.

.   .   .

One other feature of the first part of the century calls for special note. The effort to make conservation a popular movement at that time involved a very particular political philosophy. This was the doctrine of Progressivism. This was undoubtedly inevitable, since conservation was dependent on a particular group of national leaders who were committed to that doctrine. It was not a very sophisticated doctrine, indeed to call it a political philosophy is to dignify it unduly. It is worth noting briefly several of the tenets of Progressivism. In the first place, Progressivism dwelt particularly, in Pinchot's words, on "the greatest good of the greatest number in the long run." That this slogan was a very slightly amended bit of plagiarism seems never to have been appreciated by Pinchot. He was not an intellectually sophisticated man, and all the evidence indicates that he thought he had invented a scientific formula that would lead inevitably to certain and unquestionable results. The fact, of course, was that this formula, minus the bit about the long run, was the invention of an eighteenth-century English philosopher, Jeremy Bentham, and that it was ridden with ambiguity. Specifically, what *kind* of good, and for which people? Are all "goods" equal in nature? And are all desires to be placed on the same plane? Such questions never entered into Pinchot's reflections, at least insofar as we are able to determine from his autobiography, his speeches, or his teachings to his agency. He was a supremely self-assured individual.

These abstract questions would be unimportant were he a mere political philosopher. But, on the contrary, he was a powerful agency head, with something like an eighth of the surface of the United States under his command and with the formation of a whole doctrine under his pen. What this all meant in practice was that the question about the *kind* of good was answered—all goods were equal. It was simply a matter of adding them up. Ultimately, it meant that those which could be measured were to be regarded as the only values that were hard and real. It is not surprising in the American context of the highly materialistic period of the early twentieth century that the dollar proved to be the best unit of measurement. And, at a later date, it has not been surprising to find that a sort of head count (as in the number of people using a bit of wilderness) should be a major test by Pinchot's agency as to whether it was justified in setting aside the area to be unimpaired. Both tests flew in the face of the experience and history that has just been traced. The dollar test was hopelessly biased in favor of material returns—sawlogs, jobs, and so on. The head count test necessarily produced the result that wilderness was less satisfying of the greatest good than a network of logging roads paid for by the logs taken out but providing an abundance of picnic tables in however devastated a landscape. If there is any doubt about this outcome from his outlook—after all, Pinchot was a logical man—consider this authoritative statement: "The object of our forest policy is not to preserve the forests because they are beautiful . . . or because they are refuges for the wild creatures of the wilderness . . . but . . . the making of prosperous homes. . . . Every other consideration becomes secondary." He was an out-and-out materialist, and, not surprisingly, his child, the United States Forest Service, has had great difficulty in surmounting the limitations which he set for it.

This test of the greatest good, moreover, implied something else which has had great importance in the shaping of American public policy. It implied some quasi-mathematical criterion and a kind of scientism in the process of decision making. Professor Samuel P. Hays has characterized conservation in the period of Pinchot and in the tradition that followed him as "the gospel of efficiency." Standing in the tradition briefly outlined above, Pinchot's doctrine implied that when it came down to choices as to which values should be preferred in the use of National Forest land, experts should have the say and the decision. In choosing, for example, between logging and wilderness, the Forest Service should be allowed to make the determination in the light of its peculiar expertise. This might be well and good if the decisions were merely whether logs could be economically taken out at a given moment, but there is no scientific expertise that can say whether logs are better than wilderness at *any* time. The claim to the power to decide was a claim to an extreme of discretion. This claim was all the more serious for being made in the presence of a materialistic bias of which Pinchot and his followers were unquestioning, and, perhaps, unaware. This characteristic of scientism, at any rate, underlines the degree to which the "conservation movement" started by Pinchot in the early part of the century was less than a popular movement. In a quite ultimate sense it was nondemocratic, although it had pretensions as a democratic movement. But this was democratic in the sense that experts would determine what was the greatest good. Whether by the test of popular support or by that of philosophic intent, conservation in the early period of this century was not a democratic movement.

II

What we see today, what goes by the old tag of conservation movement, is a different kind of animal. We now behold a movement with a strong popular base. It is not the sort of thing that progressivism fostered, a gathering up of material demands upon the natural resources of the environment, with all demands having equal standing except as they were made by more or fewer people as measured by an elite of experts. We have, rather, a body of belief firmly grounded on a set of principles cherished by a substantial and growing segment of the public. This is a fact of the first political magnitude, one that requires explanation.

• • •

A full explanation would be complex. On the face of things it might seem that the values of great numbers of Americans have changed over the years. In the sense that values are really testable only by choices actually given effect, this is plainly true. But this is to say very little. There is a genuine possibility that recent generations have wanted different things than their predecessors, but in view of the possibility that the political system may have had a bias in validating some preferences instead of others, casting aspersions on our ancestors as a wholly materialist lot is not justified. If current Americans show more signs of caring for the nonmaterial aspects of their environment, it may well be because the political order has evolved sufficiently to allow such concern to have occasional effect.

There are good grounds for believing that this is the case. Very briefly, the United States is much more of a nation than it has been in the past. It is knit together with roads, airlines, telephones, television, and magazines to a degree difficult to foresee even a relatively few decades ago. The horizons of the average American have vastly expanded so that the inhabitants of Sauk Center and all its real counterparts now share a national culture as never before. Inevitably, this has been reflected in the workings of the political system. Many decisions that were formerly within the exclusive provinces of states and localities are now made in larger arenas, arenas in which an inevitably greater diversity of citizens participate.

Formerly, choices on the allocation of values, as for example between natural beauty and resource exploitation, was largely in the hands of localities and, in fact, was regarded as mainly a private matter. Insofar as the choice lay in the hands of a lumber or a mining company, the choice for exploitation was preordained. But the situation was more complex than this suggests. If the choice were in the hands—as it usually has been—of a locality or a state in which the lumbering or mining industry bulked particularly large, the support of the community or state would flow to the narrow interests of such industry. Some local citizens would be aggrieved at the costs in natural beauty and wilderness but their voices would be so weak in face of the seemingly monolithic determination of their neighbors as to be beneath the threshold of hearing. Indeed, the feeling of powerlessness would generally lead them not to speak at all, given the inevitability of failure and the necessity of living with those neighbors.

Thus, it has generally been true that fights for conservation have taken on an aspect of outsiders against locals. The appearance has been false in that almost any locality contains some individuals concerned for conservation. Nevertheless, these individuals could only be heard in chorus with like-minded fellows drawn from a larger constituency. The exploiters of commodities, understanding the situation at least intuitively, have persistently appealed to the strong American tradition of decentralization as a supposedly democratic principle and have sought to retain the power of decision in local hands. There have been contests in which localities have lined up for conservation, establishment of the Gila Wilderness, for example, but these have been rare. Conservation, and conservation of wilderness and scenic values especially, have depended on creation of larger constituencies. Thus it is not difficult to imagine what would have happened to the Grand Canyon if its future had been left to Arizona to decide instead of the nation; the American people as a whole have a far smaller per capita money stake in damming the canyon's potential kilowatts than do the people of Arizona. It is also understandable why officials of Humboldt County resisted creation of a Redwoods National Park, while a strong drive for the park came from San Francisco, and why opposition to the North Cascades Park was loudest in Bellingham and Wenatchee and weakest in Seattle.

The change that has come about is far from total. It is in degree only. It is, moreover, a change of some complexity. It involves a new awareness and knowledge of people in New England, the Midwest, and California about the North Cascades, many miles distant from their homes. It involves the increasing urbanization of Americans and the drift of political power to city dwellers. It involves the changing economic base of cities like Seattle, with the relative decline and position of the lumber industry. Thus, it is not inconceivable that the success of the Boeing Company may have been the essential factor in preserving the North Cascades. The change also involves the development of national conservation organizations. All of these have converged in the creation of a larger and more diverse constituency, with a consequently growing power supporting wilderness, scenic values, and environmental protection.

III

Second, a deep and general change has occurred in our national political life. This is now a rich and prosperous nation. We now have a large generation of youth that has no memory of depression. At long last, we are generally free of the incubus of fear that tomorrow the economy will collapse. This has a very profound meaning—that the substance of political and moral life is no longer almost wholly economic. Economic matters have, in the past, been highly preoccupying, simply because hitherto we have never been out of the shadow of potential famine or other economic disaster. It is highly unlikely that men have ever really believed that economic affairs are the most important department of life, but it is true that we have always so far had to give first thought to that department simply because it has had a prior urgency. As a result, our political system has been formulated to adjust economic claims, and it has worked peculiarly well. The reason for this is that economic claims are bargainable; it is almost always possible to split the difference somewhere in an economic contest so that each side is reasonably satisfied. When we respond to the injunction, "Come, let us reason together," it is to bargain and to split differences.

As the nation has become richer, however, economic values have lost their old urgency and other more important matters have emerged and taken the foreground. The values of natural beauty and wilderness are critical examples here. But these are really not bargainable. The sort of "reasoning" which has been characteristic of politics on the economic model does not apply. It is faintly conceivable, for example, that by offering a sufficiently high price to the National Museum in Amsterdam to acquire its treasure, *The Night Watch*, one could get that great painting away from the Dutch; but it is absolutely inconceivable that one could make a deal to get a two-foot square cut out of the lower left-hand quadrant of the picture for *any* price. This is just not a possible bargain.

So it is with supposed bargains offered on natural beauty and wilderness. To bargain over the Grand Canyon, the redwoods, the North Cascades, may seem eminently sensible if you are interested in kilowatts, lumber, or copper, but it is nonetheless immoral if your concern is with scenic beauty and wilderness. Such a bargain might be possible if the value of scenic beauty and wilderness could be stated in the same dollar measure as kilowatts, lumber, and copper. It would, alternatively, be bargainable if the economic developers were able to offer a new Grand Canyon, some new two-thousand-year-old redwoods, or some new North Cascades in the exchange. Unfortunately, however, this alternative has practical difficulties. The fact of the matter is that any such bargain is completely one-sided—to take away more or less of the Grand Canyon, the redwoods, or the North Cascades. The brute power of the opposition may conceivably win, but such an outcome will not be a bargain in the sense of being mutually acceptable.

This fundamental characteristic of the politics of conservation is deeply involved in what has occurred with the conservation movement. There is much evidence that Americans today have moved beyond the conception that everything of meaning in life can be stated in either dollar or head-count terms. It is evident, for example, that many Americans are willing to go to extreme lengths in their principled opposition to the Viet Nam War. It is plain that many individuals are willing to lay their lives on the line for simple human dignity. And many of our best young people are going to extremes to assert their rejection of the material calculus. Both moral and aesthetic principles are emerging everywhere as the fundamental material of politics and common life. In this setting, increasing numbers of individuals are declaring themselves for what they really believe in. It is hardly surprising that many are declaring the values of scenic beauty and wilderness; there are hardly any values less uncertain and ambiguous than these. Formerly, the sort of ridicule offered by spokesmen for firms such as the Kennecott Copper Corporation, that concern for these values is "sentimental," was effective. We were once half persuaded that such concern was soft-headed, and that these values were inferior. It is beginning to emerge that the really soft-headed sentimentalism is that attaching to money.

•   •   •

Clear Skies and Clean Rivers
EDMUND K. FALTERMAYER

The ecology movement is the result of the American people finally becoming aware of the violence they have been perpetrating against air, water, and the environment in general. Edmund K. Faltermayer, an associate editor of Fortune *magazine, has dramatically described the kinds of pollution we have inflicted upon our world. What is encouraging about Faltermayer's work is that he concludes on an optimistic note. Faltermayer believes that with the proper amount of funding, we can beat the problem of pollution—a state of affairs that at this moment seems hard to believe.*

Abridgment of "Clear Skies and Clean Rivers" from *Redoing America* by Edmund K. Faltermayer. Copyright © 1968 by Edmund K. Faltermayer, published by Harper & Row, Publishers, Inc.

The United States has begun to move against the colossal outpouring of industrial and municipal waste that defiles its air and streams. In this field, the defeatists and cynics who believe our democracy is incapable of responding to environmental deterioration are already being proved wrong, and the "impossible" is beginning to happen. The opposition from big business, which once seemed to doom any crackdown, has begun to crumble, and some corporations even boast in full-page newspaper advertisements of their pollution-abatement feats. In many parts of the country, control laws which once got nowhere are sailing through city councils and state legislatures. The reason, of course, is that the public has shaken off its apathy and has begun to demand action, and the politicians have begun to oblige. The real question, therefore, is not whether we can move against pollution, but how good a job we can do.

The answer: far better than we are doing now. By the year 2000, we can make the United States virtually free of man-made pollution for the first time since the industrial revolution, with automobiles and factories that emit no aerial contaminants whatever, and "dry" manufacturing processes that purify and reuse water instead of dumping obnoxious effluents into rivers. We cannot realize this goal in the immediate future, however. Industry has not yet developed nonpolluting cars that would meet all our transportation needs, for example, nor has it seriously attempted to design manufacturing processes that eliminate pollution completely instead of merely curtailing it. Therefore, while spurring on research to achieve these longer-range objectives, we must clean up the vehicles, the factories, and the municipal waste-disposal systems that already exist. The federal, state and local legislation enacted in recent years will barely enable most metropolitan areas to hold their own against the rising tide of pollution. We must aim during the next decade for nothing less than a massive *rollback*, and thereby restore blue skies and clear waters in our urban areas most of the time.

. . .

An astounding 139 million tons of dirt and poison are now being dumped into the United States atmosphere each year. If all this pollution could be placed on a giant scale, it would outweigh the country's annual steel production.

. . .

These pollutants are eating away at fabrics and metals. They are spoiling crops and defacing buildings and priceless art objects. Partly because of air pollution, Cleopatra's Needle in New York City's Central Park has eroded more during the past century than it did during 3,000 years in Egypt. The federal government estimates the property damage alone at about $12 billion a year—a figure that probably errs on the low side and does not take into account the depressed real-estate values in neighborhoods with second-class air or worse. Air pollution also represents a prodigious waste of potentially valuable resources. The harmful sulfur dioxide that is vented to the atmosphere each year, for example, contains about $300 million worth of sulfur at recent prices —more than is mined from the earth to supply United States industry. While medical researchers have not proved that any of these pollutants is injuring large numbers of people, the junk obviously is doing our systems no good. "There is no doubt," John W. Gardner, Secretary of Health, Education, and Welfare, has declared, "that air pollution is a contributing factor in the rising incidence of chronic respiratory diseases—lung cancer, emphysema, bronchitis, and asthma." The American Medical Association, which once took a cautious stand on the issue, has called for the "maximum feasible reduction of all forms of air pollution." Some experts see the growing pollution of the atmosphere as a threat to human life itself. Meteorologist Morris Neiburger of the University of California at Los Angeles has warned that if we continue to fill the air with gases, "the world's atmosphere will grow more and more polluted until, a century from now, it will be too poisonous to allow human life to survive, and civilization will pass away."

Besides damaging health and property and wasting resources, air pollution dejects and degrades the human spirit in ways that a civilized society need no longer tolerate. The acrid smog associated with automobile exhausts, once confined to Los Angeles but now turning up in other cities, probably does not kill people. It merely envelops them in an ugly yellow haze that blots out the view and makes the eyes smart. The pride of Denver— the prospect of the Rocky Mountains from downtown streets—is often obscured these days by a man-made cloud of pollution. In St. Louis, a survey has shown, 39 percent of the people are bothered by noisome odors. With more dust particles in the air, cities get up to 10 percent more precipitation than the surrounding countryside, and less sunshine the rest of the time. After poor schools and inadequate play space, air pollution is probably the most important single factor driving middle-class families with children to the suburbs, and a portion of the country's commuting woes must be ascribed to it.

Thus, city air that is gritty, malodorous, and menacing is helping to restrict our choices in where to live.

Though we long regarded the atmosphere as boundless, its limitations as a dumping ground have become all too apparent in recent years. At any given time, to be sure, there are 90 trillion tons of air over the forty-eight contiguous states. The annual load of pollutants, if released all at once and evenly dispersed, would amount to only 1.5 parts per million in the air. Since the contamination actually is spread over a whole year and continuously falls to the ground or is washed out by rains, the average concentration in the nation's air supply is considerably less than that. But the average means little, for half of the pollution is emitted from the 1 percent of the land area on which 50 percent of the population lives. When winds are slack, this far heavier outpouring can build up to thousands of times the national average.

Things can get worse when there is also a temperature inversion, in which a warm layer of air aloft acts as a lid atop the contaminants in the cooler surface air. This phenomenon was once thought to be peculiar to Los Angeles, where the lid drops to 500 feet or less 40 percent of the time. Actually, it occurs commonly throughout most of the United States. In New York and Philadelphia, for example, low-level inversions occur 25 percent of the time, and even more often in the fall. The only real difference is that Los Angeles' inversions tend to be lower, and are accompanied by below-average winds. But New York throws off much more nonautomotive air pollution, including the country's highest dosage of sulfur dioxide. When a temperature inversion occurs and the wind drops, as it did during New York's pollution alert of Thanksgiving, 1966, people with respiratory diseases are warned by the city to remain indoors, and heating and the burning of trash are restricted. The air above our metropolitan areas is not a limitless ocean, as we once believed. Much of the time it is a shallow, stagnant pond, and we are the fish at the bottom.

• • •

A maximum effort to reduce air pollution during the next decade would mean applying throughout the United States standards roughly comparable to those enforced in Los Angeles, which are the most stringent in the land. Faced with acute smog conditions, Los Angeles authorities helped to push through a California law that required the installation of exhaust control devices on new cars a year before the federal law took effect. They have also forced local industry to reduce its emissions by nearly 80 percent since the late 1940's; an estimated 5,000 tons of pollutants a day from stationary sources are now being kept out of the sky. "We've had to force industry to do the best job existing technology will allow," says an official of the Los Angeles County Air Pollution Control District. "Whenever there's a new breakthrough in technology, we tighten our rules."

• • •

The most compelling argument for a maximum nationwide clampdown, however, is that we can well afford it. While a precise figure is impossible to arrive at, we can get a good idea of the kind of money required by looking at the major sources of air pollution, namely key branches of industry, automobiles, and rubbish disposal.

• • •

In terms of sheer tonnage, the automobile is the country's Number 1 air polluter. According to estimates by the U. S. Department of Health, Education, and Welfare, it accounts for over four-fifths of the 86 million tons of contaminants emitted by all forms of transporation, including trucks, buses, railroads, and airlines. The three dangerous and obnoxious ingredients issuing from the nation's 75 million automobile tailpipes are carbon monoxide, unburned hydrocarbons, and oxides of nitrogen. While it can kill a man by depriving his blood of its oxygen-carrying capability, carbon monoxide is generally not dangerous in open places. Nevertheless, it can reach dangerous concentrations in heavily traveled city intersections and expressways. Biochemist A. J. Haagan-Smit of California Institute of Technology says the level frequently gets to 30 p.p.m. on the Los Angeles freeways— enough to deprive the blood of 5 percent of its oxygen capacity if inhaled for eight hours and make drivers drowsy from briefer exposures—and sometimes reaches 120 p.p.m. in traffic jams.

*   *   *

The only solution, for the next decade at least, is to clean up the internal-combustion engine. For several years the automobile industry stoutly opposed uniform, nationwide pollution-controls on cars on the unpersuasive grounds that the automobile smog problem was confined to only a few centers like Los Angeles, and that anti-pollution devices would needlessly raise new-car prices and hurt automobile sales. Once Congress approved the 1965 law giving the federal government the power to set emissions standards for all new cars, however, Detroit got behind the anti-smog program. Indeed, its actions since then show how industry can respond to an environmental challenge once it is forced to do so by legislation.

*   *   *

What all . . . figures clearly indicate is that a major cleanup of our badly soiled atmosphere is well within the country's means. To apply the best existing abatement techniques to all the plants in the three main branches of manufacturing—steel, chemicals, and petroleum refining —and effectively to curb fly-ash emissions throughout the country's present electric-generating facilities, would require an expenditure on equipment of about $1 billion during the next decade, over and above spending programs already under way. This figure, which takes into account the added cost of installing emission-curbing devices in old plants, should be doubled to include branches of industry not examined here, and doubled again to include the cost of operating the equipment. This works out to $4 billion, or about $400 million annually during the next ten years. Meanwhile, industry should increase somewhat its outlays for curbing air pollution in its new plants—presumably where much of its current spending is directed. Altogether, then, the application of the best existing technology to industry would cost about $1 billion a year, or $500 million more than corporations have recently been spending.

This is a realistic estimate. Industry in Los Angeles County, where the strictest regulations prevail, has been spending a total of about $2.30 a year for each of the area's residents, which would work out to only $450 million for the whole nation. This may understate things a bit, however, as Los Angeles does not have as much heavy industry of the air-polluting type as some other areas. But it is evident that industry can clean up without going bankrupt.

To this step-up in spending of $500 million a year must be added the $600 million it might cost to remove sulfur dioxide from the flue gases of electric power stations, the $500 million it could conceivably cost to install additional devices in automobiles, and the $200 million needed to insure soot-free disposal of municipal rubbish. A few miscellaneous items should be thrown in, such as a ban on the use of high-sulfur fuel for home heating, programs to reduce the oxides of nitrogen emitted by electric-generating plants and to curb diesel exhausts, more research, and an increase in government enforcement activities. Altogether, it adds up to an additional $2 billion a year to roll back air pollution.

This additional outlay, however, is only a sixth of the estimated $12 billion of property damage caused by air pollution. Moreover, it errs on the high side, if anything, because it makes no allowance for savings to industry from the recovery of usable products, nor does it allow for the revenue towns and cities may earn from the sale of power generated by the new incinerators now being studied. Also, it assumes there will be no major new cost-cutting breakthroughs in controlling sulfur dioxide or in cleaning up automobile emissions—an assumption that could turn out to be unduly pessimistic. This program will not buy city air as pure as that which greeted the Pilgrim Fathers at Plymouth Rock. But it would reduce total pollution by at least two-thirds within ten years, so that we would only occasionally be bothered by it.

For about 85 cents a month each, we could all breathe easier.

For another $1.25 a month, or $3 billion a year, we could also have relatively clean rivers, lakes and streams in place of the open sewers that we are forced to gaze upon—and draw our drinking water from—today.

Water pollution is a heavy and rising burden upon the United States, in both aesthetic and economic terms. The Hudson River, for example, once was called lovelier than the Rhine in one of Baedeker's travel guides, but today a fetid outpouring of municipal and industrial filth several times as great as in 1900 has made the river unfit for fishing and swimming along much of its length. The same fate has befallen Lake Erie at Cleveland, as well as the waters near hundreds of other American cities and towns. Much of Lake Erie is so saturated with accumulated wastes that it has become virtually "dead" in the biological sense. Phosphorus and nitrogen compounds in both sewage and in industrial effluent, and in the fertilizer compounds washed from farms by rains, have triggered an explosive growth of plant-like algae that have depleted much of the dissolved oxygen needed by fish and other aquatic species. These algae "blooms," which form ugly underwater growths, exude noxious odors, and leave a green scum on the surface, are turning up increasingly in other bodies of water, too.

• • •

The financing of an all-out drive against air and water pollution need not be onerous or complicated. About half the $5 billion of increased spending would go for improved local sewer systems and treatment plants and would entail some increases in local taxes. Fortunately, the new federal-grant program, if stepped up and accompanied by increased aid from state governments, could greatly lessen these local increases, which are the ones most vulnerable to opposition by householders. Except for enforcement costs, the rest of the cleanup can be paid for entirely by private enterprise and passed along to consumers in the form of higher prices. Only two items, electricity and new cars, might become noticeably more expensive. But these are so universal in the United States that price increases would be a perfectly equitable way to distribute the burden. With these two exceptions, consumers would scarcely be able to detect the costs of a cleanup in the things they buy.

• • •

With a full-scale anti-pollution drive under way during

the next decade, the United States can begin to design
an environment that will be free of man-made contamination altogether. Until now, pollution control has not been
an important factor in the design of factories or vehicles,
and most of the current methods of reducing pollution
involve the clumsy grafting of contraptions onto systems
designed when pollution was not a major worry. But the
strict enforcement of emissions standards will force industry to design future plants in which potential pollutants will be trapped or continuously reused. In the
case of air pollution, says Dean A. J. Teller of New
York City's Cooper Union School of Engineering and
Science, "we should aim for zero levels of emission." The
complete elimination of all aerial pollutants may be
impossible, but Teller, who designed some of the systems
for curbing fluoride emissions from the Florida phos-
phate plants, says that "we have already come pretty
close to this in industries where people screamed for
years and years that it couldn't be done."

• • •

Long before 1980, the country will have to begin reno-
vating water on a large scale. By that year, the daily
intake of water by households and industry is expected to
absorb all of the fresh water potentially available from
the runoff of precipitation into river basins, and extensive reuse will become necessary. Secondary sewage
treatment does not create reusable water. It removes up
to 90 percent of the suspended solid matter and the compounds that consume oxygen when sewage is dumped
raw into rivers, but gets out only about half of the nitrogen and 20 to 40 percent of the phosphorus—both of
which nourish algae blooms—and almost none of the dissolved inorganic salts. Already, a few communities with
limited fresh-water supplies are giving so-called tertiary
treatment to municipal wastes, making it as pure as

mountain spring water if not as fresh tasting. In Santee, California, kids have been swimming for several years in a lake of renovated water whose source is the local treatment plant.

•   •   •

Any longer-range attack on pollution must devise better ways to dispose of the solid refuse that is now burned or dumped somewhere. A complete systems approach is needed, and some experts foresee the day when the trashman and his noisy, smelly truck will be eliminated, and all refuse will be ground up in homes and sent through the sewer system to a treatment plant. There the materials valuable to industry will be separated out automatically, and the rest converted by bacteria into a compost that can be piped or trucked to outlying areas where it can be used as a soil conditioner. Such a system would require a complete change-over to packaging materials that can readily be separated and returned to the production cycle, or which are biodegradable and lend themselves to decomposition in treatment plants. This would mean a complete reversal of the recent trend toward the plastic bottles, nonrusting aluminum cans and no-return glass bottles that have begun to flood the country. Industry might find itself faced with two choices, either to bring back the returnable container or to develop one that can be recycled or chemically decomposed after use. The soap industry provides a precedent for the latter course. Threatened with federal legislation a few years ago when the foam from detergents began to swamp sewage treatment plants, the industry developed a biodegradable detergent—and incidentally spent $150 million to convert its manufacturing plants to make the new detergent without receiving a government subsidy.

One thing is clear: we can no longer throw things away

as we once did—into the air, the water, or the city dump —and blithely let someone else worry about their ultimate disposition. For our urban areas are becoming more crowded and, as a panel on pollution of the National Academy of Sciences said in a 1966 report, "there is no longer an 'away.' One person's trash basket is another's living space."

The Negro Revolution—Why 1963?
MARTIN LUTHER KING, JR.

The black revolution of the 1960s is still in progress, causing Americans to rethink their notions of the black man's role in society. One of the most prominent spokesmen for the civil rights cause in this century was the late Reverend Martin Luther King, Jr., who was cut down by an assassin's bullet in 1968. Ironically, King was devoted to nonviolence as the tactic to be used to achieve equality. In Why We Can't Wait *he explained why 1963 was the year that the black revolution really got off the ground.*

I

The bitterly cold winter of 1962 lingered throughout the opening months of 1963, touching the land with chill and frost, and then was replaced by a placid spring. Americans awaited a quiet summer. That it would be pleasant they had no doubt. The worst of it would be the nightmare created by sixty million cars, all apparently trying to reach the same destination at the same time. Fifty million families looked forward to the pleasure of two hundred million vacations in the American tradition of the frenetic hunt for relaxation.

It would be a pleasant summer because, in the mind of the average man, there was little cause for concern. The blithe outlook about the state of the nation was reflected from as high up as the White House. The administration confidently readied a tax-reduction bill. Business and employment were at comfortable levels. Money was—for many Americans—plentiful.

Summer came, and the weather was beautiful. But the climate, the social climate of American life, erupted into lightning flashes, trembled with thunder and vibrated to the relentless, growing rain of protest come to life through the land. Explosively, America's third revolution —the Negro Revolution—had begun.

For the first time in the long and turbulent history of the nation, almost one thousand cities were engulfed in civil turmoil, with violence trembling just below the surface. Reminiscent of the French Revolution of 1789, the streets had become a battleground, just as they had become the battleground, in the 1830's, of England's tumultuous Chartist movement. As in these two revolutions, a submerged social group, propelled by a burning need for justice, lifting itself with sudden swiftness, moving with determination and a majestic scorn for risk and danger, created an uprising so powerful that it shook a huge society from its comfortable base.

Never in American history had a group seized the streets, the squares, the sacrosanct business thorough-fares and the marbled halls of government to protest and proclaim the unendurability of their oppression. Had room-size machines turned human, burst from the plants that housed them and stalked the land in revolt, the nation could not have been more amazed. Undeniably, the Negro had been an object of sympathy and wore the scars of deep grievances, but the nation had come to count on him as a creature who could quietly endure, silently suffer and patiently wait. He was well trained in service and, whatever the provocation, he neither pushed back nor spoke back.

Just as lightning makes no sound until it strikes, the Negro Revolution generated quietly. But when it struck, the revealing flash of its power and the impact of its sincerity and fervor displayed a force of frightening intensity. Three hundred years of humiliation, abuse and deprivation cannot be expected to find voice in a whisper. The storm clouds did not release a "gentle rain from heaven," but a whirlwind, which has not yet spent its force or attained its full momentum.

Because there is more to come; because American society is bewildered by the spectacle of the Negro in revolt; because the dimensions are vast and the implications deep in a nation with twenty million Negroes, it is important to understand the history that is being made today.

II

Some years ago, I sat in a Harlem department store, surrounded by hundreds of people. I was autographing copies of *Stride Toward Freedom*, my book about the Montgomery bus boycott of 1955-56. As I signed my name to a page, I felt something sharp plunge forcefully into into my chest. I had been stabbed with a letter opener, struck home by a woman who would later be judged insane. Rushed by ambulance to Harlem Hospital, I lay in a bed for hours while preparations were made to remove the keen-edged knife from my body. Days later, when I was well enough to talk with Dr. Aubrey Maynard, the chief of the surgeons who performed the delicate, dangerous operation, I learned the reason for the long delay that preceded surgery. He told me that the razor tip of the instrument had been touching my aorta and that my whole chest had to be opened to extract it.

"If you had sneezed during all those hours of waiting," Dr. Maynard said, "your aorta would have been punctured and you would have drowned in your own blood."

In the summer of 1963 the knife of violence was just that close to the nation's aorta. Hundreds of cities might now be mourning countless dead but for the operation of certain forces which gave political surgeons an opportunity to cut boldly and safely to remove the deadly peril.

What was it that gave us the second chance? To answer this we must answer another question. Why did this Revolution occur in 1963? Negroes had for decades endured evil. In the words of the poet, they had long asked: "Why must the blackness of nighttime collect in our mouth; why must we always taste grief in our blood?" Any time would seem to have been the right time. Why 1963?

Why did a thousand cities shudder almost simultaneously and why did the whole world—in gleaming capitals and mud-hut villages—hold its breath during those months? Why was it this year that the American Negro, so long ignored, so long written out of the pages of history books, tramped a declaration of freedom with his marching feet across the pages of newspapers, the television screens and the magazines? Sarah Turner closed the kitchen cupboard and went into the streets; John Wilkins shut down the elevator and enlisted in the nonviolent army; Bill Griggs slammed the brakes of his truck and slid to the sidewalk; the Reverend Arthur Jones led his flock into the streets and held church in jail. The words and actions of parliaments and statesmen, of kings and prime ministers, movie stars and athletes, were shifted from the front pages to make room for the history-making deeds of the servants, the drivers, the elevator operators and the ministers. Why in 1963, and what has this to do with why the dark threat of violence did not erupt in blood?

III

The Negro had been deeply disappointed over the slow pace of school desegregation. He knew that in 1954 the highest court in the land had handed down a decree calling for desegregation of schools "with all deliberate speed." He knew that this edict from the Supreme Court had been heeded with all deliberate delay. At the beginning of 1963, nine years after this historic decision, approximately 9 per cent of southern Negro students were attending integrated schools. If this pace were maintained, it would be the year 2054 before integration in southern schools would be a reality.

In its wording the Supreme Court decision had revealed an awareness that attempts would be made to evade its intent. The phrase "all deliberate speed" did not mean that another century should be allowed to unfold before we released Negro children from the narrow pigeonhole of the segregated schools; it meant that, giving some courtesy and consideration to the need for softening old attitudes and outdated customs, democracy must press ahead, out of the past of ignorance and intolerance, and into the present of educational opportunity and moral freedom.

Yet the statistics make it abundantly clear that the segregationists of the South remained undefeated by the decision. From every section of Dixie, the announcement of the high court had been met with declarations of defiance. Once recovered from their initial outrage, these defenders of the status quo had seized the offensive to impose their own schedule of change. The progress that was supposed to have been achieved with deliberate speed had created change for less than 2 per cent of Negro children in most areas of the South and not even one-tenth of 1 per cent in some parts of the deepest South.

There was another factor in the slow pace of progress, a factor of which few are aware and even fewer understand. It is an unadvertised fact that soon after the 1954 decision the Supreme Court retreated from its own position by giving approval to the Pupil Placement Law. This law permitted the states themselves to determine where school children might be placed by virtue of family background, special ability and other subjective criteria. The Pupil Placement Law was almost as far-reaching in modifying and limiting the integration of schools as the original decision had been in attempting to eliminate segregation. Without technically reversing itself, the Court had granted legal sanction to tokenism and thereby guaranteed that segregation, in substance, would last for an indefinite period, though formally it was illegal.

In order, then, to understand the deep disillusion of the Negro in 1963, one must examine his contrasting emotions at the time of the decision and during the nine years that followed. One must understand the pendulum swing between the elation that arose when the edict was handed down and the despair that followed the failure to bring it to life.

A second reason for the outburst in 1963 was rooted in disappointment with both political parties. From the city of Los Angeles in 1960, the Democratic party had written an historic and sweeping civil-rights pronouncement into its campaign platform. The Democratic standard bearer had repeated eloquently and often that the moral weight of the Presidency must be applied to this burning issue. From Chicago, the Republican party had been generous in its convention vows on civil rights, although its candidate had made no great effort in his campaign to convince the nation that he would redeem his party's promises.

Then 1961 and 1962 arrived, with both parties marking time in the cause of justice. In the Congress, reactionary Republicans were still doing business with the Dixiecrats. And the feeling was growing among Negroes that the administration had oversimplified and underestimated the civil-rights issue. President Kennedy, if not backing down, had backed away from a key pledge of his campaign—to wipe out housing discrimination immediately "with the stroke of a pen." When he had finally signed the housing order, two years after taking office, its terms, though praiseworthy, had revealed a serious weakness in its failure to attack the key problem of discrimination in financing by banks and other institutions.

While Negroes were being appointed to some significant jobs, and social hospitality was being extended at the White House to Negro leaders, the dreams of the masses remained in tatters. The Negro felt that he recognized the same old bone that had been tossed to him in the past—only now it was being handed to him on a platter, with courtesy.

The administration had fashioned its primary approach to discrimination in the South around a series of lawsuits chiefly designed to protect the right to vote. Opposition toward action on other fronts had begun to harden. With each new Negro protest, we were advised, sometimes privately and sometimes in public, to call off our efforts and channel all of our energies into registering voters. On each occasion we would agree with the importance of voting rights, but would patiently seek to explain that Negroes did not want to neglect all other rights while one was selected for concentrated attention.

It was necessary to conclude that our argument was not persuading the administration any more than the government's logic was prevailing with us. Negroes had manifested their faith by racking up a substantial majority of their votes for President Kennedy. They had expected more of him than of the previous administration. In no sense had President Kennedy betrayed his promises. Yet his administration appeared to believe it was doing as much as was politically possible and had, by its positive deeds, earned enough credit to coast on civil rights. Politically, perhaps, this was not a surprising conclusion. How many people understood, during the first two years of the Kennedy administration, that the Negroes' "Now" was becoming as militant as the segregationists' "Never"? Eventually the President would set political considerations aside and rise to the level of his own unswerving moral commitment. But this was still in the future.

No discussion of the influences that bore on the thinking of the Negro in 1963 would be complete without some attention to the relationship of this Revolution to international events. Throughout the upheavals of cold-war politics, Negroes had seen their government go to the brink of nuclear conflict more than once. The justification for risking the annihilation of the human race was always expressed in terms of America's willingness to go to any lengths to preserve freedom. To the Negro that readiness for heroic measures in the defense of liberty disappeared or became tragically weak when the threat was within our own borders and was concerned with the Negro's liberty. While the Negro is not so selfish as to stand isolated in concern for his own dilemma, ignoring the ebb and flow of events around the world, there is a certain bitter irony in the picture of his country championing freedom in foreign lands and failing to ensure that freedom to twenty million of its own.

From beyond the borders of his own land, the Negro had been inspired by another powerful force. He had watched the decolonization and liberation of nations in Africa and Asia since World War II. He knew that yellow, black and brown people had felt for years that the the American Negro was too passive, unwilling to take strong measures to gain his freedom. He might have remembered the visit to this country of an African head of state, who was called upon by a delegation of prominent American Negroes. When they began reciting to him their long list of grievances, the visiting statesman had waved a weary hand and said:

"I am aware of current events. I know everything you are telling me about what the white man is doing to the Negro. Now tell me: What is the Negro doing for himself?"

The American Negro saw, in the land from which he had been snatched and thrown into slavery, a great pageant of political progress. He realized that just thirty years ago there were only three independent nations in the whole of Africa. He knew that by 1963 more than thirty-four African nations had risen from colonial bondage. The Negro saw black statesmen voting on vital issues in the United Nations—and knew that in many cities of his own land he was not permitted to take that significant walk to the ballot box. He saw black kings and potentates ruling from palaces—and knew he had been condemned to move from small ghettos to larger ones. Witnessing the drama of Negro progress elsewhere in the world, witnessing a level of conspicuous consumption at home exceeding anything in our history, it was natural that by 1963 Negroes would rise with resolution and demand a share of governing power, and living conditions measured by American standards rather than by the standards of colonial impoverishment.

An additional and decisive fact confronted the Negro and helped to bring him out of the houses, into the streets, out of the trenches and into the front lines. This was his recognition that one hundred years had passed since emancipation, with no profound effect on his plight.

With the dawn of 1963, plans were afoot all over the land to celebrate the Emancipation Proclamation, the one-hundredth birthday of the Negro's liberation from bondage. In Washington, a federal commission had been established to mark the event. Governors of states and mayors of cities had utilized the date to enhance their political image by naming commissions, receiving committees, issuing statements, planning state pageants, sponsoring dinners, endorsing social activities. Champagne, this year, would bubble on countless tables. Appropriately attired, over thick cuts of roast beef, legions would listen as luminous phrases were spun to salute the great democratic landmark which 1963 represented.

But alas! All the talk and publicity accompanying the centennial only served to remind the Negro that he still wasn't free, that he still lived a form of slavery disguised by certain niceties of complexity. As the then Vice-President, Lyndon B. Johnson, phrased it: "Emancipation was a Proclamation but not a fact." The pen of the Great Emancipator had moved the Negro into the sunlight of physical freedom, but actual conditions had left him behind in the shadow of political, psychological, social, economic and intellectual bondage. In the South, discrimination faced the Negro in its obvious and glaring forms. In the North, it confronted him in hidden and subtle disguise.

The Negro also had to recognize that one hundred years after emancipation he lived on a lonely island of economic insecurity in the midst of a vast ocean of material prosperity. Negroes are still at the bottom of the economic ladder. They live within two concentric circles of segregation. One imprisons them on the basis of color, while the other confines them within a separate culture of poverty. The average Negro is born into want and deprivation. His struggle to escape his circumstances is hindered by color discrimination. He is deprived of normal education and normal social and economic opportunities. When he seeks opportunity, he is told, in effect, to lift himself by his own bootstraps, advice which does not take into account the fact that he is barefoot.

By 1963, most of America's working population had forgotten the Great Depression or had never known it. The slow and steady growth of unemployment had touched some of the white working force but the proportion was still not more than one in twenty. This was not true for the Negro. There were two and one-half times as many jobless Negroes as whites in 1963, and their median income was half that of the white man. Many white Americans of good will have never connected bigotry with economic exploitation. They have deplored prejudice, but tolerated or ignored economic injustice. But the Negro knows that these two evils have a malignant kinship. He knows this because he has worked in shops that employ him exclusively because the pay is below a living standard. He knows it is not an accident of geography that wage rates in the South are significantly lower than those in the North. He knows that the spotlight recently focused on the growth in the number of women who work is not a phenomenon in Negro life. The average Negro woman has always had to work to help keep her family in food and clothes.

To the Negro, as 1963 approached, the economic structure of society appeared to be so ordered that a precise sifting of jobs took place. The lowest-paid employment and the most tentative jobs were reserved for him. If he sought to change his position, he was walled in by the tall barrier of discrimination. As summer came, more than ever the spread of unemployment had visible and tangible dimensions to the colored American. Equality meant dignity and dignity demanded a job that was secure and a pay check that lasted throughout the week.

The Negro's economic problem was compounded by the emergence and growth of automation. Since discrimination and lack of education confined him to unskilled and semi-skilled labor, the Negro was and remains the first to suffer in these days of great technological development. The Negro knew all too well that there was not in existence the kind of vigorous retaining program that could really help him to grapple with the magnitude of his problem.

The symbol of the job beyond the great wall was construction work. The Negro whose slave labor helped to build a nation was being told by employers on the one hand and unions on the other that there was no place for him in this industry. Billions were being spent on city, state and national building for which the Negro paid taxes but could draw no pay check. No one who saw the spanning bridges, the grand mansions, the sturdy docks and stout factories of the South could question the Negro's ability to build if he were given a chance for apprenticeship training. It was plain, hard, raw discrimination that shut him out of decent employment.

In 1963, the Negro, who had realized for many years that he was not truly free, awoke from a stupor of inaction with the cold dash of realization that 1963 meant one hundred years after Lincoln gave his autograph to the cause of freedom.

The milestone of the centennial of emancipation gave the Negro a reason to act—a reason so simple and obvious that he almost had to step back to see it.

Simple logic made it painfully clear that if this centennial were to be meaningful, it must be observed not as a celebration, but rather as a commemoration of the one moment in the country's history when a bold, brave *start* had been made, and a rededication to the obvious fact that urgent business was at hand—the resumption of that noble journey toward the goals reflected in the Preamble to the Constitution, the Constitution itself, the Bill of Rights and the Thirteenth, Fourteenth and Fifteenth Amendments.

Yet not all of these forces conjoined could have brought about the massive and largely bloodless Revolution of 1963 if there had not been at hand a philosophy and a method worthy of its goals. Nonviolent direct action did not originate in America, but it found its natural home in this land, where refusal to cooperate with injustice was an ancient and honorable tradition and where Christian forgiveness was written into the minds and hearts of good men. Tested in Montgomery during the winter of 1955-56, and toughened throughout the South in the eight ensuing years, nonviolent resistance had become, by 1963, the logical force in the greatest mass-action crusade for freedom that has ever occurred in American history.

Nonviolence is a powerful and just weapon. It is a weapon unique in history, which cuts without wounding and ennobles the man who wields it. It is a sword that heals. Both a practical and a moral answer to the Negro's cry for justice, nonviolent direct action proved that it could win victories without losing wars, and so became the triumphant tactic of the Negro Revolution of 1963.

Black Power: Its Need and Substance
STOKELY CARMICHAEL and
CHARLES V. HAMILTON

As the 1960s progressed, the black revolution moved from integration to Black Power. New figures like Malcolm X and Stokely Carmichael joined Martin Luther King as leaders in the struggle for equality. But there was a great difference between the King and Carmichael philosophies. According to Carmichael, blacks no longer wanted to be part of white society—rather they wanted to control their own destiny. Carmichael and Charles V. Hamilton, a black political scientist, define what Black Power really means in the following excerpt from their book.

The adoption of the concept of Black Power is one of the most legitimate and healthy developments in American politics and race relations in our time. The concept of Black Power speaks to all the needs mentioned in this chapter. It is a call for black people in this country to unite, to recognize their heritage, to build a sense of community. It is a call for black people to begin to define their own goals, to lead their own organizations and to support those organizations. It is a call to reject the racist institutions and values of this society.

The concept of Black Power rests on a fundamental premise: *Before a group can enter the open society, it must first close ranks.* By this we mean that group solidarity is necessary before a group can operate effectively from a bargaining position of strength in a pluralistic society. Traditionally, each new ethnic group in this society has found the route to social and political viability through the organization of its own institutions with which to represent its needs within the larger society. Studies in voting behavior specifically, and political behavior generally, have made it clear that politically the American pot has not melted. Italians vote for Rubino over O'Brien; Irish for Murphy over Goldberg, etc. This phenomenon may seem distasteful to some, but it has been and remains today a central fact of the American political system.

·　·　·

. . . black people must lead and run their own organizations. Only black people can convey the revolutionary idea—and it is a revolutionary idea—that black people are able to do things themselves. Only they can help create in the community an aroused and continuing black consciousness that will provide the basis for political strength. In the past, white allies have often furthered white supremacy without the whites involved realizing it, or even wanting to do so. Black people must come together and do things for themselves. They must achieve self-identity and self-determination in order to have their daily needs met.

Black Power means, for example, that in Lowndes County, Alabama, a black sheriff can end police brutality. A black tax assessor and tax collector and county board of revenue can lay, collect, and channel tax monies for the building of better roads and schools serving black people. In such areas as Lowndes, where black people have a majority, they will attempt to use power to exercise control. This is what they seek: control. When black people lack a majority, Black Power means proper representation and sharing of control. It means the creation of power bases, of strength, from which black people can press to change local or nation-wide patterns of oppression—instead of from weakness.

It does not mean *merely* putting black faces into office. Black visibility is not Black Power. Most of the black politicians around the country today are not examples of Black Power. The power must be that of a community, and emanate from there. The black politicians must start from there. The black politicians must stop being representatives of "downtown" machines, whatever the cost might be in terms of lost patronage and holiday hand-outs.

Black Power recognizes—it must recognize—the ethnic basis of American politics as well as the power-oriented nature of American politics. Black Power therefore calls for black people to consolidate behind their own, so that they can bargain from a position of strength.

But while we endorse the *procedure* of group solidarity and identity for the purpose of attaining certain goals in the body politic, this does not mean that black people should strive for the same kind of rewards (i.e., end results) obtained by the white society. The ultimate values and goals are not domination or exploitation of other groups, but rather an effective share in the total power of the society.

Nevertheless, some observers have labeled those who advocate Black Power as racists; they have said that the call for self-identification and self-determination is "racism in reverse" or "black supremacy." This is a deliberate and absurd lie. There is no analogy—by any stretch of definition or imagination—between the advocates of Black Power and white racists. Racism is not merely exclusion on the basis of race but exclusion for the purpose of subjugating or maintaining subjugation. The goal of the racists is to keep black people on the bottom, arbitrarily and dictatorially, as they have done in this country for over three hundred years. The goal of black self-determination and black self-identity—Black Power—is full participation in the decision-making processes affecting the lives of black people, and recognition of the virtues in themselves as black people. The black people of this country have not lynched whites, bombed their churches, murdered their children and manipulated laws and institutions to maintain oppression. White racists have. Congressional laws, one after the other, have not been necessary to stop black people from oppressing others and denying others the full enjoyment of their rights. White racists have made such laws necessary. The goal of Black Power is positive and functional to a free and viable society. No white racist can make this claim.

•   •   •

It is a commentary on the fundamentally racist nature of this society that the concept of group strength for black people must be articulated—not to mention defended. No other group would submit to being led by others. Italians do not run the Anti-Defamation League of B'nai B'rith. Irish do not chair Christopher Columbus Societies. Yet when black people call for black-run and all-black organizations, they are immediately classed in a category with the Ku Klux Klan. This is interesting and ironic, but by no means surprising: the society does not expect black people to be able to take care of their business, and there are many who prefer it precisely that way.

In the end, we cannot and shall not offer any guarantees that Black Power, if achieved, would be non-racist. No one can predict human behavior. Social change always has unanticipated consequences. If black racism is what the larger society fears, we cannot help them. We can only state what we hope will be the result, given the fact that the present situation is unacceptable and that we have no real alternative but to work for Black Power. The final truth is that the white society is not entitled to reassurances, even if it were possible to offer them.

We have outlined the meaning and goals of Black Power; we have also discussed one major thing which it is not. There are others of greater importance. The advocates of Black Power reject the old slogans and meaningless rhetoric of previous years in the civil rights struggle. The language of yesterday is indeed irrelevant; progress, non-violence, integration, fear of "white backlash," coalition. Let us look at the rhetoric and see why these terms must be set aside or redefined.

One of the tragedies of the struggle against racism is that up to this point there has been no national organization which could speak to the growing militancy of young black people in the urban ghettos and the black-

belt South. There has been only a "civil rights" movement, whose tone of voice was adapted to an audience of
middle-class whites. It served as a sort of buffer zone
between that audience and angry young blacks. It claimed
to speak for the needs of a community, but it did not
speak in the tone of that community. None of its so-called
leaders could go into a rioting community and be listened
to. In a sense, the blame must be shared—along with the
mass media—by those leaders for what happened in
Watts, Harlem, Chicago, Cleveland and other places. Each
time the black people in those cities saw Dr. Martin
Luther King get slapped they became angry. When they
saw little black girls bombed to death *in a church* and
civil rights workers ambushed and murdered, they were
angrier; and when nothing happened, they were steaming
mad. We had nothing to offer that they could see, except
to go out and be beaten again. We helped to build their
frustration.

We had only the old language of love and suffering.
And in most places—that is, from the liberals and middle
class—we got back the old language of patience and progress. The civil rights leaders were saying to the country:
"Look, you guys are supposed to be nice guys, and we
are only going to do what we are supposed to do. Why
do you beat us up? Why don't you give us what we ask?
Why don't you straighten yourselves out?" For the masses
of black people, this language resulted in virtually nothing. In fact, their objective day-to-day condition worsened.
The unemployment rate among black people increased
while that among whites declined. Housing conditions in
the black communities deteriorated. Schools in the black
ghettos continued to plod along on outmoded techniques,
inadequate curricula, and with all too many tired and
indifferent teachers. Meanwhile, the President picked up
the refrain of "We Shall Overcome" while the Congress

passed civil rights law after civil rights law, only to have them effectively nullified by deliberately weak enforcement. "Progress is being made," we were told.

Such language, along with admonitions to remain nonviolent and fear the white backlash, convinced some that that course was the *only* course to follow. It misled some into believing that a black minority could bow its head and get whipped into a meaningful position of power. The very notion is absurd. The white society devised the language, adopted the rules and had the black community narcotized into believing that that language and those rules were, in fact, relevant. The black community was told time and again how *other* immigrants finally won *acceptance:* that is, by following the Protestant Ethic of Work and Achievement. They worked hard; therefore, they achieved. We were not told that it was by building Irish Power, Italian Power, Polish Power or Jewish Power that these groups got themselves together and operated from positions of strength. We were not told that "the American dream" wasn't designed for black people. That while today, to whites, the dream may *seem* to include black people, it cannot do so by the very nature of this nation's political and economic system, which imposes institutional racism on the black masses if not upon every individual black. A notable comment on that "dream" was made by Dr. Percy Julian, the black scientist and director of the Julian Research Institute in Chicago, a man for whom the dream seems to have come true. While not subscribing to "black power" as he understood it, Dr. Julian clearly understood the basis for it: "The false concept of basic Negro inferiority is one of the curses that still lingers. It is a problem created by the white man. Our children just no longer are going to accept the patience we were taught by our generation. We were taught a pretty little lie—excel and the whole world lies open before you. . . ."

A key phrase in our buffer-zone days was non-violence. For years it has been thought that black people would not literally fight for their lives. Why this has been so is not entirely clear; neither the larger society nor black people are noted for passivity. The notion apparently stems from the years of marches and demonstrations and sit-ins where black people did not strike back and the violence always came from white mobs. There are many who still sincerely believe in that approach. From our viewpoint, rampaging white mobs and white night-riders must be made to understand that their days of free head-whipping are over. Black people should and must fight back. Nothing more quickly repels someone bent on destroying you than the unequivocal message: "O.K., fool, make your move, and run the same risk I run—of dying."

When the concept of Black Power is set forth, many people immediately conjure up notions of violence. The country's reaction to the Deacons for Defense and Justice, which originated in Louisiana, is instructive. Here is a group which realized that the "law" and law enforcement agencies would not protect people, so they had to do it themselves. If a nation fails to protect its citizens, then that nation cannot condemn those who take up the task themselves. The Deacons and all other blacks who resort to self-defense represent a simple answer to a simple question: what man would not defend his family and home from attack?

But this frightened some white people, because they knew that black people would now fight back. They knew that this was precisely what *they* would have long since done if *they* were subjected to the injustices and oppression heaped on blacks. Those of us who advocate Black Power are quite clear in our own minds that a "non-violent" approach to civil rights is an approach black people cannot afford and a luxury white people do not deserve. It is crystal clear to us—and it must become so with the white society—*that there can be no social order without social justice.* White people must be made to understand that they must stop messing with black people, or the blacks *will* fight back!

Next, we must deal with the term "integration." According to its advocates, social justice will be accomplished by "integrating the Negro into the mainstream institutions of the society from which he has been traditionally excluded." This concept is based on the assumption that there is nothing of value in the black community and that little of value could be created among black people. The thing to do is siphon off the "acceptable" black people into the surrounding middle-class white community.

The goals of integrationists are middle-class goals, articulated primarily by a small group of Negroes with middle-class aspirations or status. Their kind of integration has meant that a few blacks "make it," leaving the black community, sapping it of leadership potential and know-how. . . . those token Negroes—absorbed into a white mass—are of no value to the remaining black masses. They become meaningless show-pieces for a conscience-soothed white society. Such people will state that they would prefer to be treated "only as individuals, not as Negroes"; that they "are not and should not be preoccupied with race." This is a totally unrealistic position. In the first place, black people have not suffered as individuals but as members of a group; therefore, their liberation lies in group action. This is why SNCC—and the concept of Black Power—affirms that helping *individ-*

ual black people to solve their problems on an *individual* basis does little to alleviate the mass of black people. Secondly, while color blindness *may* be a sound goal ultimately, we must realize that race is an overwhelming fact of life in this historical period. There is no black man in this country who can live "simply as a man." His blackness is an ever-present fact of this racist society, whether he recognizes it or not. It is unlikely that this or the next generation will witness the time when race will no longer be relevant in the conduct of public affairs and in public policy decision-making. To realize this and to attempt to deal with it does not make one a racist or overly preoccupied with race; it puts one in the forefront of a significant *struggle*. If there is no intense struggle today, there will be no meaningful results tomorrow.

"Integration" as a goal today speaks to the problem of blackness not only in an unrealistic way but also in a despicable way. It is based on complete acceptance of the fact that in order to have a decent house or education, black people must move into a white neighborhood or send their children to a white school. This reinforces, among both black and white, the idea that "white" is automatically superior and "black" is by definition inferior. For this reason, "integration" is a subterfuge for the maintenance of white supremacy. It allows the nation to focus on a handful of Southern black children who get into white schools at a great price, and to ignore the ninety-four percent who are left in unimproved all-black schools. Such situations will not change until black people become equal in a way that means something, and integration ceases to be a one-way street. Then integration does not mean draining skills and energies from the black ghetto into white neighborhoods. To sprinkle black children among white pupils in outlying schools is at best a stop-gap measure. The goal is not to take black children out of the black community and expose them to white middle-class values; the goal is to build and strengthen the black community.

"Integration" also means that black people must give up their identity, deny their heritage. We recall the conclusion of Killian and Grigg: "At the present time, integration as a solution to the race problem demands that the Negro foreswear his identity as a Negro." The fact is that integration, as traditionally articulated, would abolish the black community. The fact is that what must be abolished is not the black community, but the dependent colonial status that has been inflicted upon it.

The racial and cultural personality of the black community must be preserved and that community must win its freedom while preserving its cultural integrity. Integrity includes a pride—in the sense of self-acceptance, not chauvinism—in being black, in the historical attainments and contributions of black people. No person can be healthy, complete and mature if he must deny a part of himself; this is what "integration" has required thus far. This is the essential difference between integration as it is currently practiced and the concept of Black Power.

The idea of cultural integrity is so obvious that it seems almost simple-minded to spell things out at this length. Yet millions of Americans resist such truths when they are applied to black people. Again, that resistance is a comment on the fundamental racism in the society. Irish Catholics took care of their own first without a lot of apology for doing so, without any dubious language from timid leadership about guarding against "backlash." Everyone understood it to be a perfectly legitimate procedure. Of course, there would be "backlash." Organization begets counterorganization, but this was no reason to defer.

The so-called white backlash against black people is something else: the embedded traditions of institutional racism being brought into the open and calling forth overt manifestations of individual racism. In the summer of 1966, when the protest marches into Cicero, Illinois, began, the black people knew they were not allowed to live in Cicero and the white people knew it. When blacks began to demand the right to live in homes in that town, the whites simply reminded them of the status quo. Some people called this "backlash." It was, in fact, racism defending itself. In the black community, this is called "White folks showing their color." It is ludicrous to blame black people for what is simply an overt manifestation of white racism. Dr. Martin Luther King stated clearly that the protest marches were not the cause of the racism but merely exposed a long-term cancerous condition in the society.

A Black Man's Anger

H. RAP BROWN

*By the end of the 1960s and the beginning of the 1970s
the black man's struggle had entered a still more militant
phase. The cry from leaders such as H. Rap Brown was
and is revolution. Brown sees white society as almost
totally oppressive toward blacks, and he is out to change
that situation. Some of the attitudes of the new black
militancy are shown in the selection from Brown's book*
Die Nigger Die.

My second arrest came about through a law that I know the government had to put 200 cats to work to even find, it was so old. I'd bought a rifle, which was not illegal at that time, and it was a sweet mama-jammer, too. I purchased it the same day that I was due to go to Baton Rouge to see my folks, so I carried it with me. When I got on the plane, I informed the stewardess what I had in the plastic bag I was carrying and asked her to hold it for me. There was never any secret about what I was carrying. I spent a couple of days in Baton Rouge and then went on back to New York. The night I arrived in New York I was supposed to have continued on to Cincinnati for a speaking engagement the next day. Instead, I stayed in New York with a friend, Allen Bailey (better known as the Prime Minister of Harlem). Someone came into the house around 2 A.M. and said that the neighborhood was filled with cops. During this time I was under 24-hour surveillance anyway. So, cops weren't unusual. But he said that there were 20 or 30 out there. So I went to the door to see and while standing there these two bootlicking, ass-kissing negro cops of the N.Y.P.D., who were assigned to follow me, called me out to the curb. At this time about 20 white pigs converged on me. They told me that they were from the Alcohol and Tobacco Division and that I was under arrest. Knowing that I don't drink or smoke, I said, "Man, you must have the wrong dude. I don't indulge!" They arrested me for transporting a rifle across state lines while under federal indictment. I've heard of some bullshit laws, but that is about number one. I didn't even know I was under indictment. The only thing hanging over my head was extradition hearings in Virginia. But seeing as how I was outnumbered by about twenty to one, I decided that I wasn't going to dispute the matter. I also decided that the day would come when odds didn't matter.

I was jailed in New York and held on $25,000 bond. Kunstler eventually got that reduced to $15,000 which SNCC had to raise in cash. No bondsman would handle the case. This was simply a tactic to make it more difficult for me to get out of jail. By the time I did get out of jail, however, "the man" had decided that I was going to be grounded for a while. I was sent from New York to New Orleans, where the judge said that when I went back to New York I was not to travel anywhere outside the Southern District of New York which meant that I couldn't even go to Queens or Brooklyn. I said, Damn! I'm gon' have to get the cracker's O.K. to go to the bathroom. The judge in Virginia decided that he wanted a piece of me, too, and he said that I couldn't travel anywhere in the country without getting his approval.

It was very clear that I was, in effect, under house arrest. So I said, Solid. Whatever they do to me is not going to stop the revolution. Anybody who is projected as a leader generally impedes the revolution anyway. Whether I was out there or not, I knew that the brothers were going to take care of business. A revolution doesn't depend on one person. In actuality, the revolutionary is an unknown person. He's the brother who's taking care of business, the one who's getting his head together, the one who's in the street, the one who dies in the rebellions. Like in Vietnam, he's the one who is known only to his cell leader, or his commander. He's the cat whose name never appears in history books. It ain't the dude with the natural. I'd rather see a cat with a processed head and a natural mind than a natural head and a processed mind. It ain't what's on your head; it's what's in it. You see negroes with naturals on their heads and nothing on their minds. Revolutionaries are not determined by physical characteristics. Some of the most revolutionary people in Vietnam are women, but we got muthafuckas here running around talking about let the men do it all.

So it didn't bother me that I was going to be grounded for a while. The struggle was going to go on.

In February, 1968, Kunstler went out to California and I had to go out to consult with him about one of the cases. I figured that I didn't need the court's permission to go as I could travel anywhere to consult with my attorney. While I was in California I checked out the scene and the brothers asked me to speak at a couple of meetings, which I did. I was out there for two days and then split on back to New York.

The morning after I got back, eight federal marshals knocked on my door. First they'd called my house to make sure I was there. When I picked up the phone this voice said he had the wrong number. Well, I figured who it was, but I didn't know what their next move was going to be. A few minutes after that, here comes these eight federal marshals in front of my door with their guns drawn.

I looked through the peephole in the door and saw all these honkies with their pistols and I said, "Yeah, What'cha want?" They said, "Open the door." I said, "Now come on. You got to do better than that." "We're federal marshals." "That's cool. What'cha want?" "We got a warrant for your arrest." So I said, "Well, wait a minute. I got to put some clothes on." I went and got dressed and picked up the phone to call my lawyer and let him know what was going on.

I'd left the door open, but I had a chain across it. I left it open so they could see inside and see that I wasn't preparing for no shoot-out with 'em or nothing like that.

But they decided they wanted to play cowboy and they came trying to kick the door down. I told them to stop kicking on the door. Kunstler wasn't in his New York office, but his brother who's also a lawyer was there, and he told me that it would be best to go ahead with 'em.

I took the chain off the door and all eight of 'em come rushing in, waving their guns all over the place. I sat down in a chair. "O.K., what'cha want?" I asked 'em. "We got a warrant for your arrest." I said, "Let me see it." They said it was an outstanding warrant, which meant that they didn't have it, but it was being drawn up. So I asked them, "What's the charges?" They didn't even know. Well, I started to argue with 'em but I decided that it was just too many folks there for me to argue with. But then they started looking through the house and I stopped 'em. "You got a search warrant?" One of 'em said, "You got any guns in here?" I said, "No." What kind of a fool he think I am? If I did have some guns there, I wasn't going to tell him of all people. They took me on down to the federal building and booked me. The next day I went on down to New Orleans where the warrant had been issued. The judge said I was guilty of violating bond and he set a new bond on me of $50,000.

During a recess in the hearing, before the judge set new bond, I was out in the corridor talking to some Black students who had come down to the court. This ol' negro FBI agent come walking up to me. The dude had testified against me in court, saying he had heard me speak out in California so I recognized him. Before he could get a word out of his mouth, I said to him, "I hope your children don't grow up to be a Tom like you are." I get back in court and I see this traitor on the stand telling the judge that I'd threatened his life. So the judge charged me with threatening an FBI agent and set $50,000 on that charge.

So now I had $100,000 bond on me and the judge in Virginia decided he had to get in his kicks, too. So he forfeited the bond he'd already set on me, which had been posted, and ordered that once I got out of jail in Louisiana, he wanted to see me again. This was clearly illegal as I didn't even have any charges against me in Virginia. But they had my ass and knew it and weren't about to cut me no slack.

They took me back to New Orleans where I was to remain in jail until SNCC could raise the $100,000 to get me out. This was a ridiculous bond. There was a woman in New York, Alice Crimmins, who was convicted of murdering her daughter, and they let her out on $25,000 bond, which meant that all she had to put up was $2,500 cash. I was being held on $100,000 cash and I hadn't killed nobody, robbed no bank or done anything. It was obvious that that was not bond. That was ransom!

When I got back to New Orleans I decided to go on a hunger strike. I figured that I had to draw the line. You have to resist whatever is done to you and I had no other weapon in jail except to not eat. I had to resist them muthafuckas somewhat. I may have been in their jail, but I wasn't going to accept it. So that Black people would understand, I wrote my second Letter from Jail:

February 21, 1968

Being a man is the continuing battle of one's life and one loses a bit of manhood with every stale compromise to the authority of any power in which one does not believe.

No slave should die a natural death. There is a point where caution ends and cowardice begins.

For every day I am imprisoned, I will refuse both food and water.

My hunger is for the liberation of my people.

My thirst is for the ending of oppression.

I am a political prisoner, jailed for my beliefs (that Black people must be free). The government has taken a position true to its fascist nature—those they cannot convert, they must silence. This government has become the enemy of mankind.

This can no longer alter our path to freedom. For our people, death has been the only known exit from slavery and oppression. We must open others.

Our will to live must no longer supersede our will to fight, for our fighting will determine if our race shall live. To desire freedom is not enough. We must move from resistance to aggression, from revolt to revolution.

For every Orangeburg, there must be 10 Detroits.

For every Max Stanford and Huey Newton, there must be 10 racist cops.

And for every Black death there must be a Dien Bien Phu.

Brothers and sisters, as well as all oppressed people, you must prepare yourselves both mentally and physically, for the major confrontation is yet to come. You must fight. It is the people who in the final analysis make and determine history, not leaders or systems. The laws to govern you must be made by you.

May the deaths of '68 signal the beginning of the end of this country. I do what I must out of the love for my people. My will is to fight. Resistance is not enough. Aggression is the order of the day.

Note to america

America, if it takes my death to organize my people to revolt against you,
And to organize your jails to revolt against you,
And to organize your troops to revolt against you,
And to organize your children to revolt against you,

And to organize your God to revolt against you,
And to organize your poor to revolt against you,
And to organize your country to revolt against you,
And to organize Mankind to rejoice in your destruction
and ruin,
Then, here is my Life!
But my soul belongs to my people.
Lasima Tushinde Mbilashaka *(We shall Conquer*
Without a Doubt).

Yours in Revolution,
H. Rap Brown

SNCC mimeographed the letter and got it distributed. After I got out of jail, I learned that Julius Lester, a member of SNCC's Central Committee at that time, had read the letter at an anti-war rally at the U.N. and had been booed by the white people there. This was right after the Orangeburg Massacre and if whites disapproved of what I said in the letter, it showed me once again that John Brown was the only white man I could respect and he is dead. The Black Movement has no use for white liberals. We need revolutionaries. Revolutions can use revolutionaries.

After I had fasted eleven days I wrote another Letter:

March 2, 1968
The deaths and arrests of 1968 signal more than ever
the resounding denial of human rights by this country.
Murder and human bondage made justice the after-
birth of america's immoral conception. True to the na-
ture of its birth through murder and slavery, america's
only offspring has been tyranny.
Who really violates the codes of justice? Justice upon
which all "laws" should be fabricated. This country has
shown that her "laws" are not based on justice; they are

based on politics. There is no separation of "law" from politics. Political perspective and allegiance determine human rights. The courts are a tool of the political structure. America's judiciary system serves the political one. When justice serves the "law," then there is no law, no rights, no redress of grievance; only political and judicial intercourse. This government has made a mockery of its Constitution. Freedom shares my cell on Death Row.

Our only redress of grievance is through revolution. No government is worth more than humanity. Tyrants are to be made accountable for tyranny.

When the courts are no longer an instrument of or for the people, the people must then become lawmakers and law enforcers.

If It Please the Court

Your country cheers for thee;
  My people are dying.
Giving my peers to thee;
  My people are dying.
My people tears to see;
  Our people are dying.
Your country tis of thee;
  Today you are dying.
Your country tears to see;
  No flag is flying.
My people cheers to see;
  We caused your dying.
My country tis of thee, sweet land of liberty . . .
Lasima Tushinde Mbilashaka
We Shall Conquer Without a Doubt

Yours in Revolution,
H. Rap Brown

A lot of Black people, even some in SNCC, wanted me to come off the hunger strike. They would send me messages saying that if I died, it would be just what "the man" wanted. I figured that if they didn't want me to die, they should get me out anyway they could. I was down there fighting with the only weapon I had, my life, and these folks wanted me to cop a plea. The authorities were very worried that I was going to die. I had them up tight. They figured on putting me in jail and if I was quiet, people would forget. But I fucked with 'em. I figured there wasn't no better place to die than in a united states jail. A lot of Black people, though, couldn't understand what I was doing.

• • •

The only reason that I'm willing to go before the racist courts is that it's an educational process for Black people. Black people should learn from my experiences. Every Black man shouldn't have to go before a judge to know what I'm experiencing. I was glad in Louisiana because the courtroom was filled with Black people, young Black brothers and sisters, every day. And they learned, because legally we beat the government on the first day. We made a motion to have this racist judge, "Mitch the Bitch," dismissed from the case because of prejudicial statements he made against me during some of the bond hearings we had before. The motion was made to him and he said, "Yeah, I'm prejudiced against him, but I'm not gonna dismiss myself."

The news media tries to project me as an enemy not only to the system, but to my people, and the high bail that has been set on me every time I've been arrested proves this. I'm a crazy, dangerous nigger, who hates white folks, according to the media. The news media is

one of the greatest enemies to Black people. It is con-
trolled by the ruling classes and is used to articulate
their point of view. Every day the news media says, "The
united states killed 2,000 Vietcong!" Hell, if you can
count, it's obvious that there can't be no more Vietcong
because the united states been killing them every day
by the thousands for four years now. So it's obvious that
somebody's lying somewhere. But negroes got more confidence in Huntley and Brinkley than Catholics got in
the Pope.

The media claims that I teach hate. Hate, like love, is
a feeling. How can you teach a feeling? If Black people
hate white people it's not because of me, it's because of
what white people do to Black people. If hate can be
taught, ain't no better teacher than white people themselves. I hate oppression. I am anti anybody who is anti-
Black. Now if that includes most white people in america, it ain't my fault. That's just the way the bones break.
I don't care whether or not white people hate me. It's
not essential that a man love you to live. But "the man"
has to respect you.

I believe that america loves the negro, though. It loves
for him to do its work, loves for him to stay down under
its foot. But america does not respect negroes; negroes
don't respect themselves.

America is always playing her game, though. Turning
anything and everything around to suit its own purposes.
When Jews talk about what the Germans did to them,
that's history and everybody agrees that it's history. But
as soon as Black people begin to raise the question of
what white folks have done to them and what white folks
do to them daily, they say that it's hate. But you also
got negro people walking around talking about Rap
Brown and Carmichael teaching hate. The brothers know
that if you saw a white man slap your sister down, you'd

react with hate. It's not because anybody told you to hate
the white man who slapped your sister, it's because
you're supposed to hate a muthafucka who treats you
worse than he treats his dog. The brothers knew all along
that they didn't dig slavery.

Each individual Black person decides for himself
whether or not he hates all whites. Racism in reverse is
charged when Blacks don't profess their undying love
for whites. But racism is based upon the concept of
racial superiority, which Blacks have not yet alluded to.
The Black Movement has never pushed the doctrine of
racial superiority. But what upsets the media is that we
don't say we love all white people. White folks get up
tight if the first words a Black person say don't deal
with love. That's their problem. If they haven't been
oppressing Black people then they ain't got nothing to
feel bad about. If they're fighting to destroy this racist
country, then they know that what I'm saying about oppression does not apply to them. And they also know that
I'm not talking to them. I'm talking to Black people.
They're eavesdropping.

White people got hung up on integration. Segregation
was the problem and the elimination of segregation was
the solution, not integration. It was the unequal nature
of segregation that Black people protested against in the
South, not segregation itself. Separate but equal is cool
with me. What's the big kick about going to school with
white folks? Them that want to do that should have the
chance. But that ain't no solution.

Racism stems from an attitude and it can't be destroyed under the capitalist system. You can't fight attitudes. If white people want to address themselves to
that, fine. They're the ones with the attitude, but the
Black Movement cannot address itself to attitudes. Fuck
attitudes. Fuck a muthafucka who hates me, because if

I ever get him on the wrong end of my gun he's in trouble. But Black people have always dealt with attitudes and attitudes always boil down to an individual thing. Change the laws and enforce 'em and let the attitudes take care of themselves. Because most of the laws in this country are built on attitudes, not justice, not equality, revolution is necessary. Racism, capitalism, colonialism and imperialism dominate the lives of people of color around the world—the people of Africa, Asia, Latin America, the colonized minorities who live inside the united states. Fanon says of racism, "It stares one in the face for it so happens that it belongs in a characteristic whole: that of the shameless exploitation of one group of men by another which has reached a higher stage of technical development. That is why military and economic oppression generally precedes, makes possible, and legitimatizes racism. The habit of considering racism as a mental quirk, as a psychological flaw, must be abandoned." Racism does not operate as an individual force, it is an integral part of colonial oppression. We must understand that all colonized people are victims of racism and exploitation, but that all exploited people are not colonized. For instance, inside the united states we see some whites who are oppressed and who are exploited, but they do not suffer from the racism which is forced upon Blacks by whites, they in fact form a part of the colonizing race. Some of the most racist whites are the oppressed whites.

Our job is not to convert whites. If whites are dedicated to revolution then they can be used in the struggle. However, if they impede the struggle and are proven to be a problem then it is up to us to deal with them as with all problems. Our job now is to project what should be our common goal—the destruction of a system that makes slavery profitable.

Now there're a lot of people who say that the way you

change laws is to destroy the power structure. I say you got to go beyond that. If you destroy the power structure, it can always be replaced by another power structure, whether it's white or Black. The power structure serves the system and the system is the thing which demands exploitation of people. You have to destroy the system. You can destroy the power structure and leave the system intact. But if you get the system, you got the power structure. That's the job which confronts us.

However we may twist our words and regardless of our personal, subjective feelings—the truth of the matter is that we cannot end racism, capitalism, colonialism and imperialism until the reins of state power are in the hands of those people who understand that the wealth, the total wealth of any country and the world, belongs equally to all people. Societies and countries based on the profit motive will never insure a new humanism or eliminate poverty and racism. However we may twist our words and regardless of our personal feelings—the stark reality remains that the power necessary to end racism, colonialism, capitalism and imperialism will only come through long, protracted, bloody, brutal and violent wars with our oppressors.

Liberation movements must be based upon political principles that give meaning and substance to the struggle of the masses of people, and it is this struggle that advances the creation of a people's ideology. Liberation movements from the very beginning must be dedicated to principles that speak to the needs of the poor and oppressed, or must evolve into this type of movement with these principles while the fighting is going on, for it is not evident that those who fight will assume power and implement decisions that appropriate the wealth of countries for all people. Rather to the contrary: the absence of these revolutionary political principles relates to the fact that some new rulers have settled for a new flag, a new style of dress, a seat in the UN, and/or ac-commodation with former colonial powers. A negotiated independence.

We must draw from all ideologies those principles which benefit the majority of mankind. We cannot limit ourselves to just one concept or ideology that was rele-vant in some other revolution. As Debray points out, and correctly so, in his book *Revolution Within the Revolu-tion*: "Revolutions cannot be imported nor exported." Certain changes have made even some of the most ad-vanced ideologies obsolete. For example, socialism as it exists today *ideologically* may be impractical for certain oppressed peoples. But the political principles of social-ism certainly have validity. This is why in Cuba and other liberated countries the principles of socialism are being incorporated into the ideologies of these countries. This again goes back to Fanon's observation that we must extend the Marxism analysis when we view colonialism. It is the political principles that make the ideology; as these principles are refined through struggle an ideology is created.

Many people have had these principles (principles that speak to the needs of the mass of humanity) in mind as they were waging a struggle for independence, but hav-ing failed to win independence by defeating the enemy through armed struggle, it was necessary for them to negotiate with the colonial powers. In this process of negotiation, the colonial powers granted political auton-omy but maintained economic influence, control and in-vestments. The mere act of negotiating freedom means that the control necessary to appropriate the entire wealth of the country did not fall to the new leaders. We should have learned by now from history that the process of negotiating freedom and not winning it by armed struggle has built-in limitations. We must be pre-pared to fight to the death to destroy this system known as capitalism, for it is this system that oppresses the majority of mankind.

Vanguard groups must begin to reevaluate politics. What is known as politics in this country is meaningless. People have been told that politics means the Democratic and Republican parties; federal, state and local government; the vote. History shows that politics as it is defined by america is undesirable and dangerous to Black people, for the politics of capitalism has always been human oppression and exploitation. We must begin to relate to the politics of revolution. Chairman Mao says, "Politics is war without bloodshed and war is an extension of politics." Every action that we are involved in is political, whether it is religious, artistic, cultural, athletic, governmental, educational, economic or personal. There is no separation between church and state, art and politics, or politics and individual beliefs. Everything is inherently political. The only division occurs around the question of whose political interest one will serve.

This country has always used negroes as a political tool against Blacks. Without a common Black political doctrine, america will use (and is using) Blacks against Blacks. Blackness must be political in our behalf. Individuals can no longer be immune to public political criticism because they are "Black and proud." There must be revolutionary political criticism of counter-revolutionary positions and acts. Some individuals who gain popularity in Black america are later used as tools by white america. In most cases, white political interest comes as a result of the existing popularity of the Black individuals. Understand, popularity does not reflect correctness. Blackness alone is not revolutionary.

If we examine Cleveland, Ohio, Gary, Indiana, Washington, D.C., and many other areas populated predominately by Blacks we can see a tactic being used that has often been tried in Africa, Vietnam and other oppressed countries. It is called neo-colonialism. In other words, when white structures and institutions are threatened whites protect their economic and political interests and maintain control by using members of the oppressed people as their spokesmen. They set up puppet governments headed by individuals with white interests in mind. These people oppress their own kind for their personal gain. These puppet leaders are as dangerous as those whom they represent. Remember, it was Jews who began to remove other Jews for Hitler. Even if the flunky's interest is sincere, he is powerless against the system. Individuals do not mandate the action of the system; rather, the system demands certain actions of them. The only constructive thing a Black mayor can do is to organize Blacks to destroy the system that oppresses Black people. We must never permit anyone, white or Black, to destroy with impunity the product of a single drop of the blood and sweat of our people.

White folks realize now that they can concede Blackness and still exercise control. This country says, "Yes, you may be Black; but, you must be american," which means we are as responsible for oppression as whites. This country says, "Yeah, you may have Black heroes; but, we must approve of them." So, they publicize negroes who have been beneficial to this country. The tactic of co-opting is being used to its fullest. White folks will co-opt dog shit if it's to their advantage. Today, niggers are tomming and don't even know they're tomming. We must say as Fidel Castro says, "No liberalism whatsoever! No softening whatsoever! A revolutionary people, a political people—a strong people—this is what is needed throughout these years. . . . What do the dangers or the sacrifices of a man or of a nation matter when the destiny of humanity is at stake?"

Indians Today, the Real and the Unreal
VINE DELORIA, JR.

*Another minority that has increased its efforts to achieve
an equal footing in American society is the Native American or Indian. Suffering for an even longer period than
the black population at the hands of the whites, Indians
have once again made their presence felt. Today, however, instead of using war as a means of opposing their
enemies, tribes are using combinations of tactics. Vine
Deloria, Jr., an Indian, speaks for the new Indian
militance.*

Reprinted with permission of The Macmillan Company from
Custer Died For Your Sins by Vine Deloria, Jr. Copyright © 1969
by Vine Deloria, Jr.

Indians are like the weather. Everyone knows all about the weather, but none can change it. When storms are predicted, the sun shines. When picnic weather is announced, the rain begins. Likewise, if you count on the unpredictability of Indian people, you will never be sorry.

One of the finest things about being an Indian is that people are always interested in you and your "plight." Other groups have difficulties, predicaments, quandaries, problems, or troubles. Traditionally we Indians have had a "plight."

Our foremost plight is our transparency. People can tell just by looking at us what we want, what should be done to help us, how we feel, and what a "real" Indian is really like. Indian life, as it relates to the real world, is a continuous attempt not to disappoint people who know us. Unfulfilled expectations cause grief and we have already had our share.

Because people can see right through us, it becomes impossible to tell truth from fiction or fact from mythology. Experts paint us as they would like us to be. Often we paint ourselves as we wish we were or as we might have been.

The more we try to be ourselves the more we are forced to defend what we have never been. The American public feels most comfortable with the mythical Indians of stereotype-land who were always THERE. These Indians are fierce, they wear feathers and grunt. Most of us don't fit this idealized figure since we grunt only when overeating, which is seldom. ●

●   ●   ●

During my three years as Executive Director of the National Congress of American Indians it was a rare day

when some white didn't visit my office and proudly proclaim that he or she was of Indian descent.

.   .   .

Whites claiming Indian blood generally tend to reinforce mythical beliefs about Indians. All but one person
I met who claimed Indian blood claimed it on their
grandmother's side. I once did a projection backward
and discovered that evidently most tribes were entirely
female for the first three hundred years of white occupation. No one, it seemed, wanted to claim a male Indian
as a forebear.

It doesn't take much insight into racial attitudes to
understand the real meaning of the Indian-grandmother
complex that plagues certain whites. A male ancestor has
too much of the aura of the savage warrior, the unknown
primitive, the instinctive animal, to make him a respectable member of the family tree. But a young Indian
princess? Ah, there was royalty for the taking. Somehow
the white was linked with a noble house of gentility and
culture if his grandmother was an Indian princess who
ran away with an intrepid pioneer. And royalty has always been an unconscious but all-consuming goal of the
European immigrant.

.   .   .

Those whites who dare not claim Indian blood have
an asset of their own. They *understand* Indians.

Understanding Indians is not an esoteric art. All it takes
is a trip through Arizona or New Mexico, watching a
documentary on TV, having known *one* in the service, or
having read a popular book on *them*.

There appears to be some secret osmosis about Indian
people by which they can magically and instantaneously
communicate complete knowledge about themselves to
these interested whites. Rarely is physical contact re-

quired. Anyone and everyone who knows an Indian or who is *interested,* immediately and thoroughly understands them.

You can verify this great truth at your next party. Mention Indians and you will find a person who saw some in a gas station in Utah, or who attended the Gallup ceremonial celebration, or whose Uncle Jim hired one to cut logs in Oregon, or whose church had a missionary come to speak last Sunday on the plight of Indians and the mission of the church.

. . .

It is fortunate that we were never slaves. We gave up land instead of life and labor. Because the Negro labored, he was considered a draft animal. Because the Indian occupied large areas of land, he was considered a wild animal. Had we given up anything else, or had anything else to give up, it is certain that we would have been considered some other thing.

. . .

The deep impression made upon American minds by the Indian struggle against the white man in the last century has made the contemporary Indian somewhat invisible compared with his ancestors. Today Indians are not conspicuous by their absence from view. Yet they should be.

In *The Other America,* the classic study of poverty by Michael Harrington, the thesis is developed that the poor are conspicuous by their invisibility. There is no mention of Indians in the book. A century ago, Indians would have dominated such a work.

Indians are probably invisible because of the tremendous amount of misinformation about them. Most books about Indians cover some abstract and esoteric topic of the last century. Contemporary books are predominantly by whites trying to solve the "Indian problem." Between the two extremes lives a dynamic people in a social structure of their own, asking only to be freed from cultural oppression. The future does not look bright for the attainment of such freedom because the white does not understand the Indian and the Indian does not wish to understand the white.

·   ·   ·

Over the past generation tribes have discovered that they must band together to make themselves heard. Consequently most states have inter-tribal councils, composed of the tribes in that state, that meet regularly and exchange ideas. In some areas, particularly in the Northwest, tribal representation is on a regional basis. The Northwest Affiliated Tribes is an organization made up of tribes from Montana, Idaho, Washington, and Oregon. Its counterpart, the Western Washington Inter-tribal Coordinating Council consists of tribes that live in the Puget Sound area.

Rarely do tribes overlap across state boundaries. While there are fifteen Sioux tribes, the United Sioux is an organization of only South Dakota tribes. Sioux groups in North Dakota, Nebraska, or Minnesota are not invited.

Indians have two "mainstream" organizations, the National Congress of American Indians and the National Indian Youth Council. The NCAI is open to tribes, organizations, and individuals, both red and white. Its major emphasis is on strong tribal membership because it works primarily with legislation and legislation is handled on an individual tribal basis.

The NIYC is the SNCC of Indian Affairs. Organized in 1962, it has been active among the post-college group just entering Indian Affairs. Although NIYC has a short history, it has been able to achieve recognition as a force to be reckoned with in national Indian Affairs. Generally more liberal and more excitable than the NCAI, the NIYC inclines to the spectacular short-term project rather than the extended program. The rivalry between the two groups is intense.

Lesser known but with great potential for the future are the traditional organizations. Primary among these is the oldest continuous Indian-run organization: the League of Nations, Pan American Indians. Its President, Alfred Gagne, incorporates the best of traditional Indian life and national problems into a coherent working philosophy. Should this group ever receive sufficient funding to have field workers, it could very well overturn established government procedures in Indian Affairs. It has long fought the Bureau of Indian Affairs and seeks a return to traditional Indian customs.

From the work of the League of Nations has come the alliance of the traditional Indians of each tribe. In June of 1968 they met in Oklahoma to form the National Aborigine Conference. Discussions ranging from religious prophecies to practical politics were held. From this conference is expected to come a strong nationalistic push on the reservations in the next several years.

Another group well worthy of mention is the American Indian Historical Society of San Francisco. Begun by Rupert Costo, a Cahuilla man, the society has become the publishers of the finest contemporary material on Indians. Excellent research and wide knowledge of Indian people makes it an influential voice in Indian Affairs.

Recently, during the Poor People's March, Indian participants formed the Coalition of American Indian Citizens. A loose and perhaps temporary alliance of disgruntled young people, the Coalition brought to Indian

Affairs a sense of urgency. Whether it will continue to function depends on the commitment of its members to goals which they originally stated.

Regional groups are occasionally formed around a specific issue. In the Northwest the Survivors of American Indians, Inc., works exclusively on the issue of fishing rights. In Oklahoma the Original Cherokee Community Organization has been formed to defend hunting and treaty rights of the Cherokees.

Most urban areas have urban centers or clubs composed of Indian people. For the most part these centers provide a place where urban Indians can meet and socialize. The best-known centers are in Los Angeles, Oakland, Chicago, and Minneapolis. New centers are always springing up in different cities. There are probably in excess of thirty functioning centers or clubs at any one time. The urban areas show the most potential for strong lasting organizations, however, and once the urban Indians stabilize themselves they will experience phenomenal growth.

All of these groups are primarily interested in issues and policies. The Indian Council Fire of Chicago works primarily in the field of public relations and Indian culture. The American Indian Development, Inc., works in the field of youth work and economic development of Indian communities.

•   •   •

In 1967 ABC television began its ill-fated series on Custer. The Tribal Indians Land Rights Association began the national fight to get the series banned. Eventually the NCAI and other groups protested to ABC over the series and a great Indian war was on. Custer, who had never been a very bright character, was tabbed by the NCAI as the "Adolf Eichmann" of the nineteenth century. But no one could figure out the correct strategy by which ABC could be forced to negotiate.

Finally the Yakima tribal lawyer, James Hovis, devised the tactic of getting every tribe to file for equal time against ABC's local affiliate (ABC itself was not subject to FCC regulations). As tribes in the different areas began to move, ABC, through its affiliate board, arranged a trip to California to discuss the program with the NCAI. Several tribes filed against the local affiliates of ABC and did receive some air time to present the Indian side of the Custer story during the brief run of the show. Later we heard that it would have cost ABC some three thousand dollars per complaint if every tribe had gone ahead and demanded FCC hearings on the controversy. Whether this was true or not we never learned, but once again the northwestern Indians had devised a legal strategy by which Indians as a national ethnic group could air their complaints. The series was canceled after nine episodes.

· · ·

Indian tribes are rapidly becoming accustomed to the manner in which the modern world works. A generation ago most Indians would not have known which way Washington, D.C., lay. Today it is a rare tribe that does not make a visit once a year to talk with its Congressional delegation, tour the government agencies, and bring home a new program or project from the many existing programs being funded by the federal government. Many tribes receive the Congressional Record and a number subscribe to leading national publications such as *The Wall Street Journal, Life, Time,* and *Newsweek.* Few events of much importance pass the eyes of watchful tribal groups without comment.

Tribes are also becoming very skilled at grantsmanship.

Among the larger, more experienced tribes, million-dollar programs are commonplace. Some tribes sharpened their teeth on the old Area Redevelopment Administration of the early sixties. When the Office of Economic Opportunity was created they jumped into the competition with incredibly complex programs and got them funded. One housing program on the Rosebud Sioux reservation is a combination of programs offered by some five different government agencies. The Sioux there have melded a winning hand by making each government agency fund a component of the total housing program for the reservation.

Some tribes take home upward of ten million dollars a year in government programs and private grants for their reservation people. Many tribes, combining a variety of sources, have their own development officer to plan and project future programs. The White Mountain Apaches are the first tribe to have their own public relations firm to keep tribal relations with the surrounding towns and cities on an even keel.

With a change in Congressional policy away from termination toward support of tribal self-sufficiency, it is conceivable that Indian tribes will be able to become economically independent of the federal government in the next generation. Most tribes operate under the provisions of their Indian Reorganization Act constitutions and are probably better operated than most towns, certainly more honestly operated than the larger cities.

Tribes lost some ten years during the 1950's when all progress was halted by the drive toward termination. Arbitrary and unreasonable harassment of tribal programs, denial of credit funds for program development, and pressure on tribes to liquidate assets all contributed to waste a decade during which tribes could have continued to develop their resources.

Today the Indian people are in a good position to demonstrate to the nation what can be done in community development in the rural areas. With the overcrowding of the urban areas, rural development should be the coming thing and understanding of tribal programs could indicate methods of resettling the vast spaces of rural America.

With so much happening on reservations and the possibility of a brighter future in store, Indians have started to become livid when they realize the contagious trap the mythology of white America has caught them in. The descendant of Pocahontas is a remote and incomprehensible mystery to us. We are no longer a wild species of animal loping freely across the prairie. We have little in common with the last of the Mohicans. We are TASK FORCED to death.

Some years ago at a Congressional hearing someone asked Alex Chasing Hawk, a council member of the Cheyenne River Sioux for thirty years, "Just what do you Indians want?" Alex replied, "A leave-us-alone law!!"

The primary goal and need of Indians today is not for someone to feel sorry for us and claim descent from Pocahontas to make us feel better. Nor do we need to be classified as semi-white and have programs and policies made to bleach us further. Nor do we need further studies to see if we are feasible. We need a new policy by Congress acknowledging our right to live in peace, free from arbitrary harassment. We need the public at large to drop the myths in which it has clothed us for so long. We need fewer and fewer "experts" on Indians.

What we need is a cultural leave-us-alone agreement, in spirit and in fact.

Politics and Policies of the Mexican-American Community
RALPH GUZMÁN

The Mexican-Americans, as political scientist Ralph Guz-
mán points out, have been part of this nation's history
since its beginnings. As an ethnic group they have en-
countered much discrimination, which still continues in
many quarters. But this is another segment of the popu-
lation that is now asserting its rights for first-class citi-
zenship. The excerpt that follows discusses the status of
the Mexican-Americans in the mid-1960s. Their struggle
for equality is still going on.

Ralph Guzmán, "Politics and Policies of the Mexican-American
Community," from *California Politics and Policies*, edited by
Eugene Dvorin and Arthur Misner, 1966, Addison-Wesley, Reading,
Massachusetts.

Perhaps the least known of all disadvantaged ethnic groups in the United States is the Mexican. There are more than three and one-half million people living in the southwestern states of Arizona, California, Colorado, New Mexico, and Texas who come under this disputed ethnic label. In addition, this minority group, sometimes called Mexican-American, Latin-American, Spanish-speaking, or Spanish-American, depending on the region of the Southwest, also includes an estimated 497,800 *landsmen* who live in the Midwest and other parts of the Union. Unlike the Negro, the Puerto Rican, and other minorities, the Mexican in the United States has never been the subject of comprehensive scholarly investigation. Reference is commonly made to the Mexican people in terms of *braceros* (legal contract agricultural workers from Mexico), "wetbacks" (illegal agricultural workers from Mexico), and the farm problem. Indeed, published reports of the Mexican in the United States give substance to the impression that Mexicans are (1) a predominantly rural people and (2) a recent immigrant population. There is a limited national regional awareness of the fact that Mexicans are today a largely urban people and that some, particularly in the State of New Mexico, antedate the Pilgrims. Mexicans today represent both the earliest settlers and the most recent immigrants.

• • •

. . . World War II accelerated the change from a predominantly rural to an urban orientation. Many of the young people had gone off to war. Those who stayed behind included young and old, men and women as well as citizen and noncitizen. Almost all of these people found employment in defense or related industries. The rural pursuits of the past were abandoned for better paying urban jobs.

In East Los Angeles, the *enganches*, contract labor crews, frequently organized among members of only one family, became less evident during the war. The migratory worker cycle that started in areas like Belvedere, and went north to the prune and grape country and back again to the walnut orchards of Southern California, was gradually brought to an end. The new caravans were exclusively male and were composed of Mexican nationals, contracted in Mexico under an international labor agreement between Mexico and the United States. For years to come, Mexican nationals, popularly referred to as *braceros*, were to dominate the agricultural fields where Mexican-Americans once labored.

Throughout the Southwest, the war fever of the majority group was picked up by Mexicans. War songs, the counterparts of famous American World War ballads, were composed in Spanish. One song, with an improvised arrangement of taps, the evening bugle call, began: "*Vengo a decirle adios a los muchachos porque pronto me voy para la guerra . . .*" ("I come to say goodby to all my friends because I shall soon be going off to war . . ."). When the New Mexico National Guard was trapped in Corregidor, the war was brought closer to many Mexicans. Thousands of youngsters volunteered for combat. The Marine Corps and the Paratroopers, in particular, attracted Mexicans from the urban slums of the Southwest. In California 375,000 Mexicans joined the Armed Forces during World War II. In Los Angeles, where Mexicans made up 10 percent of the total city population when Pearl Harbor was bombed, Mexicans accounted for 20 percent of all names on the war casualty lists.

Both new-found urban employment and involvement in

the armed forces contributed to the change from rural to urban life. Within the postwar urban *barrios, colonias,* or ghettos, further changes took place. Increased social interaction with non-Mexicans opened new social vistas and new ethnic goals. Unknown to many members of this minority group, the process of acculturation had increased its effect on the members of the urban Mexican community.

Social change seemed to be greatest in residential areas where Mexicans were well-integrated with other peoples, including so-called Anglos. On the other hand, neighborhoods that were predominantly Mexican reflected less rapid social change during the early postwar years. East Los Angeles provides a graphic illustration. The first significant postwar political activity took place in the Boyle Heights community, where Mexicans lived side by side with other minorities. On the other hand, social change came about more slowly in the predominantly Mexican enclave of Maravilla, located on the outskirts of the Los Angeles urban area.

• • •

. . . Increased contact with Anglo society during the War, together with the new-found urban status of the Mexican, gave rise to commensurate political activity throughout the Southwest. However, most of this activity was local and of a protest nature. Often, discrimination and other majority group pressures forced the creation of new organizations that were later to reach national prominence. One such organization was the American G.I. Forum organized in Corpus Christi, Texas after a local cemetery refused to accept the body of a Mexican serviceman who died during World War II. In California, Pomona and San Bernardino Valley veterans, ranch hands, industrial workers, and railroad laborers formed

Unity Leagues in order to deal with local problems, e.g., street lighting, sanitary conditions, street repairs, and politics. Throughout the Southwest, both old and new organizations emphasized the ballot as the most important method for bringing about social change.

Political organization was rarely exclusively Mexican in plan and execution. Considerable financial and organizational support was given to the Mexican people by sympathetic Anglos. Anglo groups like the Race Relations Council, the Industrial Area Foundation, the Fund for the Republic, the Marshall Trust Fund, and many labor and church groups made substantial contributions. In addition, minority group organizations like the Legal Redress Committee of the National Association for the Advancement of Colored People (NAACP), the Urban League, the Anti-Defamation League of B'nai B'rith, the American Jewish Committee, the Japanese-American Citizens' League (JACL), and several other groups provided funds and/or organizational knowledge to Mexican groups, particularly to the Mexican-American members of the Community Service Organization (CSO).

Mexicans were a disadvantaged people who recognized their social problems but who knew little about means for solving those problems. The concept of community organization, working together and finding allies among non-Mexicans, was not a familiar one. Invariably, community goals were defined with great difficulty. And when agreement did prevail, the implementation of proposals suffered from lack of full-time personnel and funds with which to pay them.

In California, the efforts of the American Council on Race Relations, and later the program of the Industrial Areas Foundation, emphasized (1) voter registration of Mexicans by Mexicans, (2) articulation of community needs by members of the community, and (3) continuous participation at the polls. The task was *not* how to induce a sense of community (an ethos), but rather how to organize Mexicans so as to recognize and achieve a priority of goals.

Voter registration of Mexicans by Mexicans forced community people to articulate organizational goals at the screen doors of their neighbors. Mexicans learned to walk the pavements and to ring doorbells. Many learned to sell American democracy at the doorstep in both English and Spanish. Mexican voter registrars were best equipped to establish instant rapport in the Mexican *barrios*, thus helping to bring about permanent social change.

Whereas, in the past, social workers and well-meaning private citizens had tried to articulate the ethnic goals of Mexicans, the Race Relations Council and the Industrial Areas Foundation emphasized indigenous expression. Mexican laborers, their wives, and their children learned to speak up at community meetings.

Organizational efforts were not always successful. Enormous apathy and self-denunciation blocked early postwar attempts to organize the Mexican community. Heavy clouds of cynicism, distrust of the Anglo, and fear of other Mexicans enervated the Mexican people. Anglos were suspected of ulterior motives, of trying to use the Mexicans, and of being insincere. Mexican leaders, on the other hand, were equally suspect. Too many of our leaders, the people said, betray us once they are in power.

Ultimately, postwar organizational efforts in California and in other parts of the Southwest resulted in improved relations between the Mexican people and governmental agencies, other minorities, and with the majority group. Ethnic goals became more clearly defined.

•   •   •

. . . After World War II, Mexicans tested the boundaries of the Anglo political world. Some, like Gustavo Garcia in San Antonio, ran for elective office in the school system and won. In other areas, Mexicans filed for political office, ran, and lost. Few had precinct-level experience and fewer still knew how to deal with "entrenched" Anglo politicians. Like Don Quixote, postwar Mexicans were convinced of the "justice of our cause." However, pure ethnic politics was seldom successful. Invariably, Mexicans were confronted by the majority group's political power structure, which was not always understanding and accommodating. In 1963, the Mexican community of Crystal City, Texas, aided by the Political Association of Spanish Speaking People (PASSO), the Teamsters Union, and other groups, won control of the home town's political system. Two years later, in 1965, a coalition slate of Mexicans and Anglos defeated the all-*chicano* group.

•   •   •

Portents of Change

It has been said that the majority group determines the behavior of the minority. This relationship is evident in the politics of the Southwest. The California context is different from that of Texas. In California, Mexicans were able to organize the Mexican American Political Association, an unquestionable Mexican organization with untarnished ethnic goals. On the other hand, a clear ethnic identity in Texas was possible only briefly, when the Mexican-Americans for Political Action was formed. In California, prejudice against Mexicans is considerably less than it is in Texas and in other parts of the Southwest. It is easier (and safer) to say "Mexican" in California than it is in other states. In Texas, for example,

"Mexican" has unmistakable pejorative implications derived from a heritage of conflict.

POLITICS

The political effectiveness of MAPA and PASSO is much debated by Mexicans and non-Mexicans alike. Among Mexicans it seems generally agreed that both MAPA and PASSO perform an essential gadfly function that has on occasion caused the donkey to bray and the elephant to trumpet. However, a significant section is concerned lest the image of a stoical, uncompromising Mexican supplant that of the docile *bracero*. One non-Mexican, a defeated officeholder in Mathis, Texas, said:

> I don't know what it is they want. These people on the other side have got so bitter. I asked one of the Mexican leaders, "What are you people up to? What have we done?" All he could say was, "We want to get on top."

VOTING

Mexican leaders at a 1965 meeting in Los Angeles said: "The Mexican vote, once a monolithic Democratic vote,

COMPARATIVE ESTIMATES OF TWO POTENTIAL CALIFORNIA ETHNIC VOTING POPULATIONS, BY STATE AND COUNTY*

Area	All U. S. Citizens 21 Years of Age and Over	Negro U. S. Citizens 21 Years of Age and Over	Spanish-Surname U. S. Citizens 21 Years of Age and Over
State of California	9,369,000	454,800	633,000
County of Los Angeles	3,708,000	243,400	256,800

*Data computed from 1960 Census by the Mexican-American Project. These are approximations only.

has shrunk and so has our political effectiveness." The voting strength of the Mexican in California has, indeed, dropped. Massive voter registration drives, once common in East Los Angeles, have been replaced by occasional specialized and narrowly focused efforts in selected Spanish-surname precincts. Out of a 1960 potential voting population of more than 600,000 Spanish-surname people in California, less than 20 percent were registered voters, and fewer yet were brought to the polls. In Los Angeles County a potential Spanish-surname vote of 256,000 was never activated. An estimate of comparative voting strength between Negro and Mexican voters (U.S. citizens only), based on 1960 Census data, suggests a potential Negro vote on the State level of 454,000 and a Mexican vote of 633,000. In Los Angeles County, the population of U.S. citizens in both groups is more nearly equal. Negro voters are computed at 243,400 and Mexicans (Spanish surnames) at 256,800. The combined potential of these two enormous minority groups has long been a prominent point in majority group conversation. (See Table).

RACE RELATIONS

Substantial support has been given to the Mexican people by other minority groups and by members of the Anglo majority. That Jewish organizational know-how and Jewish funds have helped the Mexican people of California is slightly known. Less known is the political and financial aid that was rendered by the Negro community.

In California, there have been two examples of Negro cooperation and assistance to the Mexican community. One involved a group of Mexican and Negro citizens from El Centro, California who, in 1955, jointly filed a class suit in a Federal district court in an effort to end school segregation in California. The case, called *Romero vs. Weakley*, was sponsored by the Alianza Hispano-Americana and the National Association for the Advancement of Colored People (NAACP). Several other organizations, among them the American Civil Liberties Union, the American Jewish Committee, and the Greater Los Angeles CIO Council, filed an *Amicus Curiae* (Friend of the Court) brief supporting the Mexican and Negro plaintiffs. A news release from the Alianza Hispano-Americana announced:

> This [case] marks the first time in U. S. history that the Negro and Mexican communities have joined hands, as American citizens, to fight for a common social problem.

Three years later, in 1958, a Negro woman lawyer, representing a coalition of Mexican and Negro politicians, nominated Henry P. Lopez, a Mexican attorney, for the office of Secretary of State at a convention in Fresno, California. That same year the Democratic Minority Conference, a predominantly Negro association, organized and financed an intensive voter registration drive among Mexican and Negro voters that netted 25,000 new voter registrations within a three month period.

Comparable cooperation between these two massive minorities no longer prevails. Mexicans and Negroes have long shared similar economic and social distress in the large urban centers of the Southwest. And yet today, meaningful dialogue between responsible Mexican and Negro leaders is not heard. However, with the increasing pressure of the Negro Civil Rights movement, it seems likely that Mexicans will eventually seek renewed contact with the Negro people.

IMMIGRATION

Outside of the Southwest, majority group members view Mexicans in the same way as they do other American immigrant groups. For example, at the 1965 White House

Conference on Education a participant commented that "Mexicans will cease to have problems when they become better acculturated, just like the Poles, the Italians, and other immigrant groups." This facile solution, unfortunately incorrect, ignores the historical factors that differentiate the Mexican from other minorities: the symbiotic relationship between the American Southwest and the Mexican northern area, and the difficulty of guarding the border. Most of all, it ignores the millions of Mexicans who have long had roots in this country. Given these conditions, it seems highly probable that the Mexican community will for a long time remain an emerging social complexity with a very real, and unresolved, heritage of conflict.

Women in the United States: Reality Behind the Myth
NANCY CARO HOLLANDER

The women's liberation movement became a reality in the late 1960s and early 1970s. Nancy Caro Hollander, who has prepared the following essay especially for this collection, is an active participant in the movement. Ms. Hollander has served as Chairwoman of the Women's Studies Program at San Diego State College—a pioneering project in women's studies—and is now teaching Latin American history at California State College, Dominguez Hills. Her article, which is certain to stir controversy, reflects her views as a woman and a historian. The analysis encompasses both sex and class as related reasons for the position of the female in today's society and should be read with the author's dedication to women's liberation in mind. This point of view reflects the criticism of the role of women in this society held by increasing numbers of women in the movement.

Woman is the nigger of the world.—Yoko Ono

The last years of the decade of the 1960s saw the birth of a vigorous and ideologically heterogeneous women's liberation movement. It was met with surprise, dismay, and contempt by many sectors of the population that include both women and men. In spite of this, the movement has continued to grow, and it is a topic of discussion in newspaper columns, television talk shows, and college classrooms. The reasons for the rise of the movement and the reasons for the reactions to it have their roots in the position of women in the United States.

Most women and men have grown up surrounded by myths that assert that women in the United States have achieved equality with men. But in reality by mere fact of having been born women, over one-half of the population is automatically channeled into inferior social, economic, and political roles because of the assumption that women's "natural" function is that of wife and mother.

It is not surprising, however, that the myth of women's equality with men continues. Since women are members of every socioeconomic class, it is often difficult to perceive the ways in which they have been discriminated against *as a group*. Although all women in this society, including those of the middle and upper classes, suffer from cultural, psychological, and sexual oppression, some —such as white working-class and third-world women— bear more economic exploitation than others. Moreover, in the most highly industrialized nation in the world, in which the lives of all citizens should have improved qualitatively and quantitatively during the last thirty years because of technological advances, women as a group have actually experienced a decline in terms of economic opportunities and social status. In this essay I shall attempt to delineate the ways in which this decline has occurred and the manner in which it is manifested in contemporary American society. The analysis that follows is the result of my research as a historian, my experiences as a woman in this society, and my participation with other women in the women's liberation movement.

Woman Defined: The Web of Ideology

Women as a group have traditionally been socialized into one role—that of housewife-mother—which has channeled them into dependent positions and has limited the control that they may exercise over their own lives. Women whose work is confined to the home are totally dependent on their husbands for economic well-being and social status. They are forced to secure their livelihood and identification vicariously through their men. Ironically, women have been taught that this oppressive condition is a privilege, something that they should strive to attain. Indeed, female children learn that their main goal in life is to become a wife and that a woman without a husband is somehow an incomplete human being.

The role of housewife-mother prescribed for women has been justified by an ideology that has pervaded American culture with the assumption that women are inferior to and therefore dependent on men. Like racism, sexism is a set of attitudes that reflects institutionalized discrimination through general stereotypes of inferiority. Stereotypes similar to those that white society has used to rationalize the exploitation of ethnic minorities have been used to justify the secondary position of women in society. The mass media continually reflect cultural values that define women as emotionally unstable, weak, inconsistent, stupid, childlike, scatterbrained, and passive. Moreover, the second-class status of women has been rationalized through assumptions that women are satisfied with their subordinate role. The popular images of the fulfilled, selfless housewife, like those of the contented, shuffling Negro, have functioned to demonstrate that both these groups are happy "in their place." Not until the past decade and a half have these prevalent images been challenged by the militant black political movement and the women's liberation movement.

Perhaps the most psychologically damaging aspect of the cultural belief that women's primary function is to service husband and children has been the ideal of true womanhood, through which women have been socialized into behavior patterns and self-concepts that have never allowed them to develop a sense of themselves as integral human beings. The symbolic female images with which women have been taught to identify have always been split. Traditionally this culture has divided women between the angelic, chaste girl on the pedestal and the evil whore of the flesh. In the past 30 years this duality has undergone a change, and the image of women is increasingly being split between the feminine woman who is primarily identified in terms of her sexuality and the career woman who, by virtue of her quest for self, is seen as a castrating, aggressive bitch who threatens all men.

This change in the symbolic image of women has emerged from the historical experience of the United States since the World War II. For while the "natural" role of women is defined in terms of their function within the family, American capitalism has always used women as a reserve labor pool. In times of crisis, women have been absorbed into the labor force, only to be sent back to the home in times of labor surplus. Thus during World

War II women worked in the industrial jobs usually re-resrved for men. Since it was in society's interest that mothers work outside the home, the federal government established a network of low-cost child care centers. Rosie the Riveter became the symbol of the working woman fighting alongside American men to preserve democracy and freedom. But with the close of the war and the return of the men from overseas, Rosie was unceremoniously fired. In order to avoid a surplus of workers on the job market, women had to be encouraged —either directly through layoffs or indirectly through mass propaganda—to return to the home.[1] The government child care facilities were dismantled, and the mass media mounted a vigorous campaign to reestablish the dominant image of woman as housewife-mother.

During the fifties and sixties, women's magazines, radio, television, and advertisements barraged the public with an ideology that defined the feminine woman as a human being totally preoccupied with the job of being a good housewife. Articles in women's magazines hardly ever touched on politics, science, education, or any other subject outside the sphere of women's "natural" interests as wives and mothers.

One of the most prevalent ideological underpinnings of this interpretation of the "natural" role of women was the popularization of the Freudian interpretation of female sexuality. Freud had observed the secondary status of women in society, but had incorrectly sought its causes in women's biological nature. He claimed that women were *by nature* passive and dependent. The mature, truly feminine woman accepted this fact and sought personal fulfillment through her role in the family and her relationship with her husband. This woman, according to Freud, manifested the ability to transfer her center of sexual eroticism from the infantile erotogenic zone of the clitoris to the mature erotogenic zone of the vagina. In contrast, the woman who aspired to define herself beyond the confines of home and husband became masculinized; this was reflected in her sexuality by her inability to achieve the so-called vaginal orgasm.[2] Although scientifically untested, this theory was uncritically accepted by psychiatrists, physicians, and other "experts" on women. During the fifties and sixties, women's magazines and marriage manuals, under the pretext of frankness, detailed in Freudian terms the sexual behavior of the "truly feminine" woman. Surveys of sexual patterns in the United States indicated that the majority of women did not experience the so-called vaginal orgasm, but many incorrectly concluded that these women were frigid and not that the theory was invalid. The tragedy of the situation lay in the terrible psychological damage done to millions of women who felt themselves to be personally inadequate and sexually immature.

Freud's theory has recently been challenged by the first comprehensive study of human sexuality (William H. Masters and Virginia E. Johnson, *Human Sexual Response*, 1966). This study demonstrates that much of Freud's thinking was incorrect and that the clitoris is the major organ of reception and transmission of female sexual excitation. The implications of this reinterpretation are manifold, but one thing is clear: the acceptance of the Freudian interpretation of women functioned at the most sophisticated intellectual level to maintain women's sexual dependency on men through the myth of the vaginal orgasm. Furthermore, it reinforced the notion that women were inferior to men and thus justified channeling them into prescribed roles that did not threaten to alter their traditional position in society.

Equally guilty of channeling women into traditional roles were the functionalists who dominated the social sciences in the intellectually repressive environment of the McCarthyite fifties.[3] Reflecting the conservatism of that period, the functionalists abdicated their responsibility to develop theoretical concepts of the process of change in society. Instead, anthropologists and sociologists questioned nothing and offered the most static interpretations of social institutions by assuming the inevitability of what already existed. The family was viewed as a functional unit, an institution composed of a complementary relationship based on the division of labor between husband and wife. It was to the benefit of society in general that the woman accept her role as wife and mother. Any woman who sought to "emulate" and "duplicate" the male role outside the home was guilty of disturbing the equilibrium of society. Popularized through the media and dominating the college sociology texts, the functionalist interpretation justified the status quo at a time when social and economic pressures were forcing women into the labor market. The result was that women were made to feel guilty if they sought through need or choice to go beyond their role of housewife-mother.

During the fifties, with the spread of credit buying, television entered a majority of homes in this country and became the most powerful vehicle reinforcing the narrow definition of women's role. Like radio and popular magazines, television portrays the ideal woman as the content, charming, selfless wife and mother constantly dedicated to cleaning, improving her home, caring for her children, and consuming the multitude of household and cosmetic products sold to her by the Madison Avenue advertisers. Women are supposed to identify with this prescribed division of labor so that they do not permanently search for other opportunities outside the home —which would aggravate an already satiated labor market—and so that unnecessary commódities produced by the giant corporations will be assured of a constantly expanding market.

The Home Economics of Women's Exploitation

There is a great contradiction between the image of the fulfilled and glamorous middle-class housewife portrayed in the media and the unhappy reality of most women's lives. During the fifties and sixties there were increasing indications that housewives were finding it impossible to feel fulfilled through daily repetitive and unimaginative tasks that, in spite of all the so-called labor-saving devices, were consuming as much time as had the housework of their grandmothers in the 1920s. Neither could women be satisfied with the limited amount of human contact realized through their relationships with their children. Indeed, during this period there were indications that women were suffering a profound sense of alienation because of the limited opportunities available to them beyond these roles. According to National Institute of Mental Health statistics, from 1950 to 1968, 223,268 more women than men were hospitalized in state and county mental hospitals. From 1964 to 1968, 125,351 more women than men were psychiatrically hospitalized and treated on an outpatient basis. These figures do not include the increasing numbers of women seeking private treatment, a phenomenon that also characterized these decades.[4] Middle-class women resorted to the psychiatrist's couch, convinced that their feelings of emptiness, insignificance, and loneliness were the result of some individual maladjustment or inadequacy.

In fact, these reactions were not the result of individual maladjustment but were the logical collective response to the oppressive reality of these women's lives. To understand their reactions, it is necessary to briefly analyze certain fundamental aspects of the function of women within the family, an institution that has bound women to a division of labor that offers little opportunity for economic autonomy or self-esteem. For example, the unpaid household labor that women perform, including child care, constitutes services that are socially necessary for the maintenance of the capitalist system in its present form. When an employer hires a wage earner, the male head of the household, he is actually buying the labor of two people. The employer, in effect, is getting the labor of the wife for free. If women did not produce these necessary services, such as cooking, laundering, house cleaning, shopping, and child care, this society would have to find other means through which these functions would be performed. Furthermore, if women were paid for their labor in the home, a mass redistribution of wealth would be the result, a process obviously not in the interest of the capitalist class.

A clear way to demonstrate the value produced by the unpaid labor of women in the home is to look at the example of the paid housekeeper. Because she is a paid worker, the housekeeper's wage is included in the annual statistics of the gross national product. But if an employer marries his housekeeper, she becomes his wife and ceases to receive wages for her labor. Thus although the GNP index would fall as a result of her change in status, she continues to perform the same labor and produce the same goods and services in the home, but without monetary remuneration. The crucial point here is that at the same time that women's unpaid labor is absolutely necessary, it receives no recognition in monetary terms because it falls outside the market economy. In the capitalist system, the value of labor is assessed in terms of the money it receives. Thus from a strictly economic point of view, because women receive no money for their services their labor is considered valueless. At the same time that women are being materially exploited, they are being taught not to view this condition as an index of oppression but as a symbol of privileged status.

A vague recognition of this contradiction is reflected in the many cultural stereotypes of the "frustrated housewife" who, having no other source of identification or little else meaningful with which to fill her time, spends the majority of her days shopping for clothes and household goods. Unfortunately, individuals who are aware of the tragic manner in which people in this society are taught to identify self-worth with the quantity of commodities they consume, incorrectly criticize women for being the major prop of the consumer society. They use as proof of this assertion the fact that most of the advertisements in the mass media are aimed at women. This view, however, misses the point completely. The advertisements merely reflect the manner in which the system exploits the insecurities from which women suffer to sell them commodities.

Furthermore, I would like to offer another perspective with which to view the relationship that women have to commodities in this society. I suggest that it is incorrect to blame women as the major consumers, since women themselves do not consume the majority of what they purchase. Technically they are but purchasing agents who expend their labor to buy the products consumed in the home by all the members of the family. Moreover, since one of the major social functions of women is to be sexually attractive, women actually do not consume the clothes and cosmetics which they purchase. Rather, they expend their labor to be the sex-objects that are consumed by men. The advertisers are constantly threatening women with the loss of their femininity and thus their husbands, homes and total identity if they do not purchase certain products. Of course, no woman can ever hope to live up to the idealized image of selfless housewife-super sex object. Therefore women are continually preoccupied with striving for an impossible goal. The result is both an all-pervasive sense of personal failure and a dreadful waste of women's energies in unproductive activities that reinforce their traditional position in society.

Women in the Marketplace of Labor

The cultural ideal of the happy housewife-mother is contradicted even more dramatically by the reality of the lives of working women. Since 1950 women have sought work in ever-increasing numbers, not necessarily out of the desire and/or opportunity for self-fulfillment, but out of pure economic need. The recessive and inflationary trends of the past twenty years and a constantly rising cost of living have made the incorporation of women into the paid work force a necessity.

In 1966, 37.3 percent of the female population of this country worked in public employment. From 1957 to 1966, women as a percentage of all workers on full-time schedules increased from 29.7 percent to 31.9 percent.[5] Before World War II, the majority of working women were unmarried and childless. In 1965, 62 percent of working women were wives and mothers, the largest proportion of whose husbands earned $5000 or less a year. Since a majority of all working women are living with their husbands, most women who work do so to help pay basic family living expenses. An even higher percentage of black women work because of low family incomes and the high unemployment rate among black men. Many women who work are heads of families; one out of every eight families in urban areas is headed by a woman. And since women earn less than men, the families headed by women suffer economically as a result. The federal government reports that families headed by women are the most frequent victims of poverty.

Although the number of working women has increased in the last twenty years, the status of the work that they perform has declined. For example, very few woman are employed at the professional level. According to the Department of Labor, women are only 1 percent of the engineers, 3 percent of the lawyers, and only 7 percent of the doctors. By far the vast majority of women are engaged increasingly in low-status clerical, service, and sales occupations. Only 20 percent of factory workers are women, and they occupy the lowest paying jobs and experience the worst working conditions. Often women are hired as part-time and temporary full-time employees because employers make more profit by not having to pay fringe benefits.

Besides being channeled into the lowest paying jobs, women receive unequal pay for equal work. That is, women doing the same jobs as men receive lower wages for their labor. Moreover, the difference between the median income received by men and women has continually increased. In 1955, the median wage of full-time women workers was 64 percent that of men, but by 1965, the relation of their median wage to men had *declined* to just under 60 percent.[6]

By far the most exploited group of individuals in the United States are women of color. They suffer double wage discrimination as shown in the following figures indicating the median annual wages in the United States for 1966:[7]

white men	$7,164
nonwhite men	4,528
white women	4,152
nonwhite women	2,949

Moreover, women are paid lower wages than men re-gardless of educational attainment. For example, the median income of women with four years of college was $4,165 in 1966, while the median income for men with only four years of high school was $6,924.[8]

That employers increase their profit rates by paying women lower wages than men is undeniable. Grace Hutchins, working from the 1950 Census and the indus-trial financial reports of the Federal Reserve Board, computed that by paying women less wages than men, manufacturing companies realized an extra profit of $5.4 billion in that year. Since the declared profits of the manufacturing sector totaled $23.2 billion, she concluded that the cheap labor of women provided 23 percent of all manufacturing profits.[9]

Working women are doubly exploited by long hours and low pay on the job and by added physical labor and psychological pressure in the home. Most women, after a full day's work, return at night to face all of the house-hold responsibilities with little help from their hus-bands. Undoubtedly women who work in the home and at a paid job work as many hours each week as house-wives, who, according to the Chase Manhattan Bank, have an average work week of 99.6 hours.[10]

This oppressive situation is exacerbated by the lack of available child care centers at a cost that working women can afford. The United States is one of the only indus-trialized nations that does not offer government-funded child care facilities with specially trained men and women to care for the children of working parents. Working women are made to feel guilty and personally responsible for being unable to provide adequately for their children because they cannot pay the high prices of the few private child care centers that do exist. These women suffer a sense of personal failure at the vast difference between their pressured, tension-filled lives and the image of the carefree, happy mother that comes into their homes every evening via the television.

The Mythology of Liberation

The relaxation of traditional sexual mores during the 1960s has usually been interpreted as a sexual revolution. More importantly, increased sexual activity on the part of women is often mistakenly equated with their liberation from the traditional roles described above. In fact, the opposite is true. During the past decade the tendency to define women primarily as sexual objects has been reinforced.

Under the pretext of sexual liberation, advertisers use female (not male) nude bodies to sell commodities, and almost every movie contains scenes, often meaningless to the plot, that feature complete female nudity. It has become a commonplace in many United States cities for cafes and nightclubs to feature topless or totally nude female waitresses and entertainers. Young women are channeled into these jobs because of the sexual objectification of women in this society and because of the lack of creative and lucrative alternatives. Thus sexual *objectification*, and not liberation, of women has increased and has only served to heighten the sense of power among men and the sense of powerlessness, competition, isolation, and insecurity among women.

Male chauvinist attitudes toward women even pervade the youth counter-culture, a phenomenon that claims to criticize traditional bourgeois values and relationships. Many of the women who form part of the counter culture are ironically tied to traditional roles: instead of baking Betty Crocker biscuits they spend their days cooking brown rice and organically grown foods. One has only to listen to the words of the "revolutionary" rock music that frames and reflects the values of the counter culture to see clearly and repeatedly the manner in which women are demeaned. For example, a recent popular song claimed that women ". . . may be stupid, but they sure are fun."

In response to the real inferior status and the demeaning image of women in this society, women have internalized both of these aspects of their oppression. Most women believe themselves to be what society says they are: emotional, irrational, passive, and unproductive. Through this internalization of sexist values, women often actively strive to maintain these traits because they are convinced that it is precisely the dependent and totally male-oriented woman that men desire. They fear that the price they will pay for any assertion of autonomy and self-definition will be the loss of the men in their lives. Often women who have achieved some degree of independence pretend that they are dependent on their men in order not to threaten their relationship. This playacting is for women a fundamental emotional and intellectual contradiction.

Conclusion

Who benefits from male chauvinism? One might say all men, but only in a limited sense. Male chauvinism, sanctioned in custom and law, provides the majority of men who have no real control over their lives in capitalist society with a modicum of power through the domination of women. The real benefactor, however, is the small percentage of people in this society who comprise the ruling class that controls North America's political and economic institutions. The capitalist system pits individuals, races, and sexes against one another through competition for jobs and status. People's awareness of this process is limited because of the way in which sexism, like racism, divides them into antagonistic groups that are scapegoated for the problems generated by the system. For example, working women are often blamed for the growing incidence of unhappy marriages, the instability and increasing competition of the job market, and the confusion of traditional sex roles that are no longer so comfortably differentiated. Moreover, women who seek to go beyond their traditional roles are often held responsible for the insecurity from which both men and women suffer in this society. In reality, the contradictions in the system itself—with its inequitable distribution of wealth and power—are responsible for this insecurity and alienation.

The contemporary Women's Liberation movement grew out of the civil rights and antiwar movements of the 1960s that sought to reform the domestic and foreign policies of American capitalism. It represented the response of women to the contradiction between the ideals of equality and the unequal treatment they received from the men who dominated these political movements. Women began to rebel at the hypocrisy and, while continuing to fight against the Vietnam war, poverty, and racism, they have begun to struggle against their own oppression as women. For the first time in history women's groups are providing women with the opportunity to break down the traditional isolation and competition from which they have suffered and to develop together a sense of solidarity and collective power. Women in the women's liberation movement are fighting to improve the quality of life for women in this society through struggles for free abortions on demand, free community-controlled child care centers funded by taxation of corporate profits, paid maternity leaves with guaranteed job security, and houseworkers' unions.

However, growing numbers of women in the movement feel that their demands for these reforms cannot be met by a system that has historically exploited and oppressed women. Through theoretical analyses of capitalism and practical experience in fighting for reforms, many women are becoming convinced that only with radical change in the system will they be able to successfully struggle for their liberation and self-determination.

Notes:

1. This fact is born out by the personal testimony of older women in my Women's Studies classes who had such experiences during World War II. Many were forced to sign contracts promising to give up their jobs at the end of the war.

2. For a detailed review of the theories of female sexuality and the Masters and Johnson study, see Mary Jane Sherfey, "The Evolution and Nature of Female Sexuality in Relation to Psychoanalytic Theory," *Journal of the American Psychoanalytic Association*, 14 (January 1966), 28–125.

3. An excellent study of the impact of functionalism on the discipline of sociology is Alvin W. Gouldner, *The Coming Crisis of Western Sociology* (New York, 1970); for specific references to the functionalist analysis of the role of women and the family, see Betty Friedan, *The Feminine Mystique* (New York, 1963), pp. 126–149.

4. Phyllis Chesler, "Men Drive Women Crazy," *Psychology Today* (July 1971), p. 18.

5. Vernon T. Clover, *Changes in Differences in Earnings and Occupational Status of Men and Women, 1947–1967* (Texas, 1970), p. 38.

6. These statistics from the U. S. Department of Labor are quoted in Ilene Winkler, *Women Workers: The Forgotten Third of the Working Class* (New York, n.d.); see also Marlene Dixon, "Why Women's Liberation?," in Deborah Babcox and Madeline Belkin, eds., *Liberation Now* (New York, 1971), pp. 19–22.

7. Elsie Adams and Mary Louise Briscoe, eds., *Up Against the Wall, Mother* (California, 1971); see section: "Women in the Labor Force," which contains statistics from the Handbook on Women Workers, published in 1969 by the Women's Bureau of the U. S. Department of Labor, pp. 339–344.

8. *Ibid.*

9. Grace Hutchins, *Women Who Work* (New York, 1952), p. 25.

10. Robin Morgan, ed., *Sisterhood is Powerful* (New York, 1970); see section: "Verbal Karate: Statistical and Aphoristic Ammunition," p. 557.

THE FOREIGN POLICY SCENE

The Sources of Soviet Conduct
GEORGE F. KENNAN

"The Sources of Soviet Conduct" appeared under the authorship of "X" in the July 1947 issue of the influential journal Foreign Affairs. Actually, "X" was George F. Kennan, a career diplomat and member of the State Department. This article, which enunciated the containment doctrine, is necessary for an understanding of the United States' foreign policy actions in the years following World War II. The implementation of Kennan's ideas by the Truman administration was already under way at the time the article was published. What makes Kennan's article seem so contemporary is that the government still seems to be following the arguments put forward in it. Containment remains America's basic foreign policy guidepost, despite the fact that Kennan, in his memoir of 1967, claimed that too much military emphasis had been placed on his theory.

Reprinted by permission from Foreign Affairs, July 1947. Copyright by the Council on Foreign Relations, Inc., New York.

The political personality of Soviet power as we know it today is the product of ideology and circumstances: ideology inherited by the present Soviet leaders from the movement in which they had their political origin, and circumstances of the power which they now have exercised for nearly three decades in Russia. There can be few tasks of psychological analysis more difficult than to try to trace the interaction of these two forces and the relative role of each in the determination of official Soviet conduct. Yet the attempt must be made if that conduct is to be understood and effectively countered.

It is difficult to summarize the set of ideological concepts with which the Soviet leaders came into power. Marxian ideology, in its Russian-Communist projection, has always been in process of subtle evolution. The materials on which it bases itself are extensive and complex. But the outstanding features of Communist thought as it existed in 1916 may perhaps be summarized as follows: (a) that the central factor in the life of man, the factor which determines the character of public life and the "physiognomy of society," is the system by which material goods are produced and exchanged; (b) that the capitalist system of production is a nefarious one which inevitably leads to the exploitation of the working class by the capital-owning class and is incapable of developing adequately the economic resources of society or of distributing fairly the material goods produced by human labor; (c) that capitalism contains the seeds of its own destruction and must, in view of the inability of the capital-owning class to adjust itself to economic change, result eventually and inescapably in a revolutionary transfer of power to the working class; and (d) that imperialism, the final phase of capitalism, leads directly to war and revolution.

The rest may be outlined in Lenin's own words: "Unevenness of economic and political development is the inflexible law of capitalism. It follows from this that the victory of Socialism may come originally in a few capitalist countries or even in a single capitalist country. The victorious proletariat of that country, having expropriated the capitalists and having organized Socialist production at home, would rise against the remaining capitalist world, drawing to itself in the process the oppressed classes of other countries." It must be noted that there was no assumption that capitalism would perish without proletarian revolution. A final push was needed from a revolutionary proletariat movement in order to tip over the tottering structure. But it was regarded as inevitable that sooner or later that push be given.

For 50 years prior to the outbreak of the Revolution, this pattern of thought had exercised great fascination for the members of the Russian revolutionary movement. Frustrated, discontented, hopeless of finding self-expression—or too impatient to seek it—in the confining limits of the Tsarist political system, yet lacking wide popular support for their choice of bloody revolution as a means of social betterment, these revolutionists found in Marxist theory a highly convenient rationalization for their own instinctive desires. It afforded pseudo-scientific justification for their impatience, for their categoric denial of all value in the Tsarist system, for their yearning for power and revenge and for their inclination to cut corners in the pursuit of it. It is therefore no wonder that they had come to believe implicitly in the truth and soundness of the Marxian-Leninist teachings, so congenial to their own impulses and emotions. Their sincerity need not be impugned. This is a phenomenon as old as human nature itself. It has never been more aptly described than by Edward Gibbon, who wrote in "The Decline and Fall of the Roman Empire": "From enthusiasm to imposture the step is perilous and slippery; the demon of Socrates affords a memorable instance how a wise man may deceive himself, how a good man may deceive others, how the conscience may slumber in a mixed and middle state between self-illusion and voluntary fraud." And it was with this set of conceptions that the members of the Bolshevik Party entered into power.

Now it must be noted that through all the years of preparation for revolution, the attention of these men, as indeed of Marx himself, had been centered less on the future form which Socialism would take than on the necessary overthrow of rival power which, in their view, had to precede the introduction of Socialism. Their views, therefore, on the positive program to be put into effect, once power was attained, were for the most part nebulous, visionary and impractical. Beyond the nationalization of industry and the expropriation of large private capital holdings there was no agreed program. The treatment of the peasantry, which according to the Marxist formulation was not of the proletariat, had always been a vague spot in the pattern of Communist thought; and it remained an object of controversy and vacillation for the first ten years of Communist power.

The circumstances of the immediate post-revolution period—the existence in Russia of civil war and foreign intervention, together with the obvious fact that the Communists represented only a tiny minority of the Russian people—made the establishment of dictatorial power a necessity. The experiment with "war Communism" and the abrupt attempt to eliminate private production and trade had unfortunate economic consequences and caused further bitterness against the new revolutionary régime. While the temporary relaxation of the effort to communize Russia, represented by the New Economic Policy, alleviated some of this economic distress and thereby served its purpose, it also made it evident that the "capitalistic sector of society" was still prepared to profit at once from any relaxation of governmental pressure, and would, if permitted to continue to exist, always constitute a powerful opposing element to the Soviet régime and a serious rival for influence in the country. Somewhat the same situation prevailed with respect to the individual peasant who, in his own small way, was also a private producer.

Lenin, had he lived, might have proved a great enough man to reconcile these conflicting forces to the ultimate benefit of Russian society, though this is questionable. But be that as it may, Stalin, and those whom he led in the struggle for succession to Lenin's position of leadership, were not the men to tolerate rival political forces in the sphere of power which they coveted. Their sense of insecurity was too great. Their particular brand of fanaticism, unmodified by any of the Anglo-Saxon traditions of compromise, was too fierce and too jealous to envisage any permanent sharing of power. From the Russian-Asiatic world out of which they had emerged they carried with them a skepticism as to the possibilities of permanent and peaceful coexistence of rival forces. Easily persuaded of their own doctrinaire "rightness," they insisted on the submission or destruction of all competing power. Outside of the Communist Party, Russian society was to have no rigidity. There were to be no forms of collective human activity or association which would not be dominated by the Party. No other force in Russian society was to be permitted to achieve vitality or integrity. Only the Party was to have structure. All else was to be an amorphous mass.

And within the Party the same principle was to apply. The mass of Party members might go through the motions of election, deliberation, decision and action; but in these motions they were to be animated not by their own individual wills but by the awesome breath of the Party leadership and the overbrooding presence of "the word."

Let it be stressed again that subjectively these men probably did not seek absolutism for its own sake. They doubtless believed—and found it easy to believe—that they alone knew what was good for society and that they would accomplish that good once their power was secure and unchallengeable. But in seeking that security of their own rule they were prepared to recognize no restrictions, either of God or man, on the character of their methods. And until such time as that security might be achieved, they placed far down on their scale of operational priorities the comforts and happiness of the peoples entrusted to their care.

Now the outstanding circumstance concerning the Soviet régime is that down to the present day this process of political consolidation has never been completed and the men in the Kremlin have continued to be predominantly absorbed with the struggle to secure and make absolute the power which they seized in November 1917. They have endeavored to secure it primarily against forces at home, within Soviet society itself. But they have also endeavored to secure it against the outside world. For ideology, as we have seen, taught them that the outside world was hostile and that it was their duty eventually to overthrow the political forces beyond their borders. The powerful hands of Russian history and tradition reached up to sustain them in this feeling.

Finally, their own aggressive intransigence with respect to the outside world began to find its own reaction; and they were soon forced, to use another Gibbonesque phrase, "to chastise the contumacy" which they themselves had provoked. It is an undeniable privilege of every man to prove himself right in the thesis that the world is his enemy; for if he reiterates it frequently enough and makes it the background of his conduct he is bound eventually to be right.

Now it lies in the nature of the mental world of the Soviet leaders, as well as in the character of their ideology, that no opposition to them can be officially recognized as having any merit or justification whatsoever. Such opposition can flow, in theory, only from the hostile and incorrigible forces of dying capitalism. As long as remnants of capitalism were officially recognized as existing in Russia, it was possible to place on them, as an internal element, part of the blame for the maintenance of a dictatorial form of society. But as these remnants were liquidated, little by little, this justification fell away; and when it was indicated officially that they had been finally destroyed, it disappeared altogether. And this fact created one of the most basic of the compulsions which came to act upon the Soviet régime: since capitalism no longer existed in Russia and since it could not be admitted that there could be serious or widespread opposition to the Kremlin springing spontaneously from the liberated masses under its authority, it became necessary to justify the retention of the dictatorship by stressing the menace of capitalism abroad.

This began at an early date. In 1924 Stalin specifically defended the retention of the "organs of suppression," meaning, among others, the army and the secret police, on the ground that "as long as there is a capitalist encirclement there will be danger of intervention with all the consequences that flow from that danger." In accordance with that theory, and from that time on, all internal opposition forces in Russia have consistenly been portrayed as the agents of foreign forces of reaction antagonistic to Soviet power.

By the same token, tremendous emphasis has been placed on the original Communist thesis of a basic antagonism between the capitalist and Socialist worlds. It is clear, from many indications, that this emphasis is not founded in reality. The real facts concerning it have been confused by the existence abroad of genuine resentment provoked by Soviet philosophy and tactics and occasionally by the existence of great centers of military power, notably the Nazi régime in Germany and the Japanese Government of the late 1930's, which did indeed have aggressive designs against the Soviet Union. But there is ample evidence that the stress laid in Moscow on the menace confronting Soviet society from the world outside its borders is founded not in the realities of foreign antagonism but in the necessity of explaining away the maintenance of dictatorial authority at home.

Now the maintenance of this pattern of Soviet power, namely, the pursuit of unlimited authority domestically, accompanied by the cultivation of the semi-myth of implacable foreign hostility, has gone far to shape the actual machinery of Soviet power as we know it today. Internal organs of administration which did not serve this purpose withered on the vine. Organs which did serve this purpose became vastly swollen. The security of Soviet power came to rest on the iron discipline of the Party, on the severity and ubiquity of the secret police, and on the uncompromising economic monopolism of the state. The "organs of suppression," in which the Soviet leaders had sought security from rival forces, became in large measure the masters of those whom they were designed to serve. Today the major part of the structure of Soviet power is committed to the perfection of the dictatorship and to the maintenance of the concept of Russia as in a state of siege, with the enemy lowering beyond the walls. And the millions of human beings who form that part of the structure of power must defend at all costs this concept of Russia's position, for without it they are themselves superfluous.

As things stand today, the rulers can no longer dream of parting with these organs of suppression. The quest for absolute power, pursued now for nearly three decades with a ruthlessness unparalleled (in scope at least) in modern times, has again produced internally, as it did externally, its own reaction. The excesses of the police apparatus have fanned the potential opposition to the régime into something far greater and more dangerous than it could have been before those excesses began.

But least of all can the rulers dispense with the fiction by which the maintenance of dictatorial power has been defended. For this fiction has been canonized in Soviet philosophy by the excesses already committed in its name; and it is now anchored in the Soviet structure of thought by bonds far greater than those of mere ideology.

II

So much for the historical background. What does it spell in terms of the political personality of Soviet power as we know it today?

Of the original ideology, nothing has been officially junked. Belief is maintained in the basic badness of capitalism, in the inevitability of its destruction, in the obligation of the proletariat to assist in that destruction and to take power into its own hands. But stress has come to be laid primarily on those concepts which relate most specifically to the Soviet régime itself: to its position as the sole truly Socialist régime in a dark and misguided world, and to the relationships of power within it.

The first of these concepts is that of the innate antagonism between capitalism and Socialism. We have seen how deeply that concept has become imbedded in foundations of Soviet power. It has profound implications for Russia's conduct as a member of international society. It means that there can never be on Moscow's side any sincere assumption of a community of aims between the Soviet Union and powers which are regarded as capitalist. It must invariably be assumed in Moscow that the aims of the capitalist world are antagonistic to the Soviet régime, and therefore to the interests of the peoples it controls. If the Soviet Government occasionally sets its signature to documents which would indicate the contrary, this is to be regarded as a tactical manœuvre permissible in dealing with the enemy (who is without honor) and should be taken in the spirit of *caveat emptor*. Basically, the antagonism remains. It is postulated. And from it flow many of the phenomena which we find disturbing in the Kremlin's conduct of foreign policy: the secretiveness, the lack of frankness, the duplicity, the wary suspiciousness, and the basic unfriendliness of purpose. These phenomena are there to stay, for the foreseeable future. There can be variations of degree and of emphasis. When there is something the Russians want from us, one or the other of these features of their policy may be thrust temporarily into the background; and when that happens there will always be Americans who will leap forward with gleeful announcements that "the Russians have changed," and some who will even try to take credit for having brought about such "changes." But we should not be misled by tactical manœuvres. These characteristics of Soviet policy, like the postulate from which they flow, are basic to the internal nature of Soviet power, and will be with us, whether in the foreground or the background, until the internal nature of Soviet power is changed.

This means that we are going to continue for a long time to find the Russians difficult to deal with. It does not mean that they should be considered as embarked upon a do-or-die program to overthrow our society by a given date. The theory of the inevitability of the eventual fall of capitalism has the fortunate connotation that there is no hurry about it. The forces of progress can take their time in preparing the final *coup de grâce*. Meanwhile, what is vital is that the "Socialist fatherland"—that oasis of power which has been already won for Socialism in the person of the Soviet Union—should be cherished and defended by all good Communists at home and abroad, its fortunes promoted, its enemies badgered and confounded. The promotion of premature, "adventuristic" revolutionary projects abroad which might embarrass Soviet power in any way would be an inexcusable, even a counter-revolutionary act. The cause of Socialism is the support and promotion of Soviet power, as defined in Moscow.

This brings us to the second of the concepts important to contemporary Soviet outlook. That is the infallibility of the Kremlin. The Soviet concept of power, which permits no focal points of organization outside the Party itself, requires that the Party leadership remain in theory the sole repository of truth. For if truth were to be found elsewhere, there would be justification for its expression in organized activity. But it is precisely that which the Kremlin cannot and will not permit.

The leadership of the Communist Party is therefore always right, and has been always right ever since in 1929 Stalin formalized his personal power by announcing that decisions of the Politburo were being taken unanimously.

On the principle of infallibility there rests the iron discipline of the Community Party. In fact, the two concepts are mutually self-supporting. Perfect discipline requires recognition of infallibility. Infallibility requires the observance of discipline. And the two together go far to determine the behaviorism of the entire Soviet apparatus of power. But their effect cannot be understood unless a third factor be taken into account: namely, the fact that the leadership is at liberty to put forward for tactical purposes any particular thesis which it finds useful to the cause at any particular moment and to require the faithful and unquestioning acceptance of that thesis by the members of the movement as a whole. This means that truth is not a constant but is actually created, for all intents and purposes, by the Soviet leaders themselves. It may vary from week to week, from month to month. It is nothing absolute and immutable—nothing which flows from objective reality. It is only the most recent manifestation of the wisdom of those in whom the ultimate wisdom is supposed to reside, because they represent the logic of history. The accumulative effect of these factors is to give to the whole subordinate apparatus of Soviet power an unshakeable stubbornness and steadfastness in its orientation. This orientation can be changed at will by the Kremlin but by no other power. Once a given party line has been laid down on a given issue of current policy, the whole Soviet governmental machine, including the mechanism of diplomacy, moves inexorably along the prescribed path, like a persistent toy automobile wound up and headed in a given direction, stopping only when it meets with some unanswerable force. The individuals who are the components of this machine are unamenable to argument or reason which comes to them from outside sources. Their whole training has taught them to mistrust and discount the glib persuasiveness of the outside world. Like the white dog before the phonograph, they hear only the "master's voice." And if they are to be called off from the purposes last dictated to them, it is the master who must call them off. Thus the foreign representative cannot hope that his words will make any impression on them. The most that he can hope is that they will be transmitted to those at the top, who are capable of changing the party line. But even those are not likely to be swayed by any normal logic in the words of the bourgeois representative. Since there can be no appeal to common purposes, there can be no appeal to common mental approaches. For this reason, facts speak louder than words to the ears of the Kremlin; and words carry the greatest weight when they have the ring of reflecting, or being backed up by, facts of unchallengeable validity.

But we have seen that the Kremlin is under no ideological compulsion to accomplish its purposes in a hurry. Like the Church, it is dealing in ideological concepts which are of long-term validity, and it can afford to be patient. It has no right to risk the existing achievements of the revolution for the sake of vain baubles of the future. The very teachings of Lenin himself require great caution and flexibility in the pursuit of Communist purposes. Again, these precepts are fortified by the lessons of Russian history: of centuries of obscure battles between nomadic forces over the stretches of a vast unfortified plain. Here caution, circumspection, flexibility and deception are the valuable qualities; and their value finds natural appreciation in the Russian or the oriental mind. Thus the Kremlin has no compunction about retreating in the face of superior force. And being under the compulsion of no timetable, it does not get panicky under the necessity for such retreat. Its political action is a fluid stream which moves constantly, wherever it is permitted to move, toward a given goal. Its main concern is to make sure that it has filled every nook and cranny available to it in the basin of world power. But if it finds unassailable barriers in its path, it accepts these philosophically and accommodates itself to them. The main thing is that there should always be pressure, unceasing constant pressure, toward the desired goal. There is no trace of any feeling in Soviet psychology that that goal must be reached at any given time.

These considerations make Soviet diplomacy at once easier and more difficult to deal with than the diplomacy of individual aggressive leaders like Napoleon and Hitler. On the one hand it is more sensitive to contrary force, more ready to yield on individual sectors of the diplomatic front when that force is felt to be too strong, and thus more rational in the logic and rhetoric of power. On the other hand it cannot be easily defeated or discouraged by a single victory on the part of its opponents. And the patient persistence by which it is animated means that it can be effectively countered not by sporadic acts which represent the momentary whims of democratic opinion but only by intelligent long-range policies on the part of Russia's adversaries—policies no less steady in their purpose, and no less variegated and resourceful in their application, than those of the Soviet Union itself.

In these circumstances it is clear that the main element of any United States policy toward the Soviet Union must be that of a long-term, patient but firm and vigilant containment of Russian expansive tendencies. It is important to note, however, that such a policy has nothing to do with outward histrionics: with threats or blustering or superfluous gestures of outward "toughness." While the Kremlin is basically flexible in its reaction to political realities, it is by no means unamenable to considerations of prestige. Like almost any other government, it can be placed by tactless and threatening gestures in a position where it cannot afford to yield even though this might be dictated by its sense of realism. The Russian leaders are keen judges of human psychology, and as such they are highly conscious that loss of temper and of self-control is never a source of strength in political affairs. They are quick to exploit such evidences of weakness. For these reasons, it is a *sine qua non* of successful dealing with Russia that the foreign government in question should remain at all times cool and collected and that its demands on Russian policy should be put forward in such a manner as to leave the way open for a compliance not too detrimental to Russian prestige.

III

In the light of the above, it will be clearly seen that the Soviet pressure against the free institutions of the western world is something that can be contained by the adroit and vigilant application of counter-force at a series of constantly shifting geographical and political points, corresponding to the shifts and manœuvres of Soviet policy, but which cannot be charmed or talked out of existence. The Russians look forward to a duel of infinite duration, and they see that already they have scored great successes. It must be borne in mind that there was a time when the Communist Party represented far more of a minority in the sphere of Russian national life than Soviet power today represents in the world community.

But if ideology convinces the rulers of Russia that

truth is on their side and that they can therefore afford to wait, those of us on whom that ideology has no claim are free to examine objectively the validity of that premise. The Soviet thesis not only implies complete lack of control by the west over its own economic destiny, it likewise assumes Russian unity, discipline and patience over an infinite period. Let us bring this apocalyptic vision down to earth, and suppose that the western world finds the strength and resourcefulness to contain Soviet power over a period of ten to fifteen years. What does that spell for Russia itself?

The Soviet leaders, taking advantage of the contributions of modern technique to the arts of despotism, have solved the question of obedience within the confines of their power. Few challenge their authority; and even those who do are unable to make that challenge valid as against the organs of suppression of the state.

The Kremlin has also proved able to accomplish its purpose of building up in Russia, regardless of the interests of the inhabitants, an industrial foundation of heavy metallurgy, which is, to be sure, not yet complete but which is nevertheless continuing to grow and is approaching those of the other major industrial countries. All of this, however, both the maintenance of internal political security and the building of heavy industry, has been carried out at a terrible cost in human life and in human hopes and energies. It has necessitated the use of forced labor on a scale unprecedented in modern times under conditions of peace. It has involved the neglect or abuse of other phases of Soviet economic life, particularly agriculture, consumers' goods production, housing and transportation.

To all that, the war has added its tremendous toll of destruction, death and human exhaustion. In consequence of this, we have in Russia today a population which is physically and spiritually tired. The mass of the people are disillusioned, skeptical and no longer as accessible as they once were to the magical attraction which Soviet power still radiates to its followers abroad. The avidity with which people seized upon the slight respite accorded to the Church for tactical reasons during the war was eloquent testimony to the fact that their capacity for faith and devotion found little expression in the purposes of the régime.

In these circumstances, there are limits to the physical and nervous strength of people themselves. These limits are absolute ones, and are binding even for the cruelest dictatorship, because beyond them people cannot be driven. The forced labor camps and the other agencies of constraint provide temporary means of compelling people to work longer hours than their own volition or mere economic pressure would dictate; but if people survive them at all they become old before their time and must be considered as human casualties to the demands of dictatorship. In either case their best powers are no longer available to society and can no longer be enlisted in the service of the state.

Here only the younger generation can help. The younger generation, despite all vicissitudes and sufferings, is numerous and vigorous; and the Russians are a talented people. But it still remains to be seen what will be the effects on mature performance of the abnormal emotional strains of childhood which Soviet dictatorship created and which were enormously increased by the war. Such things as normal security and placidity of home environment have practically ceased to exist in the Soviet Union outside of the most remote farms and villages. And observers are not yet sure whether that is not going to leave its mark on the over-all capacity of the generation now coming into maturity.

In addition to this, we have the fact that Soviet economic development, while it can list certain formidable achievements, has been precariously spotty and uneven. Russian Communists who speak of the "uneven development of capitalism" should blush at the contemplation of their own national economy. Here certain branches of economic life, such as the metallurgical and machine industries, have been pushed out of all proportion to other sectors of economy. Here is a nation striving to become in a short period one of the great industrial nations of the world while it still has no highway network worthy of the name and only a relatively primitive network of railways. Much has been done to increase efficiency of labor and to teach primitive peasants something about the operation of machines. But maintenance is still a crying deficiency of all Soviet economy. Construction is hasty and poor in quality. Depreciation must be enormous. And in vast sectors of economic life it has not yet been possible to instill into labor anything like that general culture of production and technical self-respect which characterizes the skilled worker of the west.

It is difficult to see how these deficiencies can be corrected at an early date by a tired and dispirited population working largely under the shadow of fear and compulsion. And as long as they are not overcome, Russia will remain economically a vulnerable, and in a certain sense an impotent, nation, capable of exporting its enthusiasms and of radiating the strange charm of its primitive political vitality but unable to back up those articles of export by the real evidences of material power and prosperity.

Meanwhile, a great uncertainty hangs over the political life of the Soviet Union. That is the uncertainty involved in the transfer of power from one individual or group of individuals to others.

This is, of course, outstandingly the problem of the personal position of Stalin. We must remember that his succession to Lenin's pinnacle of preeminence in the Communist movement was the only such transfer of individual authority which the Soviet Union has experienced. That transfer took 12 years to consolidate. It cost the lives of millions of people and shook the state to its foundations. The attendant tremors were felt all through the international revolutionary movement, to the disadvantage of the Kremlin itself.

It is always possible that another transfer of preeminent power may take place quietly and inconspicuously, with no repercussions anywhere. But again, it is possible that the questions involved may unleash, to use some of Lenin's words, one of those "incredibly swift transitions" from "delicate deceit" to "wild violence" which characterize Russian history, and may shake Soviet power to its foundations.

But this is not only a question of Stalin himself. There has been, since 1938, a dangerous congealment of political life in the higher circles of Soviet power. The All-Union Congress of Soviets, in theory the supreme body of the Party, is supposed to meet not less often than once in three years. It will soon be eight full years since its last meeting. During this period membership in the Party has numerically doubled. Party mortality during the war was enormous; and today well over half of the Party members are persons who have entered since the last Party congress was held. Meanwhile, the same small group of men has carried on at the top through an amazing series of national vicissitudes. Surely there is some reason why the experiences of the war brought basic political changes to every one of the great governments of the west. Surely the causes of that phenomenon are basic enough to be present somewhere in the obscurity of Soviet political life, as well. And yet no recognition has been given to these causes in Russia.

It must be surmised from this that even within so highly disciplined an organization as the Communist Party there must be a growing divergence in age, outlook and interest between the great mass of Party members, only so recently recruited into the movement, and the little self-perpetuating clique of men at the top, whom most of these Party members have never met, with whom they have never conversed, and with whom they can have no political intimacy.

Who can say whether, in these circumstances, the eventual rejuvenation of the higher spheres of authority (which can only be a matter of time) can take place smoothly and peacefully, or whether rivals in the quest for higher power will not eventually reach down into these politically immature and inexperienced masses in order to find support for their respective claims? If this were ever to happen, strange consequences could flow for the Communist Party: for the membership at large has been exercised only in the practices of iron discipline and obedience and not in the arts of compromise and accommodation. And if disunity were ever to seize and paralyze the Party, the chaos and weakness of Russian society would be revealed in forms beyond description. For we have seen that Soviet power is only a crust concealing an amorphous mass of human beings among whom no independent organizational structure is tolerated. In Russia there is not even such a thing as local government. The present generation of Russians have never known spontaneity of collective action. If, consequently, anything were ever to occur to disrupt the unity and efficacy of the Party as a political instrument, Soviet Russia might be changed overnight from one of the strongest to one of the weakest and most pitiable of national societies.

Thus the future of Soviet power may not be by any means as secure as Russian capacity for self-delusion would make it appear to the men in the Kremlin. That they can keep power themselves, they have demonstrated. That they can quietly and easily turn it over to others remains to be proved. Meanwhile, the hardships of their rule and the vicissitudes of international life have taken a heavy toll of the strength and hopes of the great people on whom their power rests. It is curious to note that the ideological power of Soviet authority is strongest today in areas beyond the frontiers of Russia, beyond the reach of its police power. This phenomenon brings to mind a comparison used by Thomas Mann in his great novel "Buddenbrooks." Observing that human institutions often show the greatest outward brilliance at a moment when inner decay is in reality farthest advanced, he compared the Buddenbrook family, in the days of its greatest glamour, to one of those stars whose light shines most brightly on this world when in reality it has long since ceased to exist. And who can say with assurance that the strong light still cast by the Kremlin on the dissatisfied peoples of the western world is not the powerful afterglow of a constellation which is in actuality on the wane? This cannot be proved. And it cannot be disproved. But the possibility remains (and in the opinion of this writer it is a strong one) that Soviet power, like the capitalist world of its conception, bears within it the seeds of its own decay, and that the sprouting of these seeds is well advanced.

IV

It is clear that the United States cannot expect in the foreseeable future to enjoy political intimacy with the Soviet régime. It must continue to regard the Soviet Union as a rival, not a partner, in the political arena. It must continue to expect that Soviet policies will reflect no abstract love of peace and stability, no real faith in the possibility of a permanent happy coexistence of the Socialist and capitalist worlds, but rather a cautious, persistent pressure toward the disruption and weakening of all rival influence and rival power.

Balanced against this are the facts that Russia, as opposed to the western world in general, is still by far the weaker party, that Soviet policy is highly flexible, and that Soviet society may well contain deficiencies which will eventually weaken its own total potential. This would of itself warrant the United States entering with reasonable confidence upon a policy of firm containment, designed to confront the Russians with unalterable counterforce at every point where they show signs of encroaching upon the interests of a peaceful and stable world.

But in actuality the possibilities for American policy are by no means limited to holding the line and hoping for the best. It is entirely possible for the United States to influence by its actions the internal developments, both within Russia and throughout the international Communist movement, by which Russian policy is largely determined. This is not only a question of the modest measure of informational activity which this government can conduct in the Soviet Union and elsewhere, although that, too, is important. It is rather a question of the degree to which the United States can create among the people of the world generally the impression of a country which knows what it wants, which is coping successfully with the problems of its internal life and with the responsibilities of a World Peace, and which has a spiritual vitality capable of holding its own among the major ideological currents of the time. To the extent that such an impression can be created and maintained, the aims of Russian Communism must appear sterile and quixotic, the hopes and enthusiasm of Moscow's supporters must wane, and added strain must be imposed on the Kremlin's foreign policies. For the palsied decrepitude of the capitalist world is the keystone of Communist philosophy. Even the failure of the United States to experience the early economic depression which the ravens of the Red Square have been predicting with such complacent confidence since hostilities ceased would have deep and important repercussions throughout the Communist world.

By the same token, exhibitions of indecision, disunity and internal disintegration within this country have an exhilarating effect on the whole Communist movement. At each evidence of these tendencies, a thrill of hope and excitement goes through the Communist world; a new jauntiness can be noted in the Moscow tread; new groups of foreign supporters climb on to what they can only view as the bandwagon of international politics; and Russian pressure increases all along the line in international affairs.

It would be an exaggeration to say that American behavior unassisted and alone could exercise a power of life and death over the Communist movement and bring about the early fall of Soviet power in Russia. But the United States has it in its power to increase enormously the strains under which Soviet policy must operate, to force upon the Kremlin a far greater degree of moderation and circumspection than it has had to observe in recent years, and in this way to promote tendencies which must eventually find their outlet in either the break-up or the gradual mellowing of Soviet power. For no mystical, Messianic movement—and particularly not that of the Kremlin—can face frustration indefinitely without eventually adjusting itself in one way or another to the logic of that state of affairs.

Thus the decision will really fall in large measure in

this country itself. The issue of Soviet-American relations is in essence a test of the over-all worth of the United States as a nation among nations. To avoid destruction the United States need only measure up to its own best traditions and prove itself worthy of preservation as a great nation.

Surely, there was never a fairer test of national quality than this. In the light of these circumstances, the thoughtful observer of Russian-American relations will find no cause for complaint in the Kremlin's challenge to American society. He will rather experience a certain gratitude to a Providence which, by providing the American people with this implacable challenge, has made their entire security as a nation dependent on their pulling themselves together and accepting the responsibilities of moral and political leadership that history plainly intended them to bear.

Korea: The War for Both Asia and Europe (1950-1951)
WALTER LaFEBER

The first shooting war in which the United States found itself after World War II occurred in Korea. Supposedly, the Truman administration acted in a swift and decisive fashion to thwart an unprovoked Soviet-sponsored attack on the Republic of South Korea. Historian Walter La-Feber of Cornell University is very critical of this explanation. He believes that much more than collective security was at stake for the United States. In his analysis America's actions in Asia are suspect and must be examined very carefully.

Excerpted from *America, Russia, and the Cold War, 1945–1966* by Walter LaFeber. Copyright © 1967, 1971 by John Wiley & Sons, Inc.

In June 1950, Korea was a Cold War-wracked country which lacked everything except authoritarian governments, illiteracy, cholera epidemics, and poverty. For nearly a century, it had been a pawn in Far Eastern power plays. In 1905, Japan, after using force to stop a Russian thrust, had established a protectorate over Korea and in 1910 annexed that country. When the Japanese surrendered Korea in 1945, it became a testing ground in the renewed battle between Russia and the United States. After setting up dependent but Korean-led governments in zones seized from the Japanese, Russia and the United States evacuated their occupation armies in 1948 and 1949, respectively. In March 1949, North Korea and the Soviets signed an agreement for economic cooperation. Russian military advisers and aid strengthened a formidable 100,000 man army. American military advisers also remained in the south, but President Truman encountered difficulty sending large amounts of aid to Syngman Rhee's government. At the end of June 1950, about $60 million of an allotted $110 million in economic aid had been shipped. Military assistance had scarcely begun. As at the turn of the century, Korea was a prize in the struggle between Russia and countries to the West; and, as in 1904, China, although now a very different China, stood apart from the conflict. Mao's regime devoted itself to internal reconstruction and drawing up plans for a probable invasion of Formosa sometime during 1950.

Mao had little cause to linger over Korean problems; South Korea itself posed no threat to his new government or, apparently, to the remainder of the Communist bloc. MacArthur and Acheson had defined Korea as beyond the perimeter of American military defenses, although not outside the realm of United Nations responsibility. It seemed possible, moreover, that without either Chinese or Russian overt pressure, the South Korean government might crumble. South Korea suffered under Rhee's authoritarian government until the State Department publicly protested his disregard of constitutional rights in early 1950. In an election in May, President Rhee's party collected only forty-eight seats as opposed to one hundred and twenty seats for the other parties; this defeat occurred despite Rhee's arrest of thirty political opponents in "anti-communist" raids just before the election was held. The Korean President pieced together a coalition government that began what promised to be a precarious, perhaps short, struggle to hold power.

On June 7 the northern government of Kim Il Sung attempted to exploit Rhee's problems by initiating an all-out campaign for peaceful reunification of the country through general elections. Rhee attempted to stop the news of this offer from circulating in the South. With that encouragement, the northern government reiterated the proposal on June 19 and intensified its political offensive.

This North Korean initiative apparently fitted within a general strategy which Stalin was designing to counter two threats. In mid-May, Truman announced that discussions on a Japanese peace treaty would receive high priority. The negotiations would particularly consider Japanese independence and the establishment of American military bases on Japan's soil under long-term agreements. The talks, American officials observed, would not be burdened with Russian representation. For Stalin this announcement opened the unhappy prospect of unity between the two greatest industrial nations in the Pacific, perhaps even the extension of a NATO-like organization on the Asian periphery of the Soviet Union. The Sino-

Soviet pact in February had singled out Japan as a potential threat to Asian Communism, and this had been followed by the Soviet press accusing Truman of attempting to "draw the Asiatic and Pacific countries into aggressive military blocs, to entangle those countries in the chains of some 'little' Marshall Plan for Asia." On May 30, the Japanese Communist party climaxed weeks of demonstrations with attacks on United States military personnel in Tokyo. If North Korea could unify the country, peacefully or otherwise, the threat of a militarized western-oriented Japan would be blunted, perhaps neutralized.

The second threat might well have caused Stalin even more concern. Mao's success had not created but probably encouraged revolutions throughout Asia, particularly in Indochina, the Philippines, and Indonesia. The possibility that some of these revolutions might triumph, perhaps following the pattern set by Mao, could weaken Stalin's two-camp premise and loosen his direction over the world Communist bloc. Stalin's view of world matters had become so rigid that he could not accept the nationalist content of these revolts without wrecking his own doctrines and tempering his grip on Soviet and satellite affairs. Malenkov had added to these troubles with his November speech, but by the spring of 1950 (that is, after the Chinese had shown their obstinacy in the Sino-Soviet negotiations and the revolutionary situation had intensified in Asia), Malenkov came back into line. In a speech in March, he no longer talked about the "friendly" nations surrounding Russia, but about a Europe, and especially Germany, which "fascist and revanchist forces," led by the United States, planned to turn into "a military-strategic bridgehead of American aggression." A speech by Molotov the same month was equally aggressive. Stalin had confined the domestic debate; a short and successful war by a Russian-controlled North Korea could intimidate Japan and check the expansive aims and reputation of Mao. On June 25, large numbers of North Korean troops moved across the 38th parallel which divided the country. They followed Soviet-built tanks which had been shipped to Korea during the previous two months.

Attending to family business in Independence, Missouri, when the attack occurred, Truman immediately returned to Washington. He and Acheson assumed the invasion was Russian-directed, perhaps the beginning of an extensive Sino-Soviet thrust. Their initial reaction, however, was carefully measured. They ordered MacArthur in Tokyo to dispatch supplies to the South Korean troops. Then, moving to contain the action, Truman ordered the American Seventh Fleet to sail between China and Formosa, and sent additional assistance to counter-revolutionary forces in the Philippines and Indochina. In a hurriedly called session of the United Nations Security Council, an American resolution branding the North Koreans as aggressors, demanding a cessation of hostilities, and requesting a withdrawal behind the 38th parallel, passed 9-0 with Yugoslavia abstaining. The Soviet Union was not represented, for Yakov Malik continued his boycott to protest the exclusion of Red China. Two days later, as the military situation worsened, Truman ordered American air and naval units into action. That same day, the 27th, the United Nations passed a resolution recommending that its members aid South Korea in restoring peace. This passed 7-1 with Yugoslavia opposing and Egypt and India abstaining. Malik still had not appeared; the rapidity and extent of Truman's reaction had taken the Soviets by surprise.

•   •   •

The United States suffered 142,000 casualties in Korea not for the sake of "collective security" or the United Nations, but because the Executive branch of the govern-

ment decided that the invasion signaled a direct threat
to American interests in both Asia and Europe. Europe,
indeed, remained uppermost in the minds of high State
Department officials. As the fighting raged in Korea,
Acheson devoted increasing amounts of time to the European situation. The State Department had long defined
Europe as having first importance. Acheson, moreover,
had gotten burned politically and diplomatically when
Korean attack raised questions about his January 12th
speech which termed the Communist threat in Asia one
of "subversion and penetration," and not "military." This
was a rare, probably traumatic, departure from his usual
reliance upon military "positions of strength," and he
moved quickly to improve the military balance in Europe.
He did so, however, not solely for military objectives.

• • •

The election occurred when American forces were advancing to greater victories in Korea. What magnifying
effects a series of battle losses would have on Republican
power and McCarthyism, Democrats did not wish to con-
template. General MacArthur had apparently removed
this possibility on September 15 with a brilliant landing
at Inchon, back of the North Korean lines, while simultaneously launching a counterattack from the shallow
perimeter at Pusan. Within two weeks the United Nations forces joined to cut off large sections of North
Korean troops. The Administration's political goals developed accordingly. In late June, Truman reported that
the main objective was the restoration of the 38th parallel; on September 1, he told the nation that the Koreans
"have a right to be free, independent, and united"; ten
days later he approved a National Security Council recommendation that MacArthur should drive the North
Koreans north of the 38th and, if encountering no Chi-

nese or Russian troops, to move north of the parallel and prepare for occupation; on September 27, Truman ordered MacArthur north of the parallel; and on October 7, the General Assembly cooperated by endorsing Truman's order 47-5. That day the lead troops of the United States First Cavalry Division crossed into North Korea.

All eyes now turned to China. Throughout July and August, the new Communist government had made little response to the conflict. Recovering from famine, a quarter century of war, and having as her top diplomatic objective the conquest of Formosa, China did not pose an immediate threat to the United Nations forces. In late August, Foreign Minister Chou En-lai made his first important move. At the United Nations, American delegate Warren Austin asked for the open door "within all parts of Korea," and later in the month, Secretary of Navy Francis Matthews applauded "a war to compel co-operation for peace." At this point, Chou reminded the world that "Korea is China's neighbor" and urged that the neighbor's problems be settled "peacefully." Mass anti-American rallies began to appear in Chinese cities. Ten days after the Inchon landing Peking warned India, which had become China's main link with the Western world, that it would not "sit back with folded hands and let the Americans come to the border." After the first remnants of the North Korean troops retreated behind the 38th, Chou formally told India in a dramatic midnight meeting on October 2 that China would attack if United Nations troops moved into North Korea. The United States discounted his threat, believing that it was aimed at influencing upcoming votes on the conflict in the United Nations. MacArthur responded by issuing an ultimatum for the complete surrender of North Korea. On October 7, as the first American troops crossed the border, Chinese troop concentrations on the Manchurian border just across the Yalu River from Korea increased from 180,000 to 320,000. On October 16, a few Chinese "volunteers" crossed the Yalu.

The Truman Administration remained convinced that China would not intervene. Emphasizing, as he had in earlier speeches, that China's immediate concern was with Russian penetration in the north, Acheson commented on national television on September 10, 1950, "I should think it would be sheer madness" for the Chinese to intervene, "and I see no advantage to them in doing it." Acheson later admitted that until late September, American intelligence considered Chinese intervention improbable. On October 9, the danger reached the boiling point when two American F-80 jets strafed a Soviet airfield only a few miles from Vladivostok, a major Russian city close to the Korean border. After the Soviets strongly protested, the United States apologized. Vexed that such a crisis could arise, and angered that he had to back down before Soviet protests just a month before national elections, Truman cancelled a trip to Independence, where he was to watch his sister installed as Worthy Matron in the Order of Eastern Star, and flew to Wake Island to check on MacArthur's policies. In the heavily-censored text of that meeting, little was implied about Russia, but the General assured the President, "We are no longer fearful of [Chinese] intervention. We no longer stand hat in hand." The Chinese, he informed Truman, possessed no air force. They might move 50,000 or 60,000 men across the Yalu, but if these troops attempted to move farther south without air cover, "there would be the greatest slaughter."

Eleven days later, on October 26, the first Chinese prisoner was captured, "so that you began to know, at that point," Acheson later commented, "that something was happening." This realization, however, made little apparent impact on American policies during the next four weeks. On November 21, advanced elements of American troops peered at Chinese sentries stationed several hundred yards across the Yalu. Three days later, MacArthur grandly announced the launching of the end-the-war offensive. At this point the United States government was still not certain whether, in Acheson's words, the Chinese "were committed to a full-scale offensive effort." Two days later, on November 26, the Chinese moved across the river in mass, trapping and destroying large numbers of United Nations troops, including 20,000 Americans and Koreans at the Chosin Reservoir; this outfit finally escaped with 4400 battle casualties and 7000 noncombat casualties, mostly severe cases of frostbite. Three weeks later the retreating United Nations forces once again fought below the 38th parallel, and now it was Chou En-lai who proclaimed his nation's intention of reunifying Korea. "They really fooled us when it comes right down to it; didn't they?" Senator Leverett Saltonstall once asked Acheson. "Yes, sir," the Secretary of State replied.

•   •   •

In Washington, Administration officials were thoroughly frightened, and Truman's response to the intervention was considerably more explicit than Stalin's. The President reiterated that the United States had no "aggressive intentions toward China," and believed that the Chinese people opposed this sending of troops by their leaders. (This remark was in line with Truman's general theory that Communism anywhere never had popular support.) Because these people could not be heard, the President continued, the aggression must be crushed or "we can expect it to spread throughout Asia and Europe to this hemisphere." As in late June, however, Truman's response was measured. He countermanded MacArthur's order to bomb Chinese troops and supplies in Manchuria. The President finally allowed only the Korean halves of the bridges crossing the Yalu to be bombed, a compromise that infuriated MacArthur and told the Chinese exactly how restrained American retaliation to their intervention would be. In a news conference of November 30, Truman showed signs of losing this restraint. He intimated that the United States would use all the power it possessed to contain the Chinese, and he explicitly did not exclude using atomic bombs.

·   ·   ·

Although the military situation steadily eroded, not even the other nations in the Western Hemisphere would offer much assistance. The Latin Americans dutifully voted with the United Nations and the Organization of American States, but in the early spring of 1951, when Truman personally appealed to Latin American Foreign Ministers to "establish the principle of sharing our burdens fairly," only Colombia responded with troops. Several other nations sent materiel, but Latin America as a whole failed to see the relevance of Korea to their own economic deprivation and political instability. Later in 1951 a shocked Administration attempted to woo its southern neighbors by extending to them the Mutual Security Program of military aid. Eight nations took the money in 1952 to protect themselves against Communist aggression; this both giver and receiver interpreted to mean preservation of the *status quo*. No other Latin American nation, however, sent men to Korea.

·   ·   ·

The President also embarked the United States upon another costly and momentous journey by committing it to developing and protecting the Western Pacific and Southeast Asia. The riches of the area made it a formidable prize: Burma, Thailand, and Indochina provided rice for much of Asia; Southeast Asia produced nearly 90 percent of the world's natural rubber, 60 percent of the world's tin, and the bulk of Asia's oil. Movements toward independence threw the area into turmoil immediately after the war, but with several exceptions (particularly Vietnam and the Philippines where an Un-Filipino Activities Committee tried to aid the Army in ferreting out the "Huk" rebels), a semblance of order appeared by 1950. Attempted Communist uprisings had been contained in most countries by nationalist elements.

Throughout Asia . . . anticolonial, nationalist movements had triumphed either peacefully or after short struggles. Vietnam was a tragic exception. There Ho Chi Minh had conducted anti-Japanese underground operations during the war and emerged in 1946 as the leading Communist and nationalist leader. Roosevelt had pressured the French to evacuate Indochina in early 1945. De Gaulle resisted that pressure until the Truman Administration reversed the American policy in order to obtain French cooperation in Europe. After a year of uneasy truce with the French, who were determined to reclaim their control over Indochina, full-scale war broke out in December 1946. The French army moved back into Vietnam carrying large numbers of American lend-lease weapons to eradicate Ho's forces. The Soviets, like the United States, refused to recognize Ho's Republic of Vietnam. Typically distrusting such revolutionaries, Stalin, like Truman, concentrated on European problems in 1946 and early 1947. By 1948 Ho was turning to the Communist Chinese for aid. He had not easily reached this decision, for the Indochinese had historically feared and distrusted their giant neighbor. On January 18, 1950, China recognized Ho's government. The Soviets followed thirteen days later.

After an intensive policy review, the United States fully

committed itself to the French cause. On February 6, four and one-half months before the Korean War began, the United States recognized the Bao Dai government which had been established by the French. On June 12, an American military advisory mission prepared to aid the French forces. As early as May, Truman discussed large-scale aid for Bao Dai, and after the Korean conflict, began to pump in aid at the rate of half a billion dollars per year. When French General de Lattre de Tassigny visited Washington in September 1951, the State Department endorsed French war aims and methods.

Although involving itself in the French struggle long before June 1950, the Korean war provided a convenient background as the United States began explaining its commitments in Vietnam. A State Department pamphlet of 1951 defined United States interests as the "much-needed rice, rubber, and tin," but added, "perhaps even more important would be the psychological effect of the fall of Indochina. It would be taken by many as a sign that the force of communism is irresistible and would lead to an attitude of defeatism." The statement concluded that "Communist forces there must be decisively conquered down to the last pocket of resistance"; to accomplish this, large amounts of American aid had been given. "Without this aid," the analysis concluded, ". . . it is doubtful whether [Bao Dai and the French] could hold their ground against the Communists."

• • •

. . . negotiations in late 1950 and 1951 determined the geographical extent of the American commitment in the Pacific. During the spring of 1951, with drama and flourishes seldom seen in American history, the military extent of that commitment was decided. In late January, United Nations forces opened a successful drive back to the 38th parallel. As the battle stalemated along the former boundary line, State Department and Pentagon officials cautiously explored the possibility of negotiations with the Chinese on March 20. Three days later General MacArthur issued a personal statement urging that the Red military commanders "confer in the field" with him on surrender; China is "doomed to imminent military collapse," the General proclaimed. Not for the first time had MacArthur undercut his superiors in Washington.

As early as July 1950, he had shown reluctance to accept Truman's decision that Chiang Kai-shek should be contained on Formosa rather than unleashed on the mainland or allowed to ship troops to Korea. A month later, MacArthur sent a message to the annual convention of the Veterans of Foreign Wars, which labeled as "appeasement" any policy that would restrain Chiang. Truman angrily demanded that this message be recalled, and MacArthur complied although it had already been published. The Wake Island conference muted these differences, but the published minutes are embarrassing in their revelation of MacArthur's incredible condescension and Truman's tittering insecurity. Once the President was back in Washington, this insecurity disappeared. After MacArthur again recommended a naval blockade of China, air attacks to level Chinese military and industrial installations, and the use of 30,000 Formosan troops in Korea, Truman patiently explained on January 13 "the political factors" involved in the "world-wide threat" of the Soviet Union which made containment of the Korean war necessary. When MacArthur issued his March 23rd ultimatum, Truman's patience, never inexhaustible, evaporated.

Only the method and timing of relieving the General remained to be decided. On April 5, Representative Joe Martin, the leading Republican in the House, read a letter from MacArthur which charged that "here we fight

Europe's war with arms while the diplomats there still
fight it with words." "We must win," the letter emphasized. "There is no substitute for victory." The Joint
Chiefs of Staff agreed with Truman that MacArthur would
have to be relieved immediately; reports from the field
indicated that the General was losing the confidence of
his men and had already lost confidence in himself. On
April 11, the President recalled MacArthur.

Truman knew the political dynamite in the decision.
Less than two weeks earlier he had agreed with top ad-
visors that an all-out speaking campaign would have to
be undertaken by Cabinet-level officers because the Administration's "'story' was not reaching the American
public." The American people preferred quick victory to
containment. This preference was dramatically demonstrated when the General returned to the greatest popular reception in American history. Senator McCarthy
expressed the feelings toward Truman of not a few Americans when with characteristic restraint he told a press
conference, "The son of a bitch ought to be impeached."
Congress warmly received MacArthur's speech before a
joint session, then in April and May settled down to investigate the case of the President versus the General.

In a battle of MacArthur versus Truman, the long-range
issues tended to be overshadowed by the personalities
involved. In MacArthur's case this was not an advantage.
Having last set foot in the United States fourteen years
before, the General seemed unable or unwilling to grasp
the political and social as well as the diplomatic views
of his country. He revealed much describing the power
he wielded in Japan between 1945 and 1950: "I had not
only the normal executive authorities such as our own
President has in this country, but I had legislative authority. I could by fiat issue directives." Although he had repeatedly advocated policies which contained the most

somber worldwide ramifications, he now admitted having only a "superficial knowledge" of NATO and European affairs.

His basic message was curiously close to Truman's and Niebuhr's in 1948: because Communism posed a threat to all civilization, "you have got to hold every place." Or again, "What I advocate is that we defend every place, and I say that we have the capacity to do it. If you say that we haven't you admit defeat." Like Acheson, he insisted on not putting military power and politics into the intellectual equivalent of a cream separator; in time of war, however, MacArthur demanded the reversal of Acheson's priority: once involved in war, the General argued, the military commander must be supreme over all military and political affairs in his theater, "or otherwise you will have the system that the Soviet once employed of the political commissar, who would run the military as well as the politics of the country." Such a remark cut across the grain of traditional American policies of subordinating military to civilian officials unless the nation was involved in total war. This MacArthur assumed to be the case. When he heard the suggestion of Assistant Secretary of State Dean Rusk that war in Korea must not become a "general conflagration," MacArthur branded it "the concept of appeasement, the concept that when you use force, you can limit the force."

The General believed that by controlling the sea and air no one could "successfully launch an effort against us," but the United States could "largely neutralize China's capability to wage aggressive war and thus save Asia from the engulfment otherwise facing it." He expressed contempt for the Chinese Communists. "Never, in our day, will atomic weapons be turned out of China. They cannot turn out the ordinary weapons." Nor was there threat of Soviet intervention. Time, however, was short. If, as MacArthur once told Forrestal, Europe was a "dying system," and the Pacific would "determine the course of history in the next ten thousand years," victory must be won immediately. The "dreadful slaughter" had to end, MacArthur pleaded; American blood as well as dust is settling in Korea, and the "blood, to some extent" rests "on me." But now, he concluded emotionally, "There is no policy—there is nothing, I tell you, no plan, or anything."

The Administration had a plan, and Acheson outlined it in his testimony after MacArthur finished. Korea must be viewed as part of a "collective security system," Acheson argued. When so viewed two things readily became apparent. First, all-out war in Korea would suck in Russian force to aid Stalin's "largest and most important satellite." "I cannot accept the assumption that the Soviet Union will go its way regardless of what we do," the Secretary of State declared. If Russia did intervene, there could be "explosive possibilities not only for the Far East, but for the rest of the world as well." Unlike MacArthur, Acheson insisted on keeping the European picture uppermost in dealing with Korea. (Truman once added a variant on this: expansion of the war could "destroy the unity of the free nations," the President declared. "We cannot go it alone in Asia and go it with company in Europe.") Second, if Europe and the prevention of Russian entry in force did comprise the main objectives, American forces were not engaged in a "dreadful slaughter," or as Acheson remarked, "a pointless and inconclusive struggle," but had "scored a powerful victory" by dealing "Communist imperialist aims in Asia a severe setback" in preventing the armed conquest of all Korea.

MacArthur lost the argument. He lost it so decisively, moreover, that while negotiations to conclude a stalemated war fitfully began in Korea during the summer of 1951, Acheson accelerated the military buildup in Europe.

The Confrontation in Cuba
THEODORE C. SORENSEN

In October 1962 it appeared that the United States and the Soviet Union stood on the brink of nuclear war. Perhaps it is somewhat ironic that this confrontation was directed by a young, liberal, Democratic President. America's actions are even more telling when one thinks back to the rhetoric of the 1950s and thinks of the lack of aggressive, overt action in that decade. Theodore C. Sorensen, a former Kennedy assistant, has retraced the events leading to the showdown between the two superpowers. In his account Kennedy comes out a hero, but it is worth asking whether this view is entirely accurate.

Abridged from Chapter XXIV in *Kennedy* by Theodore C. Sorensen. Copyright © 1965 by Theodore C. Sorensen, published by Harper & Row, Publishers, Inc.

On October 9 the President—whose personal authorization was required for every U-2 flight and who throughout this period had authorized all flights requested of him—approved a mission over the western end of Cuba. The primary purpose of the mission was to obtain information on the actual operation of Soviet SAMs. The western end was selected because the SAMs in that area—first spotted on August 29—were believed most likely to be operational. A secondary objective, inasmuch as the September flights had surveyed previously uncovered parts of the island, was to resurvey the military build-up in that sector—specifically to check two convoy observations from inside Cuba (both delayed because of the difficulty in getting reports out) which had indicated more precisely than usual the possibility of a medium-range ballistic missile site in that location. (It was not until one day after this authorization, on October 10, that Senator Keating first asserted the presence of offensive missile bases in Cuba.)

Delayed by bad weather until October 14, the U-2 flew in the early morning hours of that cloudless Sunday high over western Cuba, moving from south to north. Processed that night, the long rolls of film were scrutinized, analyzed, compared with earlier photos, and reanalyzed throughout Monday by the extraordinarily talented photo interpreters of the U.S. Government's intelligence network; and late that afternoon they spotted in the San Cristobal area the first rude beginnings of a Soviet medium-range missile base.

By Monday evening, October 15, the analysts were fairly certain of their findings. Between 8 and 10 P.M., the top CIA officials were notified and they notified in turn the

Defense and State intelligence chiefs and, at his home, McGeorge Bundy. Bundy immediately recognized that this was no unconfirmed refugee report or minor incident. He decided, however—and quite rightly, I believe—not to call the President but to brief him in person and in detail the next morning. (Over four months later, almost as an afterthought, the President asked why he didn't telephone him that night; and Bundy responded with a memorandum "for your memoirs":

> . . . Its validity would need to be demonstrated clearly to you and others before action could be taken. The [photographic] blow-ups and other elements of such a presentation would not be ready before morning. . . . [To] remain a secret . . . everything should go on as nearly normal as possible, in particular there should be no hastily summoned meeting Monday night. [Bundy, Rusk, McNamara and others were all at different dinner parties where reporters, foreign diplomats and other guests might become suspicious.] . . . This was not something that could be dealt with on the phone. . . . What help would it be to you to give you this piece of news and then tell you nothing could be done about it till morning? . . . You were tired [from] a strenuous campaign weekend, returning . . . at 1:40 Monday morning. So I decided that a quiet evening and a night of sleep were the best preparation you could have. . . .)

Around 9 A.M. Tuesday morning, October 16, having first received a detailed briefing from top CIA officials, Bundy broke the news to the President as he scanned the morning papers in his bedroom. Kennedy, though angry at Khrushchev's efforts to deceive him and immediately aware of their significance, took the news calmly but with an expression of surprise. He had not expected the Soviets to attempt so reckless and risky an action in a place like Cuba, and had accepted—perhaps too readily, in retrospect—the judgment of the experts that such a deployment of nuclear weapons would be wholly inconsistent with Soviet policy. Even John McCone had assumed that no missiles would be moved in until an operational network of SAMs would make their detection from the air difficult. (Why the Soviets failed to coordinate this timing is still inexplicable.) For weeks the President had been publicly discounting the wild refugee reports checked out by his intelligence experts and found to be inaccurate. He had criticized in a campaign speech the previous weekend (in Capehart's Indiana) "those self-appointed generals and admirals who want to send someone else's son to war." While he had at least conditioned all his public statements on the basis of information *then* available, some subordinate officials had flatly asserted that no offensive weapons were in Cuba.

• • •

Shortly thereafter, upon arriving at his office, he [the President] sent for me and told me the news. He asked me to attend the 11:45 A.M. meeting in the Cabinet Room and in the meantime to review his public statements on what our reaction would be to offensive missiles in Cuba. At the time those statements were made he may well have doubted that he would ever be compelled to act on them. But at 11 A.M., as CIA Deputy Director Marshall Carter spread the enlarged U-2 photographs before him with comments by a photo interpreter, all doubts were gone. The Soviet missiles were there; their range and purpose were offensive; and they would soon be operative.

At 11:45 A.M. the meeting began in the Cabinet Room. Those summoned to that session at the personal direction of the President, or taking part in the daily meetings that then followed, were the principal members of what would later be called the Executive Committee of the National Security Council, some fourteen or fifteen men who had little in common except the President's desire for their judgment:

STATE: Secretary Dean Rusk, Under Secretary George Ball, Latin-American Assistant Secretary Edwin Martin, Deputy Under Secretary Alexis Johnson and Soviet expert Llewellyn Thompson. (Participating until departing for his new post as Ambassador to France the following night was Charles "Chip" Bohlen.)

DEFENSE: Secretary Robert McNamara, Deputy Secretary Roswell Gilpatric, Assistant Secretary Paul Nitze and General Maxwell Taylor (newly appointed Chairman of the Joint Chiefs of Staff).

CIA: On the first day, Deputy Director Carter; thereafter (upon his return to Washington), Director John McCone.

OTHER: Attorney General Robert Kennedy, Treasury Secretary Douglas Dillon, White House aides Bundy and Sorensen. (Also sitting in on the earlier and later meetings in the White House were the Vice President and Kenneth O'Donnell. Others—such as Dean Acheson, Adlai Stevenson and Robert Lovett— sat in from time to time; and six days later USIA Deputy Director Donald Wilson, acting for the ailing Edward R. Murrow, was officially added.)

• • •

The President was somber but crisp. His first directive was for more photography. He expressed the nation's gratitude to the entire photo collection and analysis team for a remarkable job. It was later concluded that late September photography of the San Cristobal area might have provided at least some hints of suspicious activity more than three weeks earlier, but certainly nothing sufficiently meaningful to convince the OAS, our allies and the world that actual missiles were being installed. The contrast between the October 14 and August 29 photos indicated that field-type missiles had been very quickly moved in and all but assembled since their arrival in mid-September. American reconnaissance and intelligence had done well to spot them before they were operational. But now more photographs were needed immediately, said the President. We had to be sure—we had to have the most convincing possible evidence—and we had to know what else was taking place throughout the island. Even a gigantic hoax had to be guarded against, someone said. Daily flights were ordered covering all of Cuba.

Kennedy's second directive was to request that those present set aside all other tasks to make a prompt and intensive survey of the dangers and all possible courses of action—because action was imperative. More meetings were set up, one in the State Department that afternoon and another back in the Cabinet Room with him at 6:30. Even at that initial 11:45 meeting the first rough outlines of alternatives were explored. One official said our task was to get rid of the missile complex before it became operational, either through an air strike's knocking it out or by pressuring the Soviets into taking it out. He mentioned the possibilities of an OAS inspection team or a direct approach to Castro. Another said an air strike could not be limited to the missile complex alone but would have to include storage sites, air bases and other targets, necessitating thousands of Cuban casualties and possibly an invasion. Still another spoke of adding a naval blockade combined with a warning and increased surveillance. It was agreed that the U.S.-leased Naval base at Cuba's Guantánamo Bay would have to be reinforced and

all dependents evacuated. No conclusions were reached
—but all the possible conclusions were grim.

The President's third directive enjoined us all to strictest secrecy until both the facts and our response could
be announced. Any premature disclosure, he stressed,
could precipitate a Soviet move or panic the American
public before we were ready to act. A full public statement later would be essential, he said, talking in the
same vein about briefing former President Eisenhower.
There was discussion about declaring a national emergency and calling up Reserves. But for the present secrecy
was vital; and for that reason advance consultations with
the Allies were impossible. He had already given the surface impression that morning that all was well, keeping
his scheduled appointments, taking Astronaut Walter
Schirra and his family out in back to see Caroline's
ponies, and meeting with his Panel on Mental Retarda-
tion. (Praised by the Panel's chairman for his interest,
the President had responded: "Thanks for the endorse-
ment.... I'm glad to get some good news.") He had also
proclaimed the last week in November to be National
Cultural Center Week and declared storm-struck areas
of Oregon to be disaster areas.

• • •

The President's helicopter landed on the South Lawn
a little after 1:30. After he had read the draft speech, we
chatted in a relaxed fashion in his office before the decisive meeting scheduled for 2:30. I gave him my view of
the key arguments: air strike no—because it could not
be surgical but would lead to invasion, because the world
would neither understand nor forget an attack without
warning and because Khrushchev could outmaneuver any
form of warning; and blockade yes—because it was a

flexible, less aggressive beginning, least likely to precipitate war and most likely to cause the Soviets to back
down.

Our meeting at 2:30 P.M. was held once again in the
Oval Room upstairs. For the first time we were convened
formally at the 505th meeting of the National Security
Council. We arrived at different gates at different times
to dampen the now growing suspicion among the press.
The President asked John McCone to lead off with the
latest photographic and other intelligence. Then the full
ramifications of the two basic tracks were set before the
President: either to begin with a blockade and move up
from there as necessary or to begin with a full air strike
moving in all likelihood to an invasion. The spokesman
for the blockade emphasized that a "cost" would be in-
curred for whatever action we took, a cost in terms of
Communist retaliation. The blockade route, he said, appeared most likely to secure our limited objective—the
removal of the missiles—at the lowest cost. Another
member presented the case for an air strike leading to
Castro's overthrow as the most direct and effective means
of removing the problem.

At the conclusion of the presentations there was a brief,
awkward silence. It was the most difficult and dangerous
decision any President could make, and only he could
make it. No one else bore his burdens or had his perspective.

• • •

The meeting dragged on past 6 P.M. I waited outside
the door with his reading copy, angry that they should
be harassing him right up to the last minute. Finally he
emerged, a bit angry himself, and hustled over to his
quarters to change clothes for his 7 P.M. speech. As I
walked with him, he told me of the meeting, muttering,

"If they want this job, they can have it—it's no great joy to me." But in a few minutes he was calm and relaxed once again. Alone back in the Cabinet Room, we reviewed the text once more; and in a few more minutes the most serious speech in his life was on the air:

> Good evening, my fellow citizens:
>
> This government, as promised, has maintained the closest surveillance of the Soviet military build-up on the island of Cuba. Within the past week, unmistakable evidence has established the fact that a series of offensive missile sites is now in preparation on that imprisoned island. The purpose of these bases can be none other than to provide a nuclear strike capability against the Western Hemisphere. . . .
>
> This urgent transformation of Cuba into an important strategic base, by the presence of these large, long-range and clearly offensive weapons of sudden mass destruction, constitutes an explicit threat to the peace and security of all the Americas. . . .
>
> For many years, both the Soviet Union and the United States . . . have deployed strategic nuclear weapons with great care, never upsetting the precarious status quo which insured that these weapons would not be used in the absence of some vital challenge. Our own strategic missiles have never been transferred to the territory of any other nation, under a cloak of secrecy and deception. . . . American citizens have become adjusted to living daily in the bull's-eye of Soviet missiles located inside the U.S.S.R. or in submarines. . . .
>
> But this secret, swift and extraordinary build-up of Communist missiles, in an area well known to have a special and historical relationship to the United States and the nations of the Western Hemisphere, in violation of Soviet assurances, and in defiance of American

and hemispheric policy—this sudden, clandestine decision to station strategic weapons for the first time outside of Soviet soil, is a deliberately provocative and unjustified change in the status quo which cannot be accepted by this country, if our courage and our commitments are ever to be trusted again by either friend or foe.

The 1930's taught us a clear lesson: aggressive conduct, if allowed to go unchecked and unchallenged, ultimately leads to war. This nation is opposed to war. We are also true to our word. Our unswerving objective, therefore, must be to prevent the use of these missiles against this or any other country, and to secure their withdrawal or elimination from the Western Hemisphere. . . .

We will not prematurely or unnecessarily risk the costs of world-wide nuclear war in which even the fruits of victory would be ashes in our mouth, but neither will we shrink from that risk at any time it must be faced.

He went on to outline—in careful language which would guide us all week—the initial steps to be taken, emphasizing the word "initial": quarantine, surveillance of the build-up, action if it continued, our response to any use of these missiles, the reinforcement of Guantánamo, OAS and UN action and an appeal to Khrushchev and the Cuban people.

The path we have chosen for the present is full of hazards, as all paths are, but it is the one most consistent with our character and courage as a nation and our commitments around the world. The cost of freedom is always high, but Americans have always paid it. And one path we shall never choose, and that is the path of surrender or submission.

Our goal is not the victory of might, but the vindication of right; not peace at the expense of freedom, but both peace *and* freedom, here in this hemisphere, and, we hope, around the world. God willing, that goal will be achieved.

The crisis had officially begun. Some Americans re acted with panic, most with pride. A Congressional leader telephoned the President that a group of them watching together after leaving his office now understood and supported his policy more fully. A U.S. resolution was presented to that month's Security Council President, Russia's Valerian Zorin. Briefings of diplomats and the press continued at the State Department and Pentagon. Strategic Air Command and North American Air Defense units had been put on maximum ground and air alert as the President began speaking. His remarks had been broadcast around the world by the USIA in thirty-eight languages and immediately printed and distributed in many more. The OAS would meet the next day as an "organ of consultation," and the formal proclamation of the blockade would not occur until then. After a brief chat with the President, I went home to get some sleep.

*   *   *

In the UN, in Washington and in the foreign embassies, support for the U.S. position was surprisingly strong. This was due in part to the shock of Soviet perfidy, and their futile attempts to deny the photographic evidence of attempted nuclear blackmail. It was due in part to world-wide recognition that this was an East-West nuclear confrontation, not a U.S. quarrel with Cuba. It was due in part to the President's choice of a low level of force at the outset and to his forceful but restrained approach. It was due, finally, to the excellent presentations made in the UN by Ambassador Stevenson, with

Schlesinger as an emergency aide and John McCloy to lend
bipartisan stature.

• • •

Still another kind of support was essential—and forthcoming. Some Americans sought to flee, to hide or to re-
supply their fallout shelters. The stock market dropped.
But by a ratio of ten to one the telegrams received at the
White House expressed confidence and support. Reminded
that the public mail response in the 1958 Formosa crisis
had been against risking military action, Kennedy offered
no comment. But he must have inwardly taken some
satisfaction with his labors over the previous two years to
prepare the American people to face the facts. He mentioned only two telegrams to me, both sarcastically. One
came from a right-wing leader who had long urged a
tougher policy toward the insignificant Castro but now
quaked at the prospects of our confronting a nuclear
power. The other came from Mississippi's Governor Bar-
nett, who "retracted" an earlier wire complaining about
our military might being used in Mississippi instead of
the Caribbean.

• • •

A new Khrushchev-to-Kennedy letter was received at
the State Department Friday evening, October 26—long,
meandering, full of polemics but in essence appearing to
contain the germ of a reasonable settlement: inasmuch as
his missiles were there only to defend Cuba against invasion, he would withdraw the missiles under UN inspection if the U.S. agreed not to invade. Similar talk came
the same day in the UN from Zorin to U Thant and,
through a highly informal channel, from Counselor of the
Soviet Embassy in Washington Aleksander Fomin to the
ABC-TV correspondent covering the State Department,

John Scali. In Khrushchev's letter the offer was a bit vague. It seemed to vary from one paragraph to the next, and was accompanied by the usual threats and denunciations. Nevertheless it was with high hopes that the Executive Committee convened Saturday morning, October 27, to draft a reply.

In the course of that meeting our hopes quickly faded. A new Khrushchev letter came in, this time public, making no mention of the private correspondence but raising the ante: the Jupiter missiles in Turkey must be removed in exchange. In addition, we learned, Fomin and Zorin were talking about extending the UN inspection to U.S. bases. Had Khrushchev's hard-liners once again taken the lead, we speculated, or had the appearance of this same swap proposal in Washington and London newspapers encouraged the Soviets to believe we would weaken under pressure? Many Western as well as neutral leaders were, in fact, quick to endorse the Soviet position. Still another possibility was that the second, public proposal had actually been written first.

•   •   •

The most attention was given to Khrushchev's letter of the previous night. Under the President's direction, our group worked all day on draft replies. Fatigue and disagreement over the right course caused more wrangling and irritability than usual. Finally the President asked the Attorney General and me to serve as a drafting committee of two to pull together a final version. He also asked me to clear the text with Stevenson, who had skillfully advanced parallel talks at the UN. The final draft of his reply—which confined itself to the proposals made in Khrushchev's Friday letter, ignoring the Fomin and Zorin talks and any specific reference to Turkish bases— read into the Chairman's letter everything we wanted.

Stevenson feared it might be too stiff. But with two minor amendments acceptable to the President, I obtained Stevenson's clearance; and the President, in the interests of both speed and psychology, released the letter publicly as it was being transmitted to Moscow shortly after 8 P.M.

> The first thing that needs to be done . . . is for work to cease on offensive missile bases in Cuba and for all weapons systems in Cuba capable of offensive use to be rendered inoperable, under effective United Nations arrangements. [Note that, instead of arguing with Mr. K. over whether his missiles and planes were intended to be offensive, he insisted on action against those "capable of offensive use."]
> As I read your letter, the key elements of your proposals—which seem generally acceptable as I understand them—are as follows:
> 1. You would agree to remove these weapons systems from Cuba under appropriate United Nations observation and supervision; and undertake, with suitable safeguards, to halt the further introduction of such weapons systems into Cuba.
> 2. We, on our part, would agree—upon the establishment of adequate arrangements through the United Nations to ensure the carrying out and continuation of these commitments—(a) to remove promptly the quarantine measures now in effect and (b) to give assurances against an invasion of Cuba. [Note that, unlike the action to be undertaken by Khrushchev, ours was conditional upon UN arrangements.]
> . . . the first ingredient, let me emphasize . . . is the cessation of work on missile sites in Cuba and measures to render such weapons inoperable, under effective international guarantees. The continuation of this

threat, or a prolonging of this discussion concerning Cuba by linking these problems to the broader questions of European and world security, would surely lead to an intensification of the Cuban crisis and a grave risk to the peace of the world.

At the private request of the President, a copy of the letter was delivered to the Soviet Ambassador by Robert Kennedy with a strong verbal message: The point of escalation was at hand; the United States could proceed toward peace and disarmament, or, as the Attorney General later described it, we could take "strong and overwhelming retaliatory action . . . unless [the President] received immediate notice that the missiles would be withdrawn." That message was conveyed to Moscow.

•   •   •

Upon awakening Sunday morning, October 28, I turned on the news on my bedside radio, as I had each morning during the week. In the course of the 9 A.M. newscast a special bulletin came in from Moscow. It was a new letter from Khrushchev, his fifth since Tuesday, sent publicly in the interest of speed. Kennedy's terms were being accepted. The missiles were being withdrawn. Inspection would be permitted. The confrontation was over.

Hardly able to believe it, I reached Bundy at the White House. It was true. He had just called the President, who took the news with "tremendous satisfaction" and asked to see the message on his way to Mass. Our meeting was postponed from 10 to 11 A.M. It was a beautiful Sunday morning in Washington in every way.

•   •   •

John F. Kennedy entered and we all stood up. He had, as Harold Macmillan would later say, earned his place in history by this one act alone. He had been engaged in a personal as well as national contest for world leadership and he had won. He had reassured those nations fearing we would use too much strength and those fearing we would use none at all. Cuba had been the site of his greatest failure and now of his greatest success. The hard lessons of the first Cuban crisis were applied in his steady handling of the second with a carefully measured combination of defense, diplomacy and dialogue. Yet he walked in and began the meeting without a trace of excitement or even exultation.

Earlier in his office—told by Bundy and Kaysen that his simultaneous plea to India and Pakistan to resolve their differences over Kashmir in view of the Chinese attack would surely be heeded, now that he looked "ten feet tall"—he had evenly replied: "That will wear off in about a week, and everyone will be back to thinking only of their own interests."

Displaying the same caution and precision with which he had determined for thirteen days exactly how much pressure to apply, he quickly and quietly organized the machinery to work for a UN inspection and reconnaissance effort. He called off the Sunday overflights and ordered the Navy to avoid halting any ships on that day. (The one ship previously approaching had stopped.) He asked that precautions be taken to prevent Cuban exile units from upsetting the agreement through one of their publicity-seeking raids. He laid down the line we were all to follow—no boasting, no gloating, not even a claim of victory. We had won by enabling Khrushchev to avoid complete humiliation—we should not humiliate him now. If Khrushchev wanted to boast that he had won a major concession and proved his peaceful manner, that was the loser's prerogative. Major problems of implementing the agreement still faced us. Other danger spots in the world remained. Soviet treachery was too fresh in our memory to relax our vigil now.

Rejecting the temptation of a dramatic TV appearance, he issued a brief three-paragraph statement welcoming Khrushchev's "statesmanlike decision . . .an important and constructive contribution to peace." Then the President's fourth letter of the week—a conciliatory reply to the Chairman's "firm undertakings"—was drafted, discussed, approved and sent on the basis of the wire service copy of the Chairman's letter, the official text having not yet arrived through diplomatic channels.

Weeks later the President would present to each of us a little silver calendar of October, 1962, mounted on walnut, with the thirteen days of October 16 through October 28 as extra deeply engraved as they already were in our memories. But on that Sunday noon, concealing the enormous sense of relief and fatigue which swept over him, he merely thanked us briefly, called another meeting for Monday morning and rejoined his family as he had each night of the crisis.

I went down the hall to where my secretary, Gloria Sitrin, was at work as she had been day and night for almost two weeks. From her bookcase I picked up a copy of *Profiles in Courage* and read to her a part of the introductory quotation John Kennedy had selected from Burke's eulogy of Charles James Fox: "He may live long, he may do much. But here is the summit. He never can exceed what he does this day."

Roots of Intervention
TOWNSEND HOOPES

The culmination of United States post-World War II foreign policy has been its involvement in Southeast Asia. This most unpopular war has caused a crisis for decision-makers in the 1970s. However, at the time of escalation there did not seem to be any momentous decision made with respect to Vietnam. It simply seemed to the administration that America's Cold War posture had to be supported by sending increasing numbers of troops to Vietnam. In the following selection, former Under Secretary of the Air Force Townsend Hoopes explains how and why the Johnson administration committed the country to increasing involvement in the war.

What seemed in retrospect to have made large-scale military intervention all but inevitable in 1965 was a fateful combination of the President's uncertainty and sense of insecurity in handling foreign policy, and a prevailing set of assumptions among his close advisers that reinforced his own tendency to think about the external world in the simplistic terms of appeasement versus military resolve. The President seemed, from the beginning to the end, uncomfortable and out of his depth in dealing with foreign policy. His exposure to the subject as a member of relevant House and Senate Committees had been long, but superficial. For reasons which seemed to have their roots deep in his personal history, he lacked the kind of confidence in his own judgments that permitted Truman, Eisenhower, and Kennedy to overrule their principal foreign policy and military advisers on major issues. In matters of war and peace he seemed too much the sentimental patriot, lacking Truman's practical horse sense, Eisenhower's experienced caution, Kennedy's cool grasp of reality. The most exhaustive search of the Johnson record reveals no solid core of philosophical principle or considered approach to foreign policy—indeed no indication that he gave the subject much serious attention before 1964. There is only an erratic rhythm of reaction to those foreign crises that impacted upon the particular elements of domestic politics that had engaged his interest or his ambition. Philip Geyelin, in his perceptive book of mid-1966, said of President Johnson that "by political background, by temperament, by personal preference he was the riverboat man . . . a swashbuckling master of the political midstream—but only in the crowded, well-travelled familiar inland waterways of domestic politics. He had no taste and scant preparation for the deep waters of foreign policy, for the sudden storms and unpredictable winds that can becalm or batter or blow off course the ocean-going man. He was king of the river and a stranger to the open sea."

The prevailing assumptions among his close advisers were firmly grounded in the Cold War order of things, in the frame of existing pacts and alliances and alignments—above all, in the notion that the "Communist Bloc" remained an essentially cohesive international conspiracy manifesting itself primarily in military and paramilitary assaults against that other comprehensible entity, the "Free World." An important corollary was the belief that an accretion of "communist" influence *anywhere* must redound to the direct benefit of the main power centers in Moscow and Peking, for from this flowed the logic that counterthrusts in kind were everywhere and almost automatically necessary; otherwise a progressive, irreversible, unacceptable erosion of the world power balance could not be averted.

Like everyone else in the United States over forty, the President's advisers were children of the Cold War in the sense that their thinking about world strategy and world politics had been decisively shaped by that phenomenon. Still relatively young and impressionable when they emerged from the wholesale fighting of World War II, they had found that the fruit of victory was a bitter bipolar enmity stretching around the globe, and apparently restrained from the plunge into final holocaust only by a delicate balance of terror. They had lived in this political-military frame of iron for the better part of twenty years, urgently preoccupied with mortal struggle against a formidable Communist structure.

But by 1965 many of the major elements of the Cold War mosaic had undergone drastic transformation or had ceased to exist. There was an effective military balance in the center of Europe—the product of NATO counterpower sustained over twenty years—and it was a stable balance in the sense of being relatively insensitive to changes in the level and composition of forces on either side, within a fairly wide spectrum. The likelihood of deliberate Soviet attack seemed very low because it was understood on both sides that *any* dramatic attempt to alter the military balance could lead rapidly to a probably uncontrollable nuclear war. Moreover, Western Europe behind the NATO shield was no longer the weak and dispirited war refugee of 1946, but strong, prosperous, and almost confident. And on the other side of the line, time was demonstrating that not even the doctrines of Marx and Lenin could render Communism immune to the inherent traps and pitfalls of the historical process —from schism, territorial dispute, the aging process, and the effects of affluence. In combination, these factors were seriously undermining the Soviet position as the ideological fountainhead of doctrine, making a shambles of party discipline in the world movement, and sharply reducing Soviet revolutionary fervor in relation to the underdeveloped world.

·   ·   ·

It is of the greatest significance that these new perspectives did not materially alter the judgments of the men closest to President Johnson. The tenets of the Cold War were bred in the bone. In fairness, it must be said that nothing is more difficult to confront than the need to outgrow conceptions that have had undeniable validity —have been in truth basic reference points for thought and action involving the life of the nation. It is a difficulty that persists even when one is intellectually aware that the familiar conceptions no longer fully square with the facts. As the President's advisers appraised the world situation in 1965, the Russians and the Chinese still seemed to them in full pursuit of bellicose, expansionist policies across the globe, and still quite ready and able to join in the support and manipulation of proxies for purposes inimical to our own.

•   •   •

. . . the Cold War syndrome prevailing in Washington in 1965 represented no break with the Kennedy period. Indeed all of President Johnson's principal foreign policy advisers were Kennedy men. All carried in their veins the implicitly unlimited commitment to global struggle against Revolutionary Communism which had grown out of our total immersion in World War II, and which had been specifically enunciated in the Truman Doctrine of March 1947. None as yet perceived the necessity—or the possibility—of redefining U.S. interests or the U.S. role in the world in ways that would permit the drawing of more careful distinctions between those commitments and interventions that are in fact *vital* to our national security, and those that spring more or less from our deeply held view of what the world "ought" to be and of how it "ought" to be organized—that is, from our re-forming zeal and our desire for wish fulfillment. To the President's men in early 1965, there seemed no logical stopping point between isolationism and globalism.

Of the close advisers on Vietnam, Dean Rusk seemed the very embodiment of the embattled Cold Warrior with convictions rooted in the Stalinist period. An intelligent man, he could not have been unaware of the trends that were fragmenting the "Communist Bloc" and creating new problems of orientation within each Communist country. But he was careful not to allow these developments to affect his basic judgments. He was, moreover, possessed of a special mania about China and of a knack for arguing by dubious analogy. Not only in public, but in private conversations with colleagues and with President Johnson, Rusk expounded his thesis that Communist China was actively promoting and supporting aggression in Vietnam, that aggression in Vietnam was not different from Hitler's aggression in Europe, that appeasement in Vietnam could have the same consequences as appeasement at Munich. In his always articulate, sometimes eloquent, formulations, Asia seemed to be Europe, China was either Stalinist Russia or Hitler Germany, and SEATO was either NATO or the Grand Alliance of World War II. This insistent drawing on the past as a basis for meeting problems that were radically different, that presented themselves in unlike circumstances, and that involved a quite dissimilar degree of U.S. national interest could hardly fail to make a major contribution to the enormous national confusion regarding the character and meaning of U.S. involvement in the Vietnam War. Rusk thus contributed to the Administration's credibility problem—directly, because his formulations could not withstand the test of even cursory historical analysis; indirectly, because they were apt to be replayed on the President's Texas amplifier. As Philip Geyelin reported it, "The backstage Johnson . . . was quite capable of telling one of the Senate's more serious students of foreign affairs that 'if we don't stop the Reds in South Vietnam, tomorrow they will be in Hawaii, and next week they will be in San Francisco.' "

Robert McNamara had blown into Washington in 1961 like a brisk and exhilarating wind. Possessed of a swift and powerful mind, training in the analytical techniques of modern management, experience in managing a large-scale industrial enterprise, and a natural affinity for the reasoned exercise of power, he quickly excited the awe and admiration of all concerned by establishing genuine civilian control over the sprawling military bureaucracies, a feat that had proved beyond the reach of all seven predecessor Secretaries of Defense. President Kennedy spoke glowingly of "that executive operation at the Pentagon," and prized McNamara as the ablest and most versatile member of the Cabinet.

By 1965, McNamara's prodigious labors to strengthen and broaden the U.S. military posture were about completed. The land-based nuclear missile force had been expanded to one thousand modern Minutemen, and the submarine-based Polaris force was a growing reality. More relevant for Vietnam, U.S. "general purpose" forces were now organized to intervene swiftly and with modern equipment in conflicts of limited scope, well below the nuclear threshold. To this end, combat-ready Army divisions had been increased from 11 to 16; the Special Forces had been expanded from 3 to 7 groups; the Army helicopter inventory had been increased from 5500 to 8000; a fourth Marine division and a fourth Marine air wing had been raised; modern tactical airlift for troops and supplies had been expanded from 16 to 38 squadrons, providing nearly a three-fold increase in carrying capacity; and STRIKECOM, a major new command group reporting directly to the Joint Chiefs of Staff, had been established to "provide the President with tailored responses for any level of warfare" and to develop the necessary new tactical doctrines, equipment, and training for limited war.

This significant new military capability had been designed precisely to arrest or restore those deteriorating situations in the world where important or vital U.S. interests were judged to be engaged, to deal with ambiguous subversion-aggressions characterized by little warning and a low silhouette, to blunt national-liberation wars. It was now ready. To a rational activist like Mc-Namara, with a very thin background in foreign affairs, it seemed entirely logical to employ a portion of this immense U.S. power if that could arrest the spreading erosion in South Vietnam. And such a result seemed hardly more than a self-evident proposition. For there was North Vietnam, a tiny primitive country of 19 million people, and there was the United States. Surely Hanoi could not withstand the graduated pressures of a nation of 200 million who possessed the strongest economy in the world and the most powerful military forces. Surely the use of limited U.S. power, applied with care and precision, but with the threat of more to come, would bring a realistic Ho Chi Minh to early negotiations. Nearly a year before the decision to apply direct U.S. power, Mc-Namara had publicly expressed his fundamental confidence that in the end all would be well. While acknowledging the difficulties and frustrations that lay ahead in Vietnam, as well as the heavy demand of courage, imagination, and above all, patience, he said in a speech delivered in late March of 1964: "When the day comes that we can safely withdraw, we expect to leave an independent and stable South Vietnam, rich with resources and bright with prospects for contributing to the peace and prosperity of Southeast Asia and of the world."

McGeorge Bundy was a brilliant and self-assured pragmatist of the highest ability. Less a scholar than an activist thinker and problem solver, he brought to the analysis of world problems a solid grounding in foreign affairs and an interesting mix of ethical imperative, *real politik*, and a feel for the innate operational complexity and limited controlability of large undertakings in war and peace. In a fundamental sense, he was a "process man" who, aware of the unforeseeable ways in which events not yet born will impinge upon and alter preselected courses of action, believes that what is important is to get started in the right direction and then play it by ear. Oriented principally to European affairs and the complex issues of strategic nuclear defense, he came to focus on the Vietnam crisis only in late 1964. He concluded that the United States must be willing to stand and fight in Vietnam, or else lose not only Southeast Asia but also the world's faith in the U.S. will and capacity to cope with the Communist threat to the Asian area. Failure to respond in Vietnam, he judged, would lead to further bold insurgencies in Malaysia, Indonesia, Burma, and the Philippines. He strongly urged the intervention of U.S. combat forces in 1965. Skeptical, however, of claims that air interdiction could really halt the infiltration, he advocated bombing North Vietnam primarily as a means of forcing Hanoi to pay a price for its cruelties in the South, and to bolster the morale of the government of South Vietnam.

·   ·   ·

It was not without irony that Walt Rostow, whose views on Vietnam so closely paralleled those of the Secretary of State, had been in 1961 turned down as the man to head Policy Planning in that department because Rusk regarded him as a rather too liberal economist. It was ironic because this deceptively mild-mannered man, who showed a natural deference to authority, proved to be the closest thing we had near the top of the U.S. government to a genuine, all-wool, anti-Communist ideologue and true believer. An inductive thinker, he constructed theories—often with perception and ingenuity—but once the pattern of his belief was established, some automatic mental filter thereafter accepted only reinforcing data, while systematically and totally rejecting all contrary evidence no matter how compelling. In debate he showed a rare capacity for "instant rationalization" (as one colleague put it), which amounted to a compulsion for buttressing his views by a rapid culling of the evidence immediately at hand; it did not matter whether the support that such evidence could provide was frail or nonexistent. His insensitivity to the opinions of others was legendary.

As a result of Rusk's rejection, Rostow became Bundy's deputy at the White House, but was moved to the planning job at State at the end of 1961, on direct instructions from President Kennedy. As the President explained it to Michael Forrestal, "Walt is a fountain of ideas; perhaps one in ten of them is absolutely brilliant. Unfortunately, six or seven are not merely unsound, but dangerously so. I admire his creativity, but it will be more comfortable to have him creating at some remove from the White House." After four years at the State Department where Rusk studiedly ignored him most of the time, Rostow returned to the White House in early 1966, upon Bundy's departure from government, as President Johnson's principal foreign policy assistant and coordinator.

He saw the problem in Vietnam as a centrally directed and coordinated Communist challenge, a deliberate testing of the national-liberation war theory with global implications. Success for Ho Chi Minh would set off a string of revolutionary explosions in vulnerable areas all across the world from which only Communism would benefit. But if the challenge in Vietnam were met and mastered by a determined Free World countereffort, similar Communist insurgencies in other miserable and restless areas—in Asia, Africa, and Latin America—would be deterred or discouraged. He was an early and unremitting advocate of bombing North Vietnam, although this seemed inconsistent with his own "strategic concept for counterinsurgency" which stressed small units, stealth, and knives as opposed to sizable conventional formations and weapons of large-scale destruction. But he had concluded that, because the infiltration could not be totally choked off, it was necessary to strike at "the source of the aggression." A participant in the Strategic Bombing Survey after World War II, he drew analogies from American experience over Germany and Japan that led him to the conviction that tactical airpower could make the war unbearable for Hanoi. He believed, erroneously, that there were in North Vietnam important industrial targets whose destruction would cripple the operation of that economy.

General Maxwell Taylor, a distinguished soldier-scholar, played several different roles in the Vietnam affair—as consultant to President Kennedy and co-author of the Taylor-Rostow report of November 1961; as Chairman of the Joint Chiefs of Staff until June 1964; as U.S. Ambassador to South Vietnam for the next twelve months; and thereafter as consultant to President Johnson and head of the Institute for Defense Analyses in Washington. In each of these positions he was a consistent, entirely predictable advocate of unrelenting military pressure in Vietnam as the only effective means of dealing with "the communist offensive in the Asian area."

•   •   •

. . . Vietnam policy in 1964–65 was formulated by a small group, and deliberations were closely held. At the time, many officials ostensibly near the center of U.S. national security affairs knew very little. Like newspaper readers everywhere, they could only note that through a series of small, almost imperceptible, steps, the United States had become involved in large and rapidly expanding combat operations. What happened between August 1964 and March 1965 confirmed the prevailing Cold War syndrome among the close advisers; it also revealed President Johnson's passion for consensus, his instinctive feeling that foreign policy is an integral and subordinate element of domestic politics, his compulsive secrecy, and his tendency to gloss over inconvenient truth—all of the qualities that were progressively to impair his credibility and effectiveness over the next three years, and finally to bring him down.

There had been in August the quixotic (and later much disputed) attacks by North Vietnamese torpedo boats on U.S. destroyers in the Tonkin Gulf. The second attack provoked a one-shot retaliatory air strike by U.S. carrier forces. Though it was difficult, both at the time and later, to discern any clear North Vietnamese purpose in provoking the U.S. giant, President Johnson in mid-campaign had found it prudent to respond militarily, on the grounds that he could not afford to play the total dove to Goldwater's hawk. He had found it prudent also to obtain from Congress a quick resolution that authorized him "to take all necessary measures to repel any armed attack against the forces of the United States and to prevent further aggression."

.   .   .

It is significant that, during most of the 1964 political campaign, the President had been by his own deliberate choice insulated from day-to-day developments in Vietnam. The word was to keep tough decisions away from the White House, and to avoid new actions or policy initiatives that would complicate the President's campaigning. During September and October, therefore, the erosion went on in South Vietnam without being brought forcefully to his attention; mounting anxieties at the intermediate levels in Washington and throughout the U.S. establishment in Saigon were muted. When the

President finally focused on the problem, sometime around mid-November, it had swollen to apparent crisis proportions, confronting him with what his advisers believed was a basic choice between major intervention and a considered liquidation of the whole commitment. His advisers appeared to agree that the first alternative that Ball had put to de Gaulle—a purely South Vietnamese counter to the Viet Cong challenge—was fast becoming academic. There wasn't enough time.

It is my impression that two things then happened: the President's close advisers (excepting Ball) unanimously urged direct U.S. military intervention in Vietnam, in order to avoid further deterioration of "our credibility vis-à-vis the Communists." The President reluctantly accepted the recommendation, because it was nearly unanimous, because it reinforced his own instincts about Communism and the needs of U.S. prestige, because he lacked the experience and self-confidence in foreign affairs to devise a valid alternative through (or by overriding) his constitutional advisers, and because he was quickly resolved not to become "the first American President to lose a war." But operating always on the instinctive premise that foreign policy is merely a subordinate element of domestic politics, he perceived political safety in continuity. He thus imposed the condition that intervention had to be made to look as though nothing was changing, as though it all flowed inexorably from commitments made by Eisenhower in 1954 and Kennedy in 1961, as though Lyndon Johnson were essentially a victim of history, doing no more than his bounden duty. "I didn't get you into Vietnam," he had said in a campaign speech, "You have been in Vietnam ten years. President Eisenhower wrote President Diem a letter in 1954 when the French pulled out . . ."

To a President convinced he must take new actions, yet obsessed by a need to preserve the posture of continuity, no major and overt actions were possible. He could not ask Congress for a declaration of war without shattering the posture (and without providing a rather specific explanation as to why "vital" U.S. interests were, after ten years of involvement, suddenly at stake). Inhibited by a formula of his own devising, he could only exploit the actions of the other side, seize available pretexts and provocations, and thus start a process that would lead in a series of acceptable steps to the required enlargement of the U.S. military effort.

The Administration positioned itself for such a development. On February 7, 1965, when the Viet Cong attacked American installations at Pleiku, destroying additional U.S. aircraft, killing seven and wounding 109, a retaliatory air strike was immediately ordered. Three days later, an American billet in the coastal city of Qui Nhon was similarly assaulted. Another air strike was carried out. McGeorge Bundy, who was in Vietnam at the time, later told a newsman, "Pleikus are streetcars," i.e., if one waits watchfully, they come along. Thereafter, the air strikes were almost imperceptibly transformed into a systematic program of bombing the North, but without formal acknowledgment of the shift until long after it was established fact. On March 6, two reinforced U.S. Marine battalions were sent ashore at Da Nang on what was described as "limited duty" related to the perimeter defense of airfields. Both Rusk and McNamara assured the nation that the role of these units, the first to be organized for combat, would be strictly confined to "defensive operations." McNamara added that because of their narrow patrolling mission they "should not tangle with the Viet Cong." But as the spring wore on, there were broad contacts between U.S. and enemy forces, significant U.S. casualties, and the arrival of additional U.S. combat forces.

By June, with 50,000 American troops in Vietnam, the White House conceded that U.S. forces were "authorized" to engage in combat under carefully defined and limited conditions—but it insisted that this was nothing new. It was merely another small step, and wholly consistent with the Eisenhower letter to Diem of 1954. As one highly placed official said much later, "The President's posture during this period was to pretend the war was not happening."

Immediately following the February attack on Pleiku, but before retaliatory action had been ordered, Vice-President Humphrey returned urgently to Washington from a trip to Georgia, to make a last-ditch attempt to prevent escalation. He gave the President his view that bombing the North could not resolve the issue in the South, but that it would generate an inexorable requirement for U.S. ground forces in the South to protect airfields and aircraft. He thought the attempt to gain a military solution in Vietnam would take years—far beyond the end of 1967 when the President would have to position himself for reelection. His views were received at the White House with particular coldness, and he was banished from the inner councils for some months thereafter, until he decided to "get back on the team."

By moving with secret purpose behind a screen of bland assurances designed to minimize or mislead, by admitting nothing until pressed by the facts and then no more than was absolutely necessary, by stretching to the limit (and perhaps beyond) the intent of the Tonkin Gulf Resolution, the President carried a bemused and half-aware nation far beyond the Eisenhower and Kennedy positions to a radically different involvement in the

intractable Vietnam conflict. It would have to be conceded that the performance was a piece of artful, even
masterful, political craftsmanship. Unfortunately for
Lyndon Johnson and the American people, it could be
vindicated only by a quick and decisive military victory.
But when the mists of summer confusion lifted, there
were 170,000 U.S. troops in Vietnam, U.S. air forces were
bombing the North with mounting intensity, and the
enemy showed no sign of surrender or defeat. There was
the President and there was the country—waist-deep in
the Big Muddy. And the integrity, the trust, the credibility
without which the leadership of great democratic nations
cannot govern were all gravely strained by a pattern of
actions that seemed an inextricable blend of high-minded-
ness, inadvertence, and either massive self-delusion or
calculated deceit.

Bibliographical Essay

The following is not intended to be exhaustive but rather is intended as a convenient starting point for those who wish to pursue further the period since 1945. Only books are listed; students seeking articles may consult the various periodical guides found in any library.

General Surveys

Eric F. Goldman, *The Crucial Decade—and After* (1960) remains the best survey covering the years from 1945 to

1960. Another overall account is Carl Degler, *Affluence and Anxiety, 1945—Present* (1968). For the 1960s, two new books are David Burner, Robert D. Marcus, and Thomas R. West, *A Giant's Strength: America in the 1960s* (1971) and William L. O'Neill, *Coming Apart: An Informal History of America in the 1960s* (1971). Unfortunately, good surveys of the 1940s and 1950s have not as yet been written. Hopefully, this will be corrected in the future.

The Political Scene

For the Truman years one may consult Richard S. Kirkendall, ed., *The Truman Period as a Research Field* (1967), as well as Barton J. Bernstein and Allen J. Matusow, eds., *The Truman Administration: A Documentary History* (1966). Bernstein has also edited a collection of essays entitled *Politics and Policies of the Truman Administration* (1970), which presents a critical view of the administration. For a positive appraisal one can read Cabell Phillips, *The Truman Presidency: The History of a Triumphant Succession* (1966). Truman's 1948 victory is the topic of Irwin Ross, *The Loneliest Campaign: The Truman Victory of 1948* (1968).

The Eisenhower administration has not been the subject of many noteworthy accounts. Arthur Larson, *Eisenhower: The President Nobody Knew* (1968), although quite favorable, is very interesting. Dean Albertson, ed., *Eisenhower as President* (1963) is a collection of stimulating essays. David A. Frier, *Conflict of Interest in the Eisenhower Administration* (1969) is one of the first scholarly attempts to deal with the administration. Eisenhower's opponent in 1952 and 1956, Adlai Stevenson, is treated critically in Bert Cochran, *Adlai Stevenson: Patrician Among the Politicians* (1969). On McCarthyism, one can profit greatly from reading any of the following:

Richard Rovere, *Senator Joe McCarthy* (1959), which is caustic; William F. Buckley, Jr. and L. Brent Bozell, *McCarthy and His Enemies* (1954), which defends the Senator; Daniel Bell, ed., *The Radical Right* (1963), a volume presenting the status arguments concerning the nature of McCarthyism; Michael P. Rogin, *The Intellectuals and McCarthy* (1967), a study challenging traditional arguments about McCarthyism; and Robert Griffith, *The Politics of Fear: Joseph R. McCarthy and the Senate* (1970), which discusses McCarthy's hold on the United States Senate. The best collection on McCarthy is Allen J. Matusow, ed., *Joseph R. McCarthy* (1970).

The Kennedy Presidency is treated in two admirable studies by friends and advisers of the late President. Arthur M. Schlesinger, Jr., *A Thousand Days* (1965) and Theodore C. Sorensen, *Kennedy* (1965) both present a vivid picture of John F. Kennedy in office. A readable anthology is Aida DiPace Donald, ed., *John F. Kennedy and the New Frontier* (1966). The 1960 election is treated in Theodore H. White, *The Making of the President 1960* (1961). Students will also be interested in Jim F. Heath, *John F. Kennedy and the Business Community* (1969), as well as in a compilation of Kennedy's press conferences called *Kennedy and the Press* (1965), edited by Howard W. Chase and Allen Lerman.

Lyndon Johnson's presidency has been written about by Louis Heren, *No Hail, No Farewell* (1970) and Eric F. Goldman, *The Tragedy of Lyndon Johnson* (1968, 1969). Tom Wicker, *JFK and LBJ: The Influence of Personality on Politics* (1968) is perceptive on both Kennedy and Johnson. Johnson's statements and policies are examined critically in Marvin E. Gettleman and David Mermelstein, eds., *The Great Society Reader: The Failure of American Liberalism* (1967).

No adequate study of the Nixon presidency is available

at this time. The election of 1968 is objectively treated by Theodore H. White, *The Making of the President 1968* (1969) while Joe McGinniss, *The Selling of the President 1968* (1969) indicts the political system for the way in which candidates are sold to the people. Lewis Chester, et al., *An American Melodrama* (1969) is another work that can be consulted with regard to the election. Eugene McCarthy's candidacy may be viewed through Arthur Herzog, *McCarthy for President* (1969). A readable political biography of President Nixon through the 1950s is Earl Mazo, *Richard Nixon* (1959, 1960). A critical view of Nixon is Gary Wills, *Nixon Agonistes* (1970).

The Social Scene

John Brooks, *The Great Leap: The Past Twenty-five Years in America* (1966) attempts to cover the period from 1940 to 1965. The best account of the "beat" culture of the 1950s is Jack Kerouac, *On the Road* (1957). Criticisms of the 1950s are to be found in C. Wright Mills, *The Power Elite* (1957) and William H. Whyte, Jr., *The Organization Man* (1956). Ronald Berman, *America in the Sixties: An Intellectual History* (1968) is an overview of that decade. Although a survey of the 1940s is lacking, one may look at Chester E. Eisinger, ed., *The 1940s: Profile of a Nation in Crisis* (1969) with benefit. On the role of media in America, Marshall McLuhan, *Understanding Media: The Extensions of Man* (1964) is a study of primary importance. The impact of television on politics is shown in Joe McGinniss, *The Selling of the President 1968* (1969) and Kurt and Gladys Lang, *Politics and Television* (1968).

Violence in the United States is discussed in any number of books. Richard Hofstadter and Michael Wallace, eds., *American Violence: A Documentary History* (1970) is a fine collection. Hugh Davis Graham and Ted Robert Gurr, eds., *Violence in America* (1969) is a series of essays tracing violence from colonial days. The study was done under the auspices of the National Commission on the Causes and Prevention of Violence. Those interested in the upheavals of the 1960s may read the *Report of the National Advisory Commission on Civil Disorders* (1968) and *Rights in Conflict* (1968)—both of which are very important. A good recent account of America's crime problems is Ramsey Clark, *Crime in America* (1970).

A classic study of poverty in America is Michael Harrington, *The Other America: Poverty in the United States* (1962). John Kenneth Galbraith, *The Affluent Society* (1958) also pointed to the inequities that were present in the country. More recently Nick Kotz, *Let Them Eat Promises: The Politics of Hunger in America* (1969) has shown how overt hunger is in the United States. Rural poverty is discussed by Harry Caudill, *Night Comes to the Cumberlands* (1963).

Theodore Roszak, *The Making of a Counter Culture* (1969) and Charles Reich, *The Greening of America* (1970) are two books that discuss youth and revolutionary change. Jerry Rubin, *Do It* (1970) and Abbie Hoffman, *Revolution for the Hell of It* (1968) argue for revolution from a participant's point of view. Campus uprisings have been the subject of a number of studies. For Columbia's problems a student may glance at the Cox Commission, *Crisis at Columbia* (1968), James Simon Kunen, *The Strawberry Statement* (1968), or Roger Kahn, *The Battle for Morningside Heights* (1970). The Berkeley situation is examined in Seymour Martin Lipset and Sheldon S. Wolin, eds., *The Berkeley Student Revolt* (1965), and more recently by Wolin and John H. Schaar, *The Berkeley Rebellion and Beyond* (1970). San Francisco State College's turmoil is the subject of William Barlow and Peter

Shapiro, *An End to Silence: The San Francisco State Movement in the 60's* (1971). The Kent State tragedy is the focus of James Michener, *Kent State* (1971).

The environment is the subject of Eugene P. Odum, et al., *The Crisis of Survival* (1970). An interesting collection of *New York Times* articles on the plight of the cities is Nathan Glazer, ed., *Cities in Trouble* (1970). Edmund K. Faltermayer, *Redoing America* (1968) and Richard A. Cooley and Geoffrey Wandesford-Smith, eds., *Congress and the Environment* (1970) are also very helpful in the environmental area.

The writings on minority groups are already voluminous. The history of the black population in America is excellently told in John Hope Franklin, *From Slavery to Freedom* (1967), which has a fine bibliography. Martin Luther King, *Why We Can't Wait* (1963, 1964) is a statement of the goals of the civil rights movement in the early 1960s. Malcolm X, *The Autobiography of Malcolm X* (1964) indicates another strain of thought that was developing as the civil rights revolution became the black revolution. The term "Black Power" is explained by Stokely Carmichael and Charles V. Hamilton, *Black Power: The Politics of Liberation in America* (1967). Eldredge Cleaver, *Soul on Ice* (1968) and H. Rap Brown, *Die Nigger Die* (1969) both indict white society for its oppression of the black population. Other volumes of interest are Claude Brown, *Manchild in the Promised Land* (1965); Bobby Seale, *Seize the Time* (1968, 1969, 1970); Floyd Barbour, ed., *The Black Power Revolt* (1968); Eric Foner, ed., *America's Black Past: A Reader in Afro-American History* (1970); and Harold Cruse, *The Crisis of the Negro Intellectual* (1967).

The Indian population is discussed in Stan Steiner, *The New Indians* (1968). Vine Deloria, Jr., *Custer Died For Your Sins* (1969) and *We Talk, You Listen* (1970) are eloquent statements of an Indian point of view. A good collection is Roger L. Nichols and George R. Adams, eds., *The American Indian: Past and Present* (1971). The Mexican-American is the subject of Carey McWilliams, *North From Mexico* (1968) and Stan Steiner, *La Raza: The Mexican Americans* (1969). Although women are not a numerical minority in the U.S., the women's liberation movement is a minority movement at this time. Two important works are Robin Morgan, ed., *Sisterhood is Powerful* (1970) and Germaine Greer, *The Female Eunuch* (1971).

The Foreign Policy Scene

United States foreign policy since 1945 is covered by Walter LaFeber, *America, Russia, and the Cold War, 1945–1971* (1972), written from a revisionist perspective, and Paul Y. Hammond, *Cold War Years: American Foreign Policy Since 1945* (1969), written from a more traditional point of view. Three different interpretations of the Cold War are found in Lloyd C. Gardner, Arthur Schlesinger, Jr., and Hans J. Morgenthau, *The Origins of the Cold War* (1970). Important recent memoirs on this period are George F. Kennan, *Memoirs* (1967) and Dean Acheson, *Present at the Creation* (1969). On Korea, Glen D. Paige, *The Korean Decision* (1968) is a detailed account of United States intervention. The Cuban missile crisis is discussed in Robert F. Kennedy, *Thirteen Days* (1969), as well as in the previously mentioned studies by Schlesinger and Sorensen on Kennedy. The Vietnam policy of the country is traced by George McTurnan Kahin and John W. Lewis, *The United States in Vietnam* (1969). One interpretation of the decision to stop the bombing is found in Townsend Hoopes, *The Limits of Intervention* (1969). Sam Brown and Len Ackland, eds., *Why Are We*

Still in Vietnam? (1970) is a collection of critical essays. Criticism of the war is also put forth in J. W. Fulbright, *The Arrogance of Power* (1967) and Noam Chomsky, *American Power and the New Mandarins* (1969). Lyndon Johnson's memoir, *The Vantage Point: Perspectives of the Presidency, 1963–1969* (1971) contains a defense of United States actions in Vietnam.